Beyond the Single Vision:

Henry James, Michel Butor, Uwe Johnson

by

Marianne Hirsch

French Literature Publications Company
York, South Carolina
1981

Library of Congress Catalog Card Number 81-68414

ISBN 0-917786-21-1

Printed in the United States of America

For my parents and Oliver

ACKNOWLEDGEMENTS

A book that covers several countries incurs many debts. My work on this project began as a doctoral dissertation at Brown University and owes a great deal to the influence of many of my professors there. I wish to thank particularly Arnold Weinstein who insists on reading fiction so as to bring out "its finest and most numerous secrets" and who, through friendship and encouragement, has shared some of his insights with me. I am grateful to Robert Scholes, Werner Hoffmeister and John Erwin for the careful and sympathetic reading they gave my work, and for their helpful criticism and suggestions. The American Association of University Women awarded me a dissertation fellowship which enabled me to complete the writing of this study in its initial form.

I could not have revised my work without having taught some of the works which form the subject of this study, and I wish to thank the students at Dartmouth College and Vanderbilt University who took my courses in modern fiction and whose questions refined and challenged my own ideas.

I have benefited from Vivian Kogan's concrete suggestions on several revised chapters and from the help of Karen Paulson, Debbie Hodges and Victoria Grossack with the preparation of the manuscript.

My very special thanks to Uwe Johnson and Michel Butor for discussing their work with me and generously answering all my questions.

I appreciate as well the opportunity to present some parts of this book publicly: a part of Chapter 3 at the 1977 Conference of the Southern Comparative Literature Association; and some of my work on Butor at the 1978 Convention of the Midwest Modern Language Association, as a colloquium at Princeton University, and to the Darmouth faculty seminar on literary criticism.

Hanover, New Hampshire

CONTENTS

C'est, ce sera sans doute, la rivalité entre
le monde extérieur et de la représentation
que nous nous en faisons. La manière dont
le monde des apparences s'impose à nous et
dont nous tentons d'imposer au monde extérieur
notre interprétation particulière, fait le
drame de notre vie.

André Gide

Its subject will doubtless be the rivalry
between the external world and the perception we have
of it. The manner in which the world of appearances
impinges on us and in which we impose on the
external world our interpretation of it,
constitutes the drama of our lives.

André Gide

Introduction: The Single Vision

In significant ways, modern fiction has retreated into the single vision of the individual mind, abdicating its connection to public reality. In an age of epistemological malaise, where public truth and accepted value have broken down, the self remains the only viable locus for our search for meaning and order.[1] Introspection and self-exploration, psychological investigation and personal confession, are its marks. A typical image of the writer is that of an individual shut up in a small room, cut off from all contact with the public world, writing furiously for no audience other than himself, exploring passionately no world other than his own inner being. Fiction from Dostoevsky's underground man, to Proust in his cork-lined room, Humbert Humbert in his prison cell, Molloy in his mother's bedroom, to Oskar in his insane asylum, has been anchored in the individual consciousness and has ranged from psychological self-examination to inventive fabulation. The responses to the withdrawal of the imagination from the real world and the assertation of the mind's autonomy have ranged from self-loathing, impotency and bankruptcy, to irony, playfulness, and celebration. Whatever his response, the writer is in the position of the outsider, the criminal, the prisoner or mad person, the spy in an enemy country, the detective, the witness.

The severance of mind from world is not a twentieth-century phenomenon. Erich Heller's famous essay "The Artist's Journey into the Interior"[2] traces the sources of this rupture and this malady from the Romantics to Rilke, and names Hamlet, whose emotion exceeds his situation, as its hero. Hegel's distinction between classical and romantic art, according to Heller, is the distinction between the oneness of mind and matter and their separation leading to a retreat into pure subjectivity and inwardness, to a celebration of the imagination not as the reflector but as the creator of reality. Georg Lukács, also a Hegelian, makes a similar distinction between novel and epic; he sees alienation as the very source of the novel form. "The novel is the epic of an age in which the extensive totality of life is no longer directly given, in which the immanence of meaning in life has become a problem, yet which still thinks in terms of totality," and "the hero of the novel is the product of estrangement from the outside world."[3] Again, the withdrawal into the individual consciousness, into the single vision, is the result of this alienation: "The inner form of the novel has been understood as the process of the problematic individual's journey toward himself...the road from dull captivity within a present reality...towards clear self-recognition."[4]

In "The Realistic Fallacy," Heller continues his investigation into the relation of mind and world in nineteenth-century literature. Nineteenth-century realism, he says, is not a desire to copy and understand reality, but to appropriate it. At the heart of all realistic literature is a hatred of reality and a competition with it. The other realism of the turn of the century is already a departure from external reality; it is the psychological realism of the mind that has made a break with "any external connection" to withdraw into inwardness.[5] Heller's essay illustrates well the dialectics of any realist movement, the struggle between the representation and the appropriation of reality.

Even if we do not, like Heller, see the history of all literature since the late eighteenth century as a history of progressive withdrawal, we must recognize the extent of that withdrawal from the turn of our century to the present, from the psychological realism of Proust and Woolf to the fabulation of Borges and Nabokov. In contemporary fiction, the single vision has included both the totally powerless, limbless characters in Beckett's garbage can and the all-powerful, endlessly creative and controlling narrators of Borges and Nabokov. The duality is best seen in a novel such as Robbe-Grillet's *In the Labyrinth*, where the narrator, sheltered in a warm and comfortable room, dreams about a poor abandoned soldier who desperately searches for an unknown man in the cold, snowy streets of a hostile city. The narrator's voice is calm, unemotional, as he recounts the soldier's desperate tale, except at those moments when the soldier threatens to invade the narrator's own room, to establish, or to re-establish a link that has been ruptured. In severing the connection with external reality, with all mimetic responsibility, our fiction has become autonomous, hermetic, and, as Robbe-Grillet suggests, protected. We seem to accept and to foster that break. Gerald Graff has argued very convincingly in his recent book *Literature Against Itself* that, by breaking with the mimetic mode, we have eliminated the power of literature to have a significant role in our society and our lives.[6] We have, nevertheless, retained an important role for it. We perceive the structures of fiction to parallel the structures of the mind and the structures of language. Where the Romantics glorify the imaginative vision over the real, we glorify language. Our approaches to fiction implicitly accept the rupture and no longer concern themselves with representation. Structuralism and semiotics, the conversion of the world into a text, the conception of modern reality as either unreal or as itself a text, are all celebrations of the imagination.

The modern writer's retreat into his own or the character's individual consciousness and his focus on the intricate workings of that consciousness come out of the realization of the relativity of all perception and the conviction that the content of all observation is subject to the position of the individual observer. Yet the very same realization has taken some modern writers in the opposite direction, to an impulse to reach out toward others, to re-establish a basis by which to explore a broader aspect of experience, to represent within the novel a world of greater scope than the inner contours of the individual self. This book is about attempts in modern fiction to go beyond the isolation of the single vision, to break out of the prison of the individual mind and the prison of unreality, to re-establish the power of fiction to serve as an instrument of knowledge about the structures of external reality. It traces manifestations and explorations of the mimetic impulse in modern fiction.

The search for a larger scope within modern fiction has taken me to certain authors whose work deals with a confrontation of different cultures, with internationalism and voyage because, in certain ways, voyage is perhaps the best emblematic representation, not only of the attempt to break out of a monoptic perspective, but of the fictional process itself. In the words of Michel Butor:

> All fiction, then, inscribes itself in our space as a voyage, and you could say in this respect that that is indeed the fundamental theme of all narrative literature; every novel which tells us of a voyage is therefore more clear, more explicit than the one which is not capable of expressing metaphorically this distance between the place of reading and the place where the narrative takes us.[7]

The theme of voyage presents the modern writer with a means of enlarging the scope of his work beyond the single vision, beyond self-exploration: the confrontation of cultures is inherently a confrontation of a plurality of perspectives. In his analysis of first person narration, *Narcisse Romancier*, Jean Rousset defines the *roman de voyage* in this same manner:

> The formula...requires a narrator who speaks as a lateral witness, rather than as a central subject. At times he is the mocking observer of places and areas he visits...if [the *roman de voyage*] obviously precludes any focus of the self on itself.... Cast back into the frame the first person serves only as the medium of the narration, all introspection is forbidden it.[8]

Rousset speaks of seventeenth- and eighteenth-century travelogues and the formula, naturally, has changed a great deal. Henry James, for example, uses the international theme precisely for the purpose of portraying a character's self-discovery; Conrad's jungles remain symbols for the deep regions of the human soul; and Gide and Mann employ the foreign setting as a backdrop to psychological action. Kakfa's America, Rilke's Paris, Robbe-Grillet's New York are imaginary realms, projections of pre-existing myths and individual creations of the fictional imagination. For these writers the foreign setting is not the Other but the Other that already exists within the Self.

In contrast, the works I have selected as the focus of this study are very concrete and literal attempts to discover and represent a foreign culture. They are not travelogues, but novels which test the mimetic and epistemological capacities of the fictional medium. The foreign retains a metaphorical significance pertinent to modern fiction because it represents, on the one hand, all that is mysterious and elusive, and therefore dramatizes the relation of the knower and the unknown and, on the other hand, it is the emblem of division and alienation between self and society and among different societies.

What particularly interests me is the epistemological dimension of this theme. In its exploration, I shall probe what we can know and how we go about knowing, how we can represent an entire multifaceted foreign world in a medium that is essentially linear and that is subject to conventions which foster not multiplicity but singularity, sequence and continuity. Inherent in the feeling of alienation is the yearning for wholeness and unity that is the source of all art.

Each of the authors chosen for this study, Henry James, Michel Butor and Uwe Johnson, combines in his works an epistemological quest and a voyage and each sees fiction as a privileged instrument of knowledge about an external reality, as the primary means by which we deal with an increasingly complex and confusing universe. James' pre-World War I and Butor and Johnson's post-World War II worlds share the impression of complexity and confusion, fragmentation and alienation. The individual confronted with either world responds with bafflement and impotence; conflicting impressions and viewpoints compete with one another to leave the individual at a loss. Fiction thus becomes a means not only of ordering the chaos but of understanding it without appropriating, taming or falsifying it. Fiction is in fact an intricate part of our lives, as Michel Butor emphasizes: "And narrative is a phenomenon which extends considerably beyond the scope of literature; it is one of the essential constituents of our understanding of reality. From the time we begin to understand language until our death, we are perpetually surrounded by narratives."[9]

In the modern world, the text itself becomes the place where self and world interact and compete with one another. To do justice to the complexity of this confrontation, fiction is by necessity an experimental medium, as Butor goes on to emphasize in his essay "The Novel as Research": "new forms will reveal new things in reality, new connections." For this reason, literature "appears no longer as a simple pastime or luxury, but in its essential role within the workings of society, and as a systematic experiment."[10]

The duality I have set up within modern fiction between mimetic and self-referential narratives is by no means a clear-cut one; neither is the realism of James, Butor and Johnson a naive positivistic mimeticism. For these writers, reality has become so complex that it must be approached with a whole new set of fictional skills which will enable us to see and to describe the complexity. In their experimentalism, these three writers are highly self-conscious; the focus of their works is not as much the discovery of the real as a careful scrutiny of fictional methods and skills that might enable us to embark on such a discovery.

James' commitment to knowledge and awareness notwithstanding, his inclusion in a study devoted to the mimetic impulse in modern fiction, to the discovery of foreign realities, demands some justification. James, after all, is known as the artist of consciousness, as the inventor of fictional strategies that both explore and reflect the relativity of perception, both individual and cultural. The technique of point of view, the limited central consciousness, the ficelle which functions as a link between that consciousness and the reader, as well as James' insistence on focusing only on the most refined and intelligent of individuals, are the methods that foster an interest not in external reality but in reality as it is filtered and reflected in the mind. Moreover, as James' work develops, the cultural settings recede more into the background, as the responses and ruminations of the centers of consciousness occupy the novels' focus and the readers' attention. Yet each of James' important characters is not just an individual, but the product of much larger cultural forces. In such early novels as *The American* and *Lady Barbarina* those influences are much more stereotyped, and they become quite subtle and refined in *The Ambassadors* and *The Wings of the Dove*, but never do they disapper altogether. The conflict between the personal and the cultural is, in fact, an important Jamesian theme and the status of the individual must constantly be re-examined. The following exchange between Isabel Archer and Mrs. Touchett provides a good example of the conflict:

> 'Now what is your point of view?' she asked of her aunt. 'When you criticize everything here, you should have a point of view. Yours doesn't seem to be American—you thought everything there so disagreeable. When I criticize, I have mine; it's thoroughly American!"
>
> 'My dear young lady,' said Mrs Touchett, 'there are as many points of view in the world as there are people of sense. You may say that doesn't make them very numerous! American? Never in the world; that's shockingly narrow. My point of view, thank God, is personal?'[11]

Ironically, Mrs. Touchett remains the stereotypical American in the novel, whereas Isabel develops far beyond the characteristics of either America or Europe. In her case, the cultural division feeds the development of character. The conflict between what is individually and what is culturally determined in each person actually becomes a much broader conflict that permeates James' work and that explains his inclusion in this study—the conflict between self and world. James' novels, especially the later ones, each take us to the point where vision and imagination become autonomous, cut off from reality. They show us the tremendous thrill and excitement that the autonomous imagination provides; no one is more creative, more exhilarated than the narrator of *The Sacred Fount* as he makes his discoveries, confirms them, plays with them. At every point, however, the real asserts its presence and poses serious resistance to the sweeping work of the imagination, either by presenting facts which negate the characters' speculations, as in *The Sacred Fount*, or by demanding outrageous costs for the imagination's triumphs, usually the ability to live. The greatest sin any Jamesian character can commit is to imagine poorly or wrongly, yet some of the most serious misinterpretations can be led back not to flaws within the imagination but to the oversight of something real and concrete. John Marcher in *The Beast in the Jungle*, for example, is such a victim of the autonomous imagination.

James responds to the relativity of perception and the breakdown of public truth that characterizes his age by building the authority of his individual observers, enabling them to develop faculties which will let them see deeply into some things, even if that depth of vision is bought at the cost of breadth. James is not the artist of consciousness alone; he demonstrates very clearly the dangers of autonomous vision and he is therefore all the more answerable to external reality. Faced with the same dilemma, the same powerlessness and relativity, Butor and Johnson explore ways out of the impasse to which James' works lead, ways to expand and to include in their texts the multifaceted aspects of an external reality that is no longer linked to human and psychological problems, but expands to all those structures—political, sociological, geographical— that determine the lives of human individuals. Other contemporary writers, those I have called self-referential, continue the other trend already present in James, the trend of the autonomous imagination. James' work is pivotal because both formally and thematically it is at the root of both traditions.

The development of the work of James, Butor and Johnson is similar in that it represents an expansion beyond single visions and single countries, toward inclusiveness and complexity. Although the lives and works of these three writers have been consistently marked by the conflict between cultures, I shall deal not with their *oeuvre* but with a group of single works each of which I shall subject to a close scrutiny. The particular fictional strategies developed to deal with this movement of expansion can best be assessed in the analysis of individual works in a comparative context.

In the first part of the book, "Confrontation," I deal with James' *The Ambassadors* and Butor's *Passing Time*, two novels which are based on the experiences of a single individual faced with a foreign culture and are limited, therefore, to a single narrative perspective. The epistemological struggle of the two protagonists is the effort to penetrate and understand the cities of Paris and Bleston. James' Strether succeeds in forming a personal vision of the city, in fusing American duty with European grace, and even in imposing his vision, be it in a limited way, on the external environment. If there is a meeting of cultures in *The Ambassadors*, it takes place in the supple and generous mind of Lambert Strether; the individual vision is capable of expanding until it can subsume difference and resolve contradiction. The cost, however, is Lambert Strether's ability to continue leading his own life. In Butor's novel the individual has lost the power to exert control over either his own life or the surrounding scene. As his diary becomes the portrait of the city, Jacques Revel sacrifices his individuality to his function as the city's chronicler; he becomes anonymous. While the knowledge achieved in James' novel benefits an elite of author, protagonist, and reader, and outweighs Strether's suffering and loss, that of Butor's work is offered to a greater community and depends on the individual sacrifice of the central subject. While James defines a culture through its most distinguished members, Butor's definition no longer concerns a human focus; the stones and trees of Bleston are as important as its inhabitants; traditional human frames of reference can no longer account for the city's complex being.

The second part, "Interaction," considers James' *The Golden Bowl* and Johnson's *Speculations about Jakob*. Built upon several narrative perspectives, these novels are formal statements of the international conflict and of its attempted resolution, in that their very structures act out the division. The novels' polyphonic structures are attempts to create a basis for communication and collaboration; yet both novels profoundly call into question the role of the artistic process as a medium of a collective vision. *The Golden Bowl* is seriously out of balance; the two points of view converge into one, as Maggie, an artist figure and the representative of American capitalism out to buy Europe, takes over and manipulates the lives of those around her. Yet, at the end, the Prince is called upon to respond to Maggie's vision and the cultural fusion can only be the result of their communication, their marriage. Although it is suggested as a possibility, the fusion is withheld from the space of the novel, and depends, to a certain extent, on the reader's involvement. Johnson, on the other hand, uses the multiple perspective technique to piece together, out of several different testimonies, the life of one man, Jakob Abs, the victim of cultural division. His story remains fragmented, tied up in other lives and in the disruptive political systems. Even a collaborative effort by the different narrators does not succeed in bridging their disparate perceptual grids and in unifying the dead man's story. Not only art, but language itself becomes suspect and corrupted in its political subservience; it is the medium of propaganda, not of community. The polyphonic structure emphasizes fragmentation, rather than facilitating unification. In both works, fiction itself is a contaminated medium, morally and ideologically suspect.

The third part, "Expansion," focuses on yet two other attempts at inclusiveness, centered on the complex and multi-faceted subject of America. Butor's *Mobile* offers the reader (the only human viewpoint left) the disjointed elements of American culture and calls upon him to invest them with significance and order. No longer a novel, *Mobile* becomes a guidebook, a catalogue, a patchwork quilt (to use Butor's own phrases). It represents a rejection of narrative as a medium not sufficiently attuned to the complexities of modern reality. The book presents the reader with a world to explore, with the challenge to acknowledge the suppressed and forgotten realities of American culture. Johnson's *Anniversaries* is very much a novel, and yet it resembles *Mobile* in its thrust toward inclusion and totality. Committed to the narrative of a human story, Johnson approaches America through the life of Gesine Cresspahl, who becomes the point of convergence of the history, the geography, the politics and the art of a forty-year period, and whose life is determined daily by external events. Yet the novel's direction is no longer epistemological, that is, it is not based on Gesine's effort to understand New York, but it represents her effort to construct a unified life there as a foreigner and a European, to make America into the meeting place of a shattered post-war world. The novel, a dialogue between Gesine and her daughter Marie, is an effort to understand the past and to use that awareness toward a better future. In their commitment to that effort, Gesine and Marie subordinate their own lives in the construction of a supra-individual story.

Through these groupings, I intend to suggest neither a specific literary tradition, nor any particular affinity between writers. In fact, I find that these authors have vastly different approaches:

James focuses primarily on psychological and moral concerns; Johnson's interest is political, and Butor's cultural and anthropological. In this study, I wish to examine six responses to a particular situation (division and alienation), responses that are expressed by a similar theme (travel and cultural confrontation), and that experiment with similar fictional forms (single point of view, multiple perspectives, intertextuality, montage). These groupings reveal not only the difficulties inherent in penetrating and rendering a foreign reality, but also suggest the epistemological potentials of various forms of storytelling. They bring out, as well, the moral dimensions of an act of perception that is essentially reduced to conjecture, speculation and fabrication. Moreover, they redefine the relationship, in the novel, between author, character and reader.

As authorship and authority are questioned, as the single vision is supplemented by others, the reader's role becomes more crucial and more central. The reader's involvement in the world of the text makes these works realistic and didactic in a very special sense. Their realism is a realism of analogy: the reader's process of orientation in the text parallels the characters' process of orientation in their world. To learn to read is to learn to live.

This book's structure is both a linear progression and a dialectic. It traces a progression in the literature of voyage: from travelogue to international novel to guidebook, in the epistemological concern: from single authorship to collaboration and a new kind of omniscience, and in the modern novel: from psychological fiction to post-psychological writing. Yet, at every point, this progression gives way to the dialectic present in each of the works examined between singularity and multiplicity, Self and Other, centrality and expansiveness.

I. CONFRONTATION

I. *The Ambassadors:* "A Drama of Discrimination"

The confrontation of European and American civilization, what James has called the international theme, runs through all of his work, but its treatment evolves significantly between the early and the late novels. Whereas contrast between cultures is the basis of *The American*, numberous short stories and even *The Portrait of a Lady*, fusion becomes the goal of *The Ambassadors*, *The Wings of the Dove*, and *The Golden Bowl*. The change from Christopher Newman to Lambert Strether is the development from the opposition of the "distinctively American and the distinctly European outlook," from what James calls "emphasized internationalism" to the creation of an individual vision that, in combining the two, goes beyond the representative and the typical.

In the Preface to "Lady Barbarina,"[1] James outlines that ultimate and ideal point toward which his international fiction has been moving--the transcendence of all national differences:

> Behind all the small comedies and tragedies of the international, in a word, has exquisitely lurked for me the idea of some eventual sublime consensus of the educated; the exquisite conceivabilities of which, intellectual, moral, emotional, sensual, social, political--all, I mean, in the face of difficulty and danger--constitute stuff for such "situations", as may easily make many of those of a more familiar type turn pale. There, if one will--in the dauntless fusions to come-- is the personal drama of the future![2]

James announces here not only the dissolution of all discord between different cultures, but also of all struggle between an individual and his culture: the culture becomes an instrument in the formation of human beings exceptional in every conceivable area of human endeavor. International conflict thus becomes a personal drama.

James' dream of cultural fusions and international communities is a direct response to the division and dislocation he experienced throughout his lifetime and represents his effort to create a fictional medium within which feelings of cultural fragmentation might be overcome. The point of view and the center of consciousness techniques James perfected clearly reflect an intense awareness of the limitations of an individual perception shaped by cultural and personal determinants, a vision further and further removed from the consensus of nineteeth-century realism. James takes on the international theme precisely to confront the limitations of individual perception in the effort to achieve, within those limitations, a vision that might transcend that of the single individual.

I would like to argue that this ideal vision of the international is manifested in *The Ambassadors*, a novel which acts out the process of achieving the "sublime consensus of the educated" on the level of a single consciousness. This novel is particularly seminal because, concentrating on an individual American confronting the culture of Europe, it presents the drama of the single mind which finds itself in the position of breaking out of its own limited vision to embrace and comprehend an entirely foreign world.

The Ambassadors represents the "drama of discrimination" or the "process of vision" that characterizes the confrontation between the knower, Lambert Strether, and the object to be known, Paris and European civilization. Through the protagonist's central consciousness, the novel demonstrates both the limitations of individual perception and the intricate complexities that result when such an exceptional figure as Lambert Strether engages a foreign reality. *The Ambassadors* creates a character who experiences the limitation of the single vision and who then transcends it, who grows beyond the provincial and the national to the point of subsuming cultural difference, contradiction and contrast.[4] In this chapter, I shall explore the development of Strether's personal vision of Europe, examining the parameters of Strether's success in terms of both the thematic international conflict and the point of view technique, and concentrating on the moral premises that underly this form of the single vision.

Lambert Strether is one of the most finely drawn characters in fiction, and the entire novel, as it depicts Strether's education, is devoted to portraying his growth as a character. In the preface, James takes great pains to stress the uniqueness of Strether, a true "man of imagination," a "hero so mature, who would give me thereby the more to bite into," (*Art*, p. 310) and elsewhere "a mirror verily of miraculous silver and quite pre-eminent" (*Art*, p. 70). In Gloriani's garden Strether explains how he, like each one of us, has been shaped by his culture:

> The affair—I mean the affair of life—couldn't, no doubt, have been different for me; for it's at the best a tin mould, either fluted and embossed, with ornamental excrescences, or else smooth and dreadfully plain, into which, a helpless jelly, one's consciousness is poured—so that one, takes, the form, as the great cook says, and is more or less compactly held by it; one lives in fine as one can. (p. 138)[5]

It is significant and paradoxical that Strether uses this strong deterministic statement as an argument for freedom in his advice to Little Bilham: "Still, one has the illusion of freedom; therefore don't be like me, without the memory of that illusion....Live!" (p. 138). Strether ultimately frees himself from the bounds of his New England upbringing. Unlike the Pococks who are so trapped that they are unable even to see Europe, unlike Waymarsh who even in Paris remains the "grand old American" (p. 79), unlike Chad who, as a creature of Woollett, cannot be fundamentally changed even by Mme. de Vionnet and will ultimately return to the family business, Strether, without violating his integrity or his principles, is able to understand profoundly the Parisian civilization he encounters and to incorporate all that it represents into his vision of life. The novel becomes the story of Strether's education, the broadening and deepening of his vision beyond the cultural determinants that have shaped his character.

Strether arrives in Europe at middle age, full of vague regret about his past, his wife and child, full of dissatisfaction with the American mercantilistic spirit, full of nostalgia for a life he feels he has missed. He has come to Europe "too late" to participate in its life, but not too late to observe it, understand it, learn from it. His ambassadorial function affords him no more than an indirect participation in the European scene and in the interacton of European and American values. His experience is mediated through Chad, the young man he has come over to save from Europe's destructive influence, but who, ironically, seems to be leading the very life Strether feels he has missed.

Strether remains throughout his European adventures an "observer of manners," as Chad calls him. In the Shakespearean indentification of life with a theatrical stage, Strether does not play the role of actor but rather that of spectator. When he visits a London theater with Maria Gostrey in the very beginning of this stay, he realizes that the show extends beyond the confines of the stage to such an extent that "the figures and faces in the stalls were interchangeable with those on the stage. He felt as if the play itself penetrated him with the naked elbow of his neighbour" (p. 44). Even as an observer, however, he is limited by his age and status in this theater in which "his seat had...fallen to somebody else" (p. 65).

Exactly how much the activity of observation actually involves the observer in the action remains open to question: "Were they, this pair, of the 'great world?'–and was he himself, for the moment and thus related to them by his observation, *in* it?" (p. 139). The images describing Strether's status, the theater, the balcony, the glass of the shopwindow or the picture frame, emphasize distance and mediation. Allowed no more than "hungry gazes through clear plates behind which lemon-colored volumes were as fresh as fruit on the tree" (p. 64), Strether is twice removed from the immediacy of experience. And yet, Strether's primarily mental activity is also described by images which give it the gravity of a real and perilous event, an adventure on a battefield, in a jungle, on the high seas. [6] James continues to dramatize the most uneventful of plots: Strether is sent to Europe by Chad's mother to convince Chad to return home. Upon meeting the woman who keeps Chad in France, Strether is convinced that their attachment is not only "virtuous" but also good for Chad. He eventually recognizes that there is more to their liaison than he had wanted to admit and, even with that realization, he abandons his mission and returns to America. The process of vision is the only "action" of the novel.[7] For Strether, living and seeing are synonymous. Although his advice to Little Bilham is "live," the latter's interpretation of that advice equates living with seeing: "Didn't you adjure me, in accents I shall never forget, to see, while I've a chance, everything I can?" (p. 172).

In the Preface, James contemptuously reviews and rejects the current myth of Paris, making it clear that his own vision transcends such a stereotyped conception of the city:

> There was the dreadful little old tradition, one of the platitudes of
> the human comedy, that people's moral scheme *does* break down in
> Paris; that nothing is more frequently observed; that hundreds of
> thousands more or less cynical persons annually visit the place

for the sake of the probable catastrophe, and that I came late in the day to work myself up about it.... The revolution performed by Strether under the influence of the most interesting of great cities was to have nothing to do with any *bêtise* of the imputably 'tempted' state. (*Art*, p. 316).

At the time of his arrival, Strether conceived of Chad as of someone whose "moral scheme" had broken down in Paris, but in London already Woollett's distinctions appear too simple. In his meeting with Maria the weight of Woollett is dubbed "the failure to enjoy" (p. 25). As Maria begins to help Strether throw off that weight and acclimatize himself, Europe is identified with an ability to enjoy, to let oneself go, to concentrate on each individual moment, and thereby free oneself from what Strether characterizes as the typically American "obsession of the other thing" (pp. 26-27). His impulsive acquaintance with Maria Gostrey, their exchanged confidences and Strether's intense pleasure at the physical sights of Chester are all signs of a beginning acclimatization to the spirit of Europe.

The obvious poverty of Woollett's categories emerges when they are confronted with Maria's refined powers of discrimination. Even while fearing and mistrusting the quality of her vision, Strether promptly identifies with it—their recognition is mutual as each sees the other in a particularly perceptive and profound way. It is this vision that becomes the meaning of Europe, much more than its sensual and material pleasures. Strether's education is twofold: it must combine material pleasure with an intense activity of reflection and discrimination. In an 1899 letter to Edward Wharton, James suggests these two meanings in a beautiful description of Paris: "It strikes me as a monstrous massive flower of national decadence, the biggest temple ever built to material joys...(yet) with a deal of beauty still in its expansive symmetries and perspectives—and such a beauty of light." This light fosters a privileged quality of vision. It is the same light that Miss Barrace means when she says: "in the light of Paris one sees what things resemble" (p. 132).

Whether living and seeing are ever harmoniously combined remains doubtful. The important point is that Strether believes in the possibility of a harmonious coexistence, and that such characters as Gloriani seem, at least in Strether's vision, to embody it.[8] On the one hand, he sees Gloriani as "the glossy male tiger, magnificently marked" (p. 139). On the other, he notices Gloriani's eyes first and foremost: "He wasn't soon to forget them, was to think of them, all unconscious, unintending, preoccupied though they were, as the source of the deepest intellectual sounding to which he had ever been exposed" (p. 125); "...he had never seen a person look at anything, he thought, just as Gloriani" (p. 162).

Strether's education begins with an incipient appreciation of material objects and his growing enjoyment and desire for them is like a current whose force he is unable to stay (p. 38). He soon moves from the relatively passive activities of looking at shopwindows and buying gloves to an immersion into the physical pleasures represented by the dinner and theater visit with Maria. Comparing it with a theater visit in Boston, he notes that there "there had been no little confronted dinner, no pink lights, no whiff of vague sweetness, as a preliminary" (p. 42). It is significant that, though the sensual pleasures of the evening are great—"had anything to his mere sense ever been so soft?" (p. 42)—they ultimately serve as the instruments of even greater intellectual pleasures. These range from the sudden "uncontrolled perceptions" to which Strether is subject all evening, to the triumph of a simile on which, as Strether remarks, "no gentleman of his age at Woollett could ever...have embarked" (p. 43) and which compares Maria with her red velvet ribbon to Mary Stuart, and Mrs. Newsome with her ruche to Queen Elizabeth. In this combination of the sensual and the intellectual, Strether comes to see the ideal of Europe.

Continuing his "sensual education," Strether begins giving dinners, a fact which Maria interprets as a symbol of his conversion. He furthermore learns to appreciate the beauty of houses and furnishings, the charm of Parisian streets, the glory of Notre Dame. His education culminates, no doubt, in the lunch with Mme. de Vionnet; it is a moment of triumph over what he calls "his odious ascetic suspicion of any form of beauty," in that it is a moment of both surrender and pure enjoyment:

> How could he wish it to be lucid for others, for any one, that he, for the hour, saw reasons enough in the mere way the bright clean ordered waterside life came in at the open window?—the mere way Madame de Vionnet, opposite him over their intensely white table-linen, their *omelette aux tomates*, their bottle of strawcolored Chablis, thanked him for everything almost with the smile of a child, while her grey eyes moved in and out of their talk, back to the quarter of the warm spring air, in which early summer had aready

> begun to throb, and then back again to his face and their human
> questions. (p. 184)

At the same time, however, his sensation of drowning, his
unsettling awareness of a complete loss of control–(Mme. de
Vionnet sees him as "a man in trouble"(p. 185)–make it a moment of
horror. during their lunch, Strether realizes how senseless his
puritanical reluctance to see her had been, but he also realizes to
what dangers he should be exposed if he should see her. During this
lunch Strether's fear of experience, represented by images of
drowning, plunging, touching bottom, and losing control, begins to
manifest itself in its most concrete form. Herein lies the underside
of the discriminatory powers Strether admires and tries to acquire,
the risk that if he allows himself to see depths, they might be
bottomless and uncontrollable.

Instead of finding in Paris the morally decadent civilization he
expected, Strether comes upon rich surfaces, enticing shopwindows,
beautiful people, and magnificent interiors. From these, Strether
infers a moral essence that corresponds to the visual perfection.[9]
When Maria asks Strether on what basis he founded his judgment
of Mme. de Vionnet's virtue, he answers, "Well, her beauty of
everything. The impression she makes. She has such variety and yet
such harmony" (p. 350). We feel intimations of the fallacy of this
correspondence, however, as Strether senses horrors lurking
underneath the elegant exteriors. These are expressed by means of
an intricate pattern of jungle imagery: "there was something in the
great world covertly tigerish" (p. 139). When he hears of Jeanne's
engagement, Strether is truly horrified: "He had allowed for depths,
but these were greater: and it was as if, oppressively–indeed,
absurdly–he was responsible for what they had now thrown up to the
surface. It was–through something ancient and cold in it–what he
would have called the real thing" (p. 251).

The strongest seduction of Paris lies precisely in its complexity,
suggested in one of the most beautiful images ever used to describe
this city:

> It hung before him this morning, the vast bright Babylon, like some
> huge irridescent object, a jewel brilliant and hard, in which parts
> were not to be discriminated nor difference comfortably marked. It
> twinkled and trembled and melted together, and what seemed all
> surface one moment seemed all depth the next. (p. 66)

Here Paris is described as an object of perception and interpretation whose intricacy requires a vision refined and precise, incisive and prodigious. Strether's response to the city's demands comes to approach the art of the city, itself: "the air had a taste of something mixed with art, something that presented nature as a white-capped master-chef" (p. 60). It is a vision based on a rich and exciting history, of a life that values tradition and art and thereby enriches daily life with a sense of beauty. It is a vision that equates physical with moral beauty, that sees the aesthetic as the creator of the moral. The absence of business and monetary concerns differentiates Paris profoundly from the Woollett he begins to despise. His is a vision which grows daily, incorporating new evidence and responding in a particularly expansive way to all the seductions of the city.

Ultimately, it is a vision that is proven wrong, as Strether intimates horrors beneath the beautiful surfaces, as he realizes that the truth of Paris is much closer to what he "came out to find," as he suspects, perhaps, that the civilized life of Chad is only made possible by the money of Woollett. On the morning of his last visit to Mme. de Vionnet, Strether feels he is participating in the real day-to-day existence of Paris. He goes to the post office, sends a *pneumatique* which connects him to the vast network that runs through the city and, related to the other people who send such messages, he discovers himself "on the side of the fierce, the sinister, the acute" (p. 333). He is forced to admit that Paris is no more than a "typical tale," perhaps not that different from Woollett's stereotype. Moreover, in the charged atmosphere of an electric storm, still full of the historic sense that had been loyal to him ever since his arrival, Strether hears the "vague voice" of the city which expresses not grandeur and beauty, but suffering: "Thus and so, on the eve of the great recorded dates, the days and nights of revolution, the sounds had come in, the omens, the beginnings broken out. They were the smell of the revolution, the smell of the public temper—or perhaps simply the smell of blood" (p. 335).[10] Eventually Strether learns to be taken in by deceptive surfaces no longer, but to discriminate between the physical and the moral reality of Paris, and to reevaluate that morality according to broader standards.

It is apparent that Strether did not just go the long way around to arrive back where he started. The "typical tale" of Paris is not the one imagined in Woollett, but one arrived at through interpretation and reinterpretation, and through the suffering that such an adjustment of vision implies. After having sounded out all the ramifications, he arrives at a vision broad, deep and generous enough to account for the city's unsettling contradictions. The destruction of Strether's personal conception is but another facet in the city's neverending complexity, and although his personal adjustment is exceedingly painful, his aesthetic sense is full of the satisfaction derived from the achievement of a more complete vision. Throughout this novel, aesthetic achievements compensate for Strether's personal losses until seeing and creating come more and more to substitute for living, rather than to complement it.

F.O. Matthiessen has pointed out that James' cities are very different from those of Balzac and Joyce.[11] *The Ambassadors* represents a very limited view of the great modern city when compared to other novels of the last two centuries. As a human psychodrama, it concentrates on all that forms the refined society in which Strether moves, and ignores those elements of the modern city that diminish and crush the human.

In fact, Strether learns to see and to understand the city's complexities not by struggling with the realities of Paris but by getting to know its human representative, Mme. de Vionnet. Mme. de Vionnet's complexity and mystery match that of Paris: "there was always more behind what she showed, and more and more again behind that" (p. 340). She is forever enticing. Here again the physical beauty of the surface is translated into an implied moral beauty, and Strether, caught as he is in the moral and verbal code of Woollett, not only misinterprets Little Bilham's phrase "virtuous attachment," but continues to apply the Woollett terminology to a being so foreign to it: "Is her life without reproach?" As Strether's moral categories are expanded, he learns to see other meanings of "virtuous" and "beyond reproach."

The foreign reality of Paris and Mme. de Vionnet is mysterious and elusive; it provokes endless attempts at response and its mystery has erotic overtones. The act of discovery, moreover, is the only eroticism Strether will know in the novel.

The recognition of the "typical tale" of Paris is paralleled by a recognition of Mme. de Vionnet's typicality, just as Strether's insight into the suffering of Paris is matched by his insight into her pain. During his last visit, he sees her no longer as Cleopatra or a Victor

Hugo heroine, no longer as a "goddess still partly engaged in a morning cloud," or "a sea-nymph waist-high in the summer surge" (p. 168), but as Mme. Roland approaching the scaffold, and, worse, a maidservant crying for her young man. The recognition is cruel: "it was like a chill in the air to him, it was almost appalling, that a creature so fine could be, by mysterious forces, a creature so exploited" (p. 341). Here Strether not only recognizes that his heroine is no different from other women, that in her despair she does not hesitate to use him and has perhaps used him all along, but he recognizes as well the price paid for Chad's magnificent transformation.[12] A similar price is paid for Strether's ultimate knowledge of Paris, for his brief and partial immersion into experience and physical enjoyment.[13]

More than any other woman in the novel, Mme. de Vionnet forces Strether to transcend his stereotyped vision. Initially idealized, transformed into numerous mythological, historical and literary figures, she finally emerges as both lover and mother, both young and very old, both unique and very common. Initially violated by Strether's fixed image of her, she is finally recognized as a compendium of different and even contradictory images, as a far from perfect human being. Strether can accept her as such only on the condition that he stop seeing her.

The development of Strether's vision to this point, its suppleness and versatility, its almost infinite expansion, can be most fully seen in the scene of Strether's trip to the country. Here Strether is at the very height of his speculative activity, at the point where he becomes more than a spectator or an observer, where he becomes an artist in his own right. At this point, the material and the moral reality of Europe give way to Strether's all-absorbing imagination.

It could appear, at first, that this day is for Strether a step away from observation and toward participation because he manages to step into the picture frame of a beloved Lambinet painting. I would suggest that, on the contrary, Strether creates an autonomous artistic structure which he opposes to the life going on around him. He molds the rural landscape to fit the Lambinet painting he desired in his youth and populates the scene with characters from Maupassant. No longer a spectator at the theater, he has become the playwright as the distant Parisian drama begins to take shape on the stage of his mind:

> ...though he had been alone all day, he had never yet so struck him-
> self as engaged with others and in the midstream of his drama.... For
> this had been all day at bottom the spell of the picture—that it was
> essentially more than anything else a scene and a stage, that the very
> air of the play was in the rustle of the willows and the tone of the
> sky. The play and the characters had, without his knowing it till
> now, peopled all his space for him, and it seemed somehow quite
> happy that they should offer themselves, in the conditions so
> supplied, with a kind of inevitability. (p. 323)

As Strether orders dinner at the small rural inn after having
spent an elating and satisfying day, we begin to have the sense of the
artist in him at work. We witness his mind as it absorbs, digests,
condenses, transforms and brings forth the artifact in finished form,
beautiful, complex, and yet palatable, fusing the rural landscape
with the moral drama of Paris and Woollett. Art becomes alchemy; it
literally becomes an object of human consumption:

> "The" thing was the thing that implied the greatest number of other
> things of the sort he had had to tackle.... Not a single one of his ob-
> servations but somehow fell into a place in it; not a breath of the
> cooler evening that wasn't somehow a syllable of the text...the
> picture and the play seemed supremely to melt together in the good
> woman's broad sketch of what she could do for her visitor's
> appetite. (p. 324)

Here Strether the artist takes elements of the visible scene—
James says that "art plucks its material in the garden of life" (*Art*, p.
312)—mixes them with the situation he has both experienced and
imagined and shapes all this into what he calls "the text," a text
which exists not as a fixed form, but as a process which continually
changes to accomodate new facts, such as the young couple in the
boat.

In a parody of the early balcony scenes (he is standing in a raised
pavillion which overlooks the river), Strether gradually realizes that
the boat is Mme. de Vionnet's, that he is not in it, and that it is not a
metaphor but a real boat, just as the heroes of his idyll turn out to be
real people. He also realizes that he is seen by those in the boat and
that they pretend, for a few moments, not to see him. He realizes
finally that the relationship of Chad and Mme. de Vionnet is not
innocent, as he had supposed, but that it includes the physical
intimacy which is, as he says, "so much like lying" (p. 331). The

glimpse of the boat threatens to overthrow the magnificent structure Strether has just built up.

But Strether recovers from the shock. He is able to accept their intimacy, at least intellectually, and so he asks Chad to remain in Paris. Nevertheless, there is profound disenchantment, as Strether realizes that life can never measure up to the image of it created by the prodigious imagination. Somehow, Strether's theory about the relationship was richer, more attractive than the truth. His imagination had embellished the facts by taking them out of the ordinary: " 'What I see, what I saw,' Maria returned, 'is that you dressed up even the virtue. You were wonderful–you were beautiful' " (p. 349). We have the sense of a vision sustained desperately and stubbornly in the face of a great deal of contradictory evidence. "I had phases. I had flights" (p. 350).

Philip Weinstein has remarked that Strether, at the end of the novel, abandons life rather than his commitment to his vision. I would qualify this statement. At the climax of his education Strether realizes the precariousness of his conception and, going one step further, he accepts the truth. He can deal with that truth on an intellectual level only; he cannot live it.

Thus we can see that Strether's rich, supple and generous vision of Europe and the "sublime consensus" of European and American values he personally achieves by the end of the novel are bought at tremendous costs. I would argue that it is precisely those cost that make it possible for Strether to see so much and so well. The primary cost is Strether's withdrawal into a mental realm, his ultimate abandonment of the physical pleasures and even the physical presence of Europe, even as he remains within its mental climate. As the book progresses, Strether's imaginative visions and projections are continually confronted with real events, checked and measured against an often brutal reality. At the end, however, as he leaves Paris so changed as to be incapable of accepting Woollett, Strether will have no receptacle for the prodigious knowledge he has acquired but the equally prodigious instrument of that knowledge, his imagination. It is an imagination nourished by the real, made to grow through error, disappointment and real pain, but it is ultimately a mental realm. If James' "sublime consensus" ever comes to be, it is only within the mind of Lambert Strether and that of the characters who join him in his discussions and projections.

The imaginative act of reading and interpretation in which Strether is engaged is rarely performed alone. There is an entire network of observers in which Strether participates. He himself is never as passionate as in the encounter with these other observers, when he has the chance to see the Parisian scene reflected in the eyes of others. The novel is, in fact, dominated by dialogue.

Several critics, including Ian Watt[14] and Charles Feidelson, have commented on James' need for mirrors, his need to see experience filtered through several different minds. Although *The Ambassadors* has a single center of consciousness, several minds are present at every point. Strether is fascinated by watching others as they watch him, and he uses the eyes of Waymarsh, Chad, and Gloriani as his mirrors. The narrator is another such mirror. Although our vision is for all intents and purposes limited to Strether's, it is significant that the language of the novel is not his. In the Preface, James justifies the existence of an external narrator by warning against "the terrible fluidity of self-revelation" (*Art*, p. 321) that characterizes first—person narratives. Strether, in contrast, is "encaged and provided for" by the external narrator who creates an atmosphere of order and safety absent from James' first—person narratives.[15] The external narrator serves to give authority to Strether's experience, to objectify and corroborate his thoughts and perceptions, as well as to translate them into more general and representative terms. Ian Watt observes that the dual narrative perspective of *The Ambassadors* combines the intensely personal with the broadly social and gives Strether's vision a broader significance.[16]

Within the novel, as well, Strether receives a great deal of help, especially from Maria Gostrey, the most imaginative and intelligent of his companion observers. Maria, we have seen, introduces him to the mysteries of Europe, as she has done for many others. Helping him to read and interpret the signs, she becomes Strether's most important educator. In so far as knowledge in James' world is reduced to the interpretation of appearances–"What more than a vain appearance does the wisest of us know?" (p. 129), says Little Bilham–and in so far as we have seen just how deceptive those appearances can be, how wide the gap between surface and depth often is, Strether and Maria actually have a great amount of freedom to refine their powers of discrimination.

Their sessions together resemble a contest, a guessing game, a matching of wits. In the privacy of Maria's apartment, quite removed from the Parisian streets and drawing rooms, they create people and situations: here Strether undergoes the training that transforms him from spectator to artist. The interest that lies in such creation, the satisfaction it affords which seems to surpass that of direct discovery, are expressed in connection with the small article manufactured in Woollett. Maria greatly prefers not knowing its identity so as to be able to invest it with her imaginative capacity. An insignificant article takes on mysterious and symbolic significance through the elaborate speculative process that goes on around it. Similarly, Strether ignores any evidence that might interfere with his desired view of things. Only thus could he have overlooked the true nature of the relationship between Chad and Mme. de Vionnet for so long, ignoring even quite obvious signs, such as their repeated common absence from town.

Strether and Maria's speculative activity proceeds with a virtuosity that knows no bounds and quickly surpasses its objects. Soon the activity of acquiring and playing with knowledge becomes far more interesting than the objects to be known. James has remarked that it is art that makes life, that the formal order of art improves on "fumbling life at her stupid work." The processes of the mind reveal intimations of beauty, complexity and meaning foreign to reality.[17] "To sit there was, as he had told his hostess before, to see life reflected for the time in ideally kept pewter; which was somehow becoming, improving to life, so that one's eyes were held and comforted" (p. 361).

Strether and Maria's speculations are performed in an isolation that make their activity border on solipsism. Consider, for example, their discussion about Mme. de Vionnet before she actually appears on the scene. They have heard that Chad is involved with a mother and daughter pair and, on the basis of that information, of Little Bilham's statement about a "virtuous attachment" and of Chad's transformation, they proceed to conjure up the figures. Their theories are far from the truth. Strether hopes that they are Polish; he assumes in turn that Chad wants to marry the daughter, that the mother is a young widow, that Chad has not yet made up his mind which of the two he prefers, and so on. This is the imagination operating in a vacuum, willfully disregarding information–Strether refuses to hear their name–and freely manipulating the lives of other people.

These speculative sessions of Strether and Maria are dominated by the image of the game, a game that observes strict rules; asking for information, for example, is considered unethical, only deductions from appearances count. The object is to see as fully as possible beyond these appearances, to "see a good deal in it," as they so often say. Its purpose, then, is the cultivation of vision as divination and prophecy. Other characters are eager to join Strether (and Maria) in their important activity: ". . . she had quitted the other room, forsaken the music, dropped out of the play, abandoned, in a word, the stage itself, that she might stand a minute behind the scenes with Strether and so perhaps figure as one of the famous augurs replying, behind the oracle, to the wink of the other" (p. 277). The image of the oracle beautifully suggests not only the development of vision as divination, but also the peculiar power of the observer to influence the central action.

In Strether and Maria's artistic activity, aesthetic considerations outweigh any moral ones. Complexity is of the utmost value and the development of a particularly intricate theory offers the supreme satisfaction. The engagement of Jeanne caused Strether a horror about whose nature we may wonder. Is Strether genuinely concerned for the girl's welfare or is his outrage directed at the new complication in his theory? The announcement of the engagement by Mme. de Vionnet "affected him on the spot as a move in a game" (p. 249), he says.

What Strether does not realize, however, is that the game he plays with Maria is no less serious and no less manipulative than the game of high society. The various dialogues which dominate the novel never lead to a genuine exchange, even less to a consensus of viewpoints. Instead, they are designed to bolster and to shelter Strether himself. Strether is never exposed and hardly ever alone; all the novel's devices are meant to protect him from involvements which might limit his vision, make it less supple, less generous. As James himself says, Strether is "encaged and provided for" through the narrative technique. The narrative encages him in a network of helpers. It traps him, moreover, in a mental world and provides for him the greatest pleasures that that world can afford.

There is real pain in *The Ambassadors* but it is never Strether's. He avoids deep involvement, hides behind the spectacles of the observer in order to escape the possibility of suffering. Strether may plead suffering, may claim that he takes things very hard, but his agonies are unconvincing. Certainly the pain of relinquishing a certain viewpoint is grave but it is of a mental, an intellectual variety. I am not forgetting that Strether loses a great deal, loses three great and admirable women as a result of his changed perspective. I would suggest, however, that Strether calculates his losses, that he never quite relinquishes control of his situation. Mrs. Newsome, perhaps the most powerful fictional character who remains absent from the story, changes quite radically in his estimation and he gives her up consciously. As a result of his experiences in Europe, Strether sees her as a narrow mind who is unable to accommodate her vision to new facts and who cannot admit surprises. She is accused, by Strether and Maria, of the worst possible sin, of having imagined stupidly and ignorantly. Mme de Vionnet is Chad's mistress and Strether's renunciation of any continuing relationship with her is due to a mixture of hopelessness and general fear. Giving up Maria is more complicated. Perhaps he still loves Mme. de Vionnet, perhaps his own puritanical reason is accurate, perhaps he has just been frightened off by the image of experience he witnesses in Paris, by the suffering of Mme. de Vionnet and all that it represents. But, as I have suggested, there is a gain on an intellectual and aesthetic level for every loss on the level of "the lived life."

What Strether does not realize is that someone suffers for him, just as Mme. de Vionnet suffers for Chad. His withdrawal from experience into the imagination is revealed as no less harmful, no less perilous than Chad's actual sexual and emotional involvement.[18] Just as Marie de Vionnet sacrifices herself in favor of Chad and his formation, so Maria initiates Strether into European society, becomes instrumental in the expansion of his vision, but is ultimately left behind. In both relationships we see the "Sacred Fount theory" at work: the growth of one person occurs at the expense of another. James calls Maria "the most unmitigated and abandoned of ficelles," (*Art*, p. 322) and when Strether, during their first talk asks her, "How do we reward you?", Maria prophetically answers, "You don't!" (p. 26).[19] The evolution of their relationship can be illustrated by citing the two references to the unnamed object of Woollett, the first occurring in the first chapter, the second in the last. "In ignorance she could humour her fancy, and that proved a useful freedom" (p. 49); ". . . she not only had no wish to know, but she wouldn't know for the world. She had done with the products of Woollett—for all the good she had got from them" (p. 362). While the first statement reveals the joy of speculation, the second reveals the disappearance of all joy and the real pain, as well as the damage she has incurred during their association.

Strether's self-transcendence is not a reaching out toward another person, toward Maria, but a narcissistic and self-serving expansion of his own mind to the point where he can understand and appreciate both Paris and Woollett. The global vision at which Strether arrives, a vision which on the level of a single mind fuses two disparate cultures, necessitates a great deal of sacrifice and refinement. It entails the service of the physical scene which is co-opted into mental images and it requires the service and sacrifice of other people. Strether may seem timid and retired but he emerges as one of the more powerful and manipulative characters in fiction. His attraction can in fact be attributed to the enormity of an imagination which is both wonderfully creative and monstrous in its ultimate isolation.

James carefully builds up the authority of Strether's personal and often erroneous vision. It does not remain, like that of the narrator of *The Sacred Fount*, isolated and eccentric, but is frequently authenticated by others, if not always by corroboration of fact, then at least by their respect and admiration. Just as Mme. de Vionnet, with Strether's help, builds a precarious but wonderful Chad, so Strether builds a composite and complex image of Paris and the people he encounters there. Through his creative power, his vision actually comes alive and is experienced by others, if only for a short period of time. His vision incurs a number of alterations and it can withstand threats from outsiders who refuse to see as he does:

> Did he live in a false world, a world that had grown simply to suit him, and was his present slight irritation . . . but the alarm of the vain thing menaced by the touch of the real? Was this contribution of the real possibly the mission of the Pococks?—had they come to make the work of observation, as *he* had practised observation, crack and crumble, and to reduce Chad to the plain terms in which honest minds could deal with him? (p. 223)

As his vision achieves the kind of presence that can seduce others, such doubts vanish. His mind may not be "honest" but it is prodigious. When he wonders whether Chad has not told Mme. de Vionnet about Woollett and his family, she answers, "Not as you do. You somehow make me see them—or at least feel them".[20] Strether uses the term "to do" for his descriptions; he "does" people and events for the benefit of others and the response he gets is more than any artist could want: " 'Ah,' returned Chad as they parted, 'you're exciting' " (p. 360). During this final scene Strether confronts Chad with the fullness of his conception of Chad's life and defies him to destroy it.

Perhaps now we can better understand Strether's power over and use of others, as well as the demands of such an education as his.[21] The disoriented stranger is actually capable of imposing a personal order on the society he encounters, and when this precarious order is destroyed, he can develop a vision even broader, more accurate, a vision which is both closer and further separated from life. There is in the creation of such a hero a statement of a tremendous belief in the power of the human imagination; an imagination responsive to reality, but ultimately not responsible to it.

The refinement of Strether's vision to this point entails a solitary existence. Strether's education stops at personal enrichment acquired through the absorption of external reality. It consists of a feeding of the self, often at the expense of other beings. It employs dialogue as its method but is refined beyond any possible exchange. According to James' "Project of Novel," Strether "revises and imaginatively reconstructs, morally reconsiders. . . civilization."[22] Unable to live in the civilizations he encounters, Strether creates an ideal one, different from Paris and Woollett; he demonstrates its nature by means of the refined processes of his mind, but its refinement dooms him to remain its only member.

Strether's personal vision which is able to combine the viewpoints and values of Paris and Woollett is a strong assertion of individuality in the face of the typical and stereotyped social roles into which either society wishes to force him.[23] By insisting on Chad's duty toward Mme. de Vionnet, Strether imposes an American value on the Parisian scene and succeeds in convincing the Parisians of it. Yet by believing in the value of their relationship Strether adopts a Parisian point of view against that of Woollett. The mixture is a personal, moral stance that is proven not to be a livable alternative in Strether's world. Thus Strether, unlike for example the narrator of *The Sacred Fount*, understands what he has missed in life, but he cannot make up for it.

James expands the viewpoint of the self as far as possible in this novel. His world is populated with exceptional characters and the most exceptional of these are enabled, to refine their minds to the point of including two entire cultures. I have said a great deal about the capacities of the individual in this novel, capacities which have included the creation of an autonomous reality, real and believable to others, as well as the ability to cope with a rich, confusing and complex external reality. The educational process portrayed in this novel is profoundly egocentric; the external world becomes the individual's object of consumption. Thus, the two cultures examined can be reduced to abstract mental qualities—America is "the bustling business,. . . the mercantile mandate, the counter, the ledger, the bank, the 'advertising interest,' " Paris, "the charm of civilization"[24]– and Strether's ability to cope is also only mental and therefore necessarily partial. James has carefully fitted the elements of his world to the needs of his characters; it is a world that is severely limited.

Ultimately Strether is a lonely figure. His step toward individuality can only be taken alone and finally, Strether's dialogue is with himself. He is doomed to a habit of self-reflection. As James says, "He sees and understands and such is the force in him of his alien and awkward tradition, that he has, almost like a gasping spectator at a thrilling play, to *see* himself, see and understand."[25]

The form of *The Ambassadors* develops and refines the individual's single vision to a point where it becomes almost perverse, to the edge of solipsism. The central intelligence which makes James' novels so intricate, complex and subtle also takes them beyond the power James hopes so much to give them, the power to serve as a medium of community and exchange. In *The Golden Bowl*, James again tries to institute the "sublime consensus of the educated," this time by expanding the novel's focus, by dividing it between two central consciousnesses which interact and compete.

In the next chapter on Butor's *Passing Time*, we shall see the failure of the Jamesian aesthetic, the defeat of a protagonist who is no longer protected like Lambert Strether. The single vision of Jacques Revel is revealed as insufficient and impotent, as totally incongruous in a world whose center is no longer human. The power of the human imagination becomes the object of nostalgia.

2. *Passing Time:* "Ruins of an Unfinished Building"

James' work, as *The Ambassadors* demonstrates, places the exploration of the cultural realities of Europe and America in the service of a human psychodrama. Ironically, all his attempts at a resolution of cultural differences takes James further and further away from the realities of the societies he explores and lead him deeper into the psychological drama of the human mind. The only reconciliation he can envisage manifests itself on the individual level. The cosmopolitan civilization of which he dreams comes to be defined specifically by an elite of individuals able to effect that "sublime consensus." These characters' highly developed intellects and sensibilities are bought at the expense of "the lived life." Plot and setting are placed in a secondary and instrumental position to character development. Thus, as James suggests, the political, social, sensual and emotional aspects of culture all combine to feed the moral and intellectual ones; these latter alone ultimately interest him. Yet, in a typically Jamesian paradox, their development seems to depend on the diminution of the others. Thus, the international theme is an absolutely essential element of James' work; only the initial cultural differences to be overcome make possible the very special characters able to bridge them. The initial conflict presents the occasion for the characters' self-transcendence.

Yet the intricate fusion Strether develops entails a withdrawal into the individual mind and prevents him from participating in the community James envisioned. Strether's desire for an imagined world is not fully realized, but his imagination has the capacity of adjusting to the world he finds. His reward is a vision more intricate, more subtle, more complex than his initial one. The Europe he leaves is, for the reader, a world influenced, if not shaped, by Strether's miraculous imagination, a world that has been molded by his desire, just as his desire has been molded by it. Chad and Madame de Vionnet are, in part, his creations and they want to live up to his expectations.

In the novel's resolution there is a profound belief in the power of the human imagination to mold reality, yet as we see Strether withdraw from both Paris and Woollett, we understand that the cost of that power is the ability to live. The commitment to vision exceeds the commitment to life, and its costs put James' presuppositions and resolutions into question.

This same commitment to knowledge and understanding characterizes the work of Michel Butor, as well, and he uses a Jamesian phrase in stating it:

> I don't write novels to sell them but to obtain a form of unity in my life; writing is for me a spinal column; and, to reiterate a statement by Henry James: A novelist is "one of the people on whom nothing is lost."[1]

But for Butor and the world he inhabits the methods of knowledge used by James are no longer appropriate. For him the writer's relentless vigilance is necessitated by an increasing complexity and multiplicity which rules our lives and which cannot, at this point, be contained by old fictional and epistemological tools.

Butor, like James, envisages an enlightened society which could understand this multiplicity and alter its myths to accommodate it. In his important essay on Ezra Pound, Butor outlines his goal:

> We must invent new ways of expression in order to be able to master the mental complexity in which we are struggling, these meetings of civilizations in our minds, their contrast, their mixture, to resolve all these problems, to find beyond them the ground, the truth, a reasonable society.[2]

Understanding is the only solution to cultural division and a condition of our participation in our own civilization. Butor conceives it as the writer's duty to serve as a guide in the cultural confusion in which we live. Understanding is not limited to an intellectual elite, since the help of such books as Butor's should make it attainable for everyone. Butor's essays continue to stress the importance of knowing the configuration of our space and the role of the book in charting it. The following statement, in its imperative mode, can be read as a kind of *ars poetica:*

> To grasp all that, to act knowingly in this space, to modify it by this object a book is among the other movable objects, movable *par*

excellence, mobile among the static buildings.[3] *

Butor conceives of the novel, or of the book (his later works can no longer be called novels) as an epistemological tool which should facilitate our apprehension of reality and therefore must be attuned to its complexities. He is a committed realist dedicated to an exploration of reality which can both suggest and contain the chaotic intricacies of the modern world. However this task cannot be accomplished with traditional narrative techniques but rather necessitates formal experimentation:

> Literature . . . comes to appear no longer as simple relaxation or
> luxury, but in its essential role within the social structure, and as a
> form of methodical experimentation.[4]

As a writer, Butor, like James, feels compelled to deal with his culture in its totality, to "fully illuminate the structure of our space."[5]

Although the feelings of division and fragmentation that emerge in the works are undoubtedly similar, Butor's vision of a consensus of cultures is profoundly different from James'. As culture clearly transcends the dimension of the human, new methods of orientation are necessary. Butor's early novels depict the epistemological search of a human subject in a world where he no longer occupies the center, where the Jamesian faith in the power of the human mind has broken down, but where that breakdown has not yet given rise to new epistemological tools.

For Butor, a place is defined, not like James' Paris, by its individuality, but by its manifold relations to other places: "Each place is the home of a sky-line of other places," Butor says. "Today we never live in a unique place; we always have a complicated localization, that is to say that when we are somewhere, we always also think about what might be going on somewhere else, we have some information about the outside."[6] It is this configuration of localities present in each single place that he seeks to understand and illuminate for his reader. The complexity of these geographical interrelations necessitates for him the theme of voyage as a fundamental concern in his work.

---

*Saisir tout cela, agir 'sciemment' dans cet espace, le modifier par cet objet qu'est un livre parmi les autres meubles, 'meuble' par excellence, 'mobile' parmi les immeubles.

Yet in many of Butor's works, as his critics repeatedly emphasize, there is an echo of a past mythical moment in which the world had a center, a human center, in which the human race was unified. The Rome of *La Modification* is potentially such a place, but has lost its unifying capacity in the course of its history. *Description de San Marco* deals in detail with Babel and the moment of division. As Jean Roudaut points out, the theft on which the basilica is based is not only the theft of Marc's body but that of our common pre-Babel language by the Judaeo—Christian God.[7] Modern Venice, a cosmopolitan city which attracts tourists from the whole world, demonstrates the difference between lost unity and a new goal: not the recreation of what has been lost but the creation of a new-found continuity. Here people have found a new cosmopolitan language, although, as the scraps of dialogue that are interspersed through the book demonstrate, it demands new standards of evaluation. An awareness of the composite structure of our civilization, reached in a new literature which aspires to the status of myth, is the only possible compensation for this lost unity: ". . . we have the most urgent need . . . to invent new songs and new tales thanks to which, little by little, our entire tribe could find each other, recognize and know each other."[8] This is a very different version of James' "sublime consensus"; by Jamesian standards Butor's Venice is stereotyped, banal, impersonal. Butor's vision of a multi-cultural community is based on a continued search, on a commitment to knowledge and a necessary vigilance. The sense of urgency that permeates his literary and critical writings comes out of a conviction that our present conceptions of ourselves and our world can only lead to our being submerged and eclipsed by the setting in which we live.[9] Thus, for Butor, it is not a question of transcending cultural difference so as to enrich ourselves, but of a very basic form of orientation, of survival in a world that is no longer and probably never has been anthropocentric.[10]

Passing Time, like *The Ambassadors*, confronts a single individual with the realities of a foreign city. Jacques Revel is a young Frenchman who spends a year training in a British office in the city of Bleston. In his efforts to live in the city, to understand it and his own reactions to it, Revel relies on the Jamesian faith, on the belief that the human imagination—his own and that of the writers and thinkers he consults—can understand, illuminate and master the environment. His belief in depth, meaning, and order is at the basis of novelistic structure: the novel tells human stories, and expresses human needs for order and meaning which, even if a given novel reveals their lack, are still confirmed as values. Revel's own efforts at finding/creating a human order in the chaos of Bleston meet with failure at every step: he is simply playing by the wrong rules. In this chapter, I shall read *Passing Time* in relation to *The Ambassadors* with the aim of exploring the insufficiency of the Jamesian individual-centered novel form in the face of Butor's world and his beginning efforts to replace this form with other modes of orientation.

Both novels immediately present their protagonists' efforts at orientation in a foreign place. Strether is comfortably installed in a Chester hotel. Directed inward, his questions concern an ambivalent attitude toward his friend Waymarsh, complicated feelings toward the European adventure in which he is engaged, as well as the complex meaning Europe holds for him. In an uncomfortable and dirty train compartment, Jacques Revel unenthusiastically and sleepily interrogates the first signs of the strange city in which he is to spend a year. He minutely describes his first steps into Bleston, the feeling of the new ground under his feet, of the new air in his nostrils. Both protagonists feel a great distance from their origin. While for Strether that distance is exhilarating and adventurous, for Revel it constitutes a painful separation from all that is familiar and symbolizes the impossibility of escaping from a city which immediately inspires him with dread and hatred. Strether is initially alone by choice, for the purpose of examining and savoring his feelings. Revel is alone because he missed his train and was not met at the station by his employer. The confusion they both exhibit in these first few scenes has profoundly different sources: Strether feels queer in his new surroundings and does not quite understand his contradictory feelings about his friend Waymarsh; Revel's disorientation is much more basic. Having missed the right train, broken the strap of his suitcase, being half asleep and having nowhere to go in a city whose language he does not master, he has hardly the luxury to examine his feelings and desires. The focus of the beginning chapter of *The Ambassadors* is on Strether, while that of *Passing Time* is on the city whose physical reality usurps his complete attention.

When Strether arrives in Europe he is welcomed and guided by acquaintances, housed in a comfortable hotel, introduced to one pleasure after another. Revel, in contrast, is lost, humiliated, reduced to the status of a laughable and inarticulate figure who, when first seeing a young woman who is to be one of the few people about whom he cares in Bleston, slips on the mud and tumbles down the stairs of the cathedral.

Stylistically, as well, the two first scenes exhibit their protagonists' difficulties. James' first paragraph is abstract, involuted, hypotactic and thus an image of Strether's complicated feelings. An external narrator articulates the intricate details of Strether's every emotion. Revel narrates his own story and his difficulty lies in keeping the different time segments of his stay in Bleston distinct. He must abstract a distant scene from all that has happened since, while still signaling subsequent changes and relating the scene to a contemporary self. The stylistic complexity, then, is due to problems of articulation and orientation and not to the complexity of emotion:

> I realize now that the broad street I had taken on the left was Brown Street; on the map I have bought from Ann Bailey I can retrace all my wanderings of that night; but during those bewildered minutes I did not even look for a name at the street corner, because the inscriptions I longed to see were 'Hotel,' 'Boardinghouse,' 'Bed and Breakfast'—those inscriptions which I have since seen on going past those houses by daylight, in bright enamel letters on first- or second-floor windows, but which were then so completely hidden in the gloom of ine small hours (p. 6).*

The basic message of this sentence is simple: Revel emphasizes that he now knows and notices things that he ignored at the moment of his arrival. Yet his difficulty of keeping time levels separate necessitates a great deal of syntactic involution: relative clauses, participial constructions, all aiming toward clarity but immersing Revel more and more in his murky prose. The pale powerless lights reflected in a myriad of raindrops on a dirty window represent the many possible, fragmented informations and meanings to which Revel is exposed and which he must try to read and to interpret.

Both Lambert Strether and Jacques Revel are confronted with realities that are foreign and therefore disorienting. Whereas Strether concentrates on his moral and intellectual reactions to his new environment, Revel is forced to respond to the concrete physical and sensual reality of Bleston. Whereas Strether's efforts

---

* Je sais maintenant que la grande rue que j'ai prise à gauche, c'est Brown Street; je suis, sur le plan que je viens d'acheter à Ann Bailey, tout mon trajet de cette nuit-là; mais en ces minutes obscures, je n'ai même pas cherché à l'angle les lettres d'un nom, parce que les inscriptions que je désirais lire, c'étaient 'Hôtel,' 'Pension,' 'Bed and Breakfast,' ces inscriptions que j'ai vues depuis, repassant de jour devant ces maisons, éclater en émail sur des vitres au premier ou second étage, alors si bien cachées dans l'ombre de cette heure indue. (p. 12)

are built up and supported by an external narrator, Revel grapples himself with the recording and organization of his own story, a story he begins to write as a means of survival in an environment which threatens to submerge him. Whereas *The Ambassadors* is enclosed in the conventional medium of past-tense narration, *Passing Time* records at every moment the relationship of the past and an ever-changing present which in turn modifies that past. As the titles at the top of each page indicate, the two levels of the novel interact at all times. Revel arrives in October, but only begins writing in May: thus the nature of his quest changes profoundly. At first concentrating merely on survival, he gradually becomes more and more interested in understanding, and realizes finally that understanding is the only possible means of survival.

Facing the first page of *Passing Time* is a map of the city, an aid to organization designed to supplement instruments of cognition which seem to be insufficient: Revel's eyes are always blurred, his ears are unable to understand English. In the society of James' Paris, eyes have a peculiar sharpness, a perspicacity that pierces through appearances to their hidden meanings, to the inner core of the person or thing in their power. The Paris light, moreover, fosters this penetrating vision by revealing the true nature of things. How different is the light of Bleston first encountered in the reflection on a dirty windshield! Incapable of seeing by this opaque light, Revel must learn to see in spite of it, and it is in this effort that his struggle consists. His eyes, since he entered the city, serve only to blind him, his skin is covered by a "layer of mud," and his spirit is contaminated by the apathy of the city:

> I walked through your streets, Bleston, with my eyes veiled by scaly lids, which I have now begun to lift but which are ready to close again because of my fatigue and inattention and your undying cunning.
>
> In me and all around me, in yourself, Bleston, lie hidden count-less sources of mist, so that while I stare at the objects in my room I cannot see them properly; huge obstacles seem to separate me from them, even from this sheet of white paper on which I write, from the very sentence I am writing. (p. 281)*

---

* Je me promenais dans tes rues, Bleston, mes pupilles couvertes par toutes sortes de paupières et d'écailles que je relève maintenant une par une, mais qui à chaque instant risquent de retomber à cause de la fatigue, de l'inattention, de tes ruses qui se survivent.

En moi et tout autour de moi, en toi, Bleston sont tapies d'innombrables sources de brumes, de telle sorte que ces objets mêmes qui peuplent ma chambre et que je regarde, je ne parviens pas à les voir suffisament, que d'immenses obstacles m'en séparent me séparent, même de cette feuille blanche sur laquelle j'écris, de cette phrase même que je suis en train d'écrire. (pp. 270-271)

When all other efforts at a clear vision of his situation and all other attempts at escape from the city fail, Revel begins to write so as to find or to create a light by which one could see and understand. Revel wishes to illuminate and interpret his experience, to find within it and within the city a form of order and significance.

"In its totality as well as in its details, the world is a cipher," says Butor in his essay on Jules Verne.[12] It is as a cipher that Revel regards Bleston and it is by a process of decipherment that he seeks to understand its nature. He begins by sensually examining the city's surface, its air, for example:

> I sniffed the air, I tasted it, knowing I was now condemned to breathe it for a whole year, and I realized it was laden with those insidious fumes which for the past seven months have been choking me, submerging me in that terrible apathy from which I have only just roused myself. (p. 4)[*]

Unlike Strether who works at understanding the spirit of Paris, its moral and intellectual reality, Revel learns to orient himself in the city's physical structure, to discriminate one street from another, to find his way in the complex bus system. He tastes its indigestible food. He painfully learns the language and tries to meet people in order to learn how they live in this city. All these basic attempts to understand the city have the purpose of helping Revel to make his stay endurable, to overcome the inertia he feels almost as soon as he arrives. As he writes about them seven months later, he tries to interpret each one according to a broader vision, as the passage quoted above demonstrates.

The next step is to deepen his knowledge, to try to get beyond the surface of the city. Like Strether, Revel believes that the appearances of the surface must correspond to a deeper significance. In the face of chaotic Bleston, Revel succumbs to our basic need for order and meaning. While Strether merely infers the depth from the appearances of the surface and always prefers to ignore disagreeable truths, Revel conceives of knowledge as archaeology and begins to dig into the layers of Bleston's history. While Strether attributes

---

* Cet air auquel j'étais désormais condamné pour tout un an, je l'ai interrogé par mes narines et ma langue, et j'ai bien senti qu'il contenait ces vapeurs sournoises qui depuis sept mois m'asphyxient, qui avaient réussi à me plonger dans le terrible engourdissement dont je viens de me réveiller. (p. 10)

moral qualities to the surfaces of Paris, equating truth and beauty, Revel discovers concrete depths, the archaeological remnants of Bleston's history, Roman sarcophagi under a modern building. Culture is defined not by mental attributes, but by physical stones. Underlying his activity is a belief in continuity and depth, his own as well as the city's. Every finding must fit into the scheme Revel invents and which he tries to refine on the basis of his observations.

Like Strether, he applies mediators from the realm of art as metaphors to his experience. He begins to see Bleston through the windows of the Old Cathedral, through the tapestries in the museum, and most importantly, through the detective story with The ambiguous title "Le Meurtre de Bleston" ("The Murder of Bleston").* He sees himself as the Theseus and the Oedipus of the museum tapestries, as the Cain of the Cathedral windows; he tries to live the story of "The Murder of Bleston." Like Strether's Lambinet painting, these neat ready-made patterns are more blinding than clarifying. Abortive efforts, they never lead to the truth he seeks, but enmesh him instead in a mazy network of correspondences:

> Through a newspaper poster I had discovered J.C. Hamilton's detective story *The Murder of Bleston*; through reading this I had discovered the Murderer's Window, which in its turn had given rise to this conversation with its closing words of advice to visit the New Cathedral. It was as though a trail had been laid for me, at each stage of which I was allowed to see the end of the next stage, a trail which was to lead me hopelessly astray. (p. 82)**

The above passage is a good example of Revel's tendency to humanize the forces of the city. It is more reassuring for him to assume a malevolent force behind the surfaces of Bleston than no meaningful force at all, more comforting to find a plot against himself than no plot at all.

His writing is both a search for and the creation of such a plot:

---

* I prefer this translation to Jean Stewart's *The Bleston Murder* because it preserves the ambiguity of the French; I have taken the liberty of changing it in her translations.

** Une affiche de journal m'avait mené vers le roman policier de J.C. Hamilton, 'Le Meurtre de Bleston,' et la lecture de celui-ci vers le Vitrail du Meurtrier qui, lui-même, avait provoqué cette conversation dont les derniers mots me conseillaient d'aller vers la Nouvelle Cathédrale; c'était comme une piste tracée à mon intention, une piste où à chaque étape, on me dévoilait le terme de la suivante, une piste pour mieux me perdre. (pp. 81-82)

> Then I decided to write in order to get things straight, to cure my-
> self, to explain to myself what had happened to me in this hateful
> town, to offer some resistance to its evil spell, to shake myself awake
> from the torpor it instilled in me . . . in order not to become like
> those sleepwalkers who passed me in its streets, in order that the
> grime of Bleston should not seep into my blood, into my bones, into
> the lenses of my eyes; I decided to erect around me this rampart of
> writing. (p. 208)*

Revel connects the act of writing with the sun and with the kind of
light which has the capacity to illuminate. He intends to use the
white pages as a filter and a trap. A more powerful flame than the
purely destructive fire of Horace Buck, his writing, "that slow
relentless flame issued from your own innards" (p. 307), has,
according to the detective novel writer's, George Burton's,
definition, the capacity of arriving at a truth which would transform
reality by its acuity. This is how Burton defines the goal of the
detective:

> The aim of his whole existence is that tremendous moment in which
> the power of his explanations, of his disclosure, of the words by
> which he tears off veils and masks, uttered generally in a tone of
> grave melancholy as if to soften the terrible, dazzling light they
> shed, so welcome to those whom it sets free but so cruel, so
> appalling, so blinding too, the power of his speech actually destroys
> the criminal, achieves that death that confirms and crowns his
> work--that moment when reality is transformed and purified by the
> sole power of his keen and accurate vision (p. 153).**

It is toward the transforming power of the detective's revelation
that Revel's journal desperately strives.

The image of alchemy is used by both James and Butor.
Strether's beautiful transforming vision has the capacity to improve

---

* Alors j'ai décidé d'écrire pour m'y retrouver, me guérir pour éclaircir ce qui m'était arrivé dans cette ville haïe, pour résister à son envoûtement, pour me réveiller de cette somnolence . . . pour ne pas devenir semblable à tous ces sommeilleux que je frôlais, pour que la crasse de Bleston ne me teigne pas jusqu'au sang, jusqu'aux os, jusqu'aux cristallins de mes yeux. (p. 199)

* Toute sa vie est tendue vers ce prodigieux moment où l'efficacité de ses explications, de sa révélation, de ces mots par lesquels il dévoile et démasque, prononcés le plus souvent sur un ton solennellement triste comme pour en atténuer le terrible éclat, la lumière dont ils sont chargés, si douce pour ceux qu'elle délivre, mais si cruelle, si consternante, si aveuglante aussi, où l'efficacité de sa parole va jusqu'à l'anéantissement du coupable, jusqu'à cette mort dont il a besoin, . . où il transforme la réalité, la purifie par la seule puissance de sa vision perçante et juste. (p. 147)

on life, though not as much by its truth as by the aesthetic harmony
of its form. Revel too is called on to reorganize the matter of Bleston
with the power of his mind. Tied to the reality of the decidedly non-
harmonious city, his task is much more difficult:

> I see you now, Bleston streets, I see your walls and your inscriptions
> and your faces; in the depths of your seemingly vacant stares I see
> the gleam of a precious raw material from which I can make gold;
> but how deep I must plunge to reach it, what efforts I must make to
> secure and collect all that dust! (p. 281)*

While Strether, after digesting, absorbing, and transforming
the raw material of his perception brings forth a finished artifact,
Revel never completes the process and must forego the satisfaction
of a completed vision.

Passing Time deconstructs the very basis of detective fiction, of
alchemy, and of mythic paradigm—that there is a truth to be
uncovered, that time is sequential and that logic and causality, that a
scientific method, provide valid analytic tools, that analogy and
contrast are significant. Each one of the metaphoric aids used by
Revel seems almost right but eventually emerges as too simple.
Neither the murder plot nor the Theseus or the Cain myths provide
the grid which helps Revel to understand himself in relation to the
city.

In contrast, *The Ambassadors* celebrates the primacy of the
human imagination. Strether is sufficiently detached from the
reality around him to enjoy the freedom of invention and
manipulation. His games reach the point of frivolity. The harmony
of his personal vision is not even destroyed when the truth discredits
its validity; Strether is able to survive several such shocks. Revel's
mistake is that he firmly believes what James so firmly establishes:
the power of the human mind to improve on the real, to infuse it
with meaning. Butor seriously questions this assumption. While
James implies that the scene is mere digestible décor, Butor knows it
is real, perhaps more real than the human phantoms of the city.
While Strether's mental activity is elevated to the status of
adventure and is able to surpass all external difficulties, Revel's

---

* Je vous vois maintenant, rues de Bleston, vos murs, vos inscriptions et vos visages; je vois briller pour moi, au
fond de vos regards apparemment vides, la précieuse matière première avec laquelle je puis faire l'or; mais quelle
plongée pour l'atteindre, et quel effort pour la fixer, la rassembler, toute cette poussière! (p. 271)

speculations remain devoid of any status or credibility. He notices for example, a strange resemblance between Mrs. Jenkins and the statues of the New Cathedral; at the same time, Mrs. Jenkins seems to be very partial to that edifice. Revel, trying as usual to put two and two together, proceeds to call her the daughter of the architect, and even imagines James' perfectly neutral reaction to his "What an astonishing resemblance!" as an encouragement. The structures of Revel's imagination receive no authority in the novel; Revel is the caricature of a Strether. Powerless to give the desired shape even to his own thoughts and words, Revel is certainly not in a position to manipulate events, places or people. His one feeble attempt at manipulation, his betrayal of Burton's identity, his one moment of prestige in the eyes of others, has perhaps the grave result of endangering the life of another. Revel feels helplessly controlled by the events, the city, even his own writing; the participation in his own existence is a struggle: ". . . I am the helpless plaything of a mighty secret power" (p. 144). The image of a swamp gradually enveloping him poignantly dramatizes his lack of control as well as the desperation with which he attempts, day after day, to stop its progress and get the better of the patterns in which he is enmeshed by understanding them:

> . . . to understand myself, before it's too late, before things have taken their course without my will.
>
> I feel all around me the threads of the warp weaving into the weft; soon my hands will be caught up in the cloth and I myself, imprisoned within the loom, unable to find the right lever to change the pattern. (p. 227)*

In James' novels the harmonious forms of the human imagination have the almost magic power if not to ward off then at least to conceal what Maggie Verver calls "the horror of the thing hideously behind." James' characters make patterns, rather than being enmeshed by them. People no longer have this capacity in the work of Butor. The mechanical structuring devices which abound in his works, the twelve chapters representing twelve hours in *Passage de Milan*, for instance, or the alphabetical order of *Mobile*, are perhaps attempts to contain the impending chaos. Butor is too

---

* . . . me comprendre avant qu'il soit trop tard, avant que les choses se soient décidées sans moi. Je sens, tout autour de moi, les fils de la chaine envahir la trame comme une marée; bientôt mes mains seront prises dans cette toile, et moi, tout enfermé dans ce métier, je ne réussis pas à découvrir le levier à mouvoir qui changerait le point. (p. 218)

honest not to recognize the feebleness of these devices, however; they are no more apt to impose an order than the map of Bleston can contain the city. While Strether's intricate imagination creates complexity, Revel tries to control an existing complexity which threatens to crush him.

Revel, unlike Strether, is viscerally tied to the routines of the city and cannot escape even for a moment. His illusions, his theories and speculations either repeatedly knock up against hard facts and are destroyed, like his dreams about Ann and Rose, or else, like his theory about Mrs. Jenkins, they are never corroborated. One disappointment follows another in *Passing Time* and the progressive revelation on which the novel seems to be structured initially quickly becomes a progressive dissolution with Revel's deep investments at stake; the loss of each pattern, the annihilation of each vision causes unending pain, and the dissolution of the identity Revel tries so desperately to construct.

What makes this pain particularly poignant is Revel's exposure in the first-person narration of *Passing Time*. Unlike Strether, he is fully open to the "terribly fluidity of self-revelation" of that form, and no screen mediates his pain and suffering for the reader. Moreover, Butor exposes the conventions of first-person past-tense narration by showing us his narrator at work, by revealing his present life and its influence on the past he is narrating.

Writing takes up time. He becomes more deeply engaged in the project of charting his experience in Bleston and gradually he is forced to cease participating in the life of the city. While Revel returns to his room night after night to write, Lucien goes to see Rose, and James meets Ann. If Revel, like Strether, is unable both to know and to live, it is not because these represent two irreconcilable stances as they do in James, but because Revel literally does not have the time to pursue both. James represents Strether's separation from the immediacy of experience by such metaphors as the theater, the shopwindow, the balcony. It is by the pages he fills with words, by the ever-growing number of words on those pages that Revel is rendered incapable to act.

Writing to stay awake, yet forced to write in the evenings, Revel must combat sleep with every sentence he sets down. The apathy of Bleston is a constant impediment. Limited to only five months of

writing, Revel desperately works against the clock to cover the
twelve months of his stay. His memory, moreover, resembles the city
in its unfathomed depths and labyrinthine structure. Revel's
writing is a "search," an "excavation," and a "dredging"; as much as
a constant fight against the city, it is a struggle against the
inexactness and the distortions of memory. Archaeology functions
in both realms. Since there are initially seven months between the
events he describes and the time of writing, it becomes clear that
subsequent events throw a different light on former ones. His
writing thus requires constant revision and Revel cannot keep up.
Revel is helplessly caught in the structure of progressive revelation
that characterizes the detective story as he comes to experience so
very painfully that "the events that happen to us shed light
progressively on what has led up to them" (p. 291). Since he writes,
rereads his journal and, of course, continues living, the structure of
his journal becomes increasingly chaotic; his sentences which refer
to five different months are more and more difficult to untangle,
and his story becomes more and more complicated. Since he never
stops living, he is unable to gain a retrospective overview and his
corrections must go on endlessly. As Revel progresses with his story,
clarity seems more and more unreachable; the journal comes to
resemble the city:

> The rope of words that uncoils down through the sheaf of papers
> and connects me directly with that moment on the first of May
> when I began to braid it, that rope of words is like Ariadne's thread,
> because I am in a labyrinth, because I am writing in order to find my
> way about in it, all these lines being the marks with which I blaze
> the trail: the labyrinth of my days in Bleston, incomparably more
> bewildering than that of the Cretan palace, since it grows and alters
> even while I explore it. (p. 195)*

Revel's prose is haunting, incantatory, tortured; unsure of
which pattern to follow, ignorant of what may yet emerge in the
future, he attempts to keep track of every moment in case it should
prove significant later on. Still hoping that some meaningful
pattern will emerge, Revel continues, until his last moments in
Bleston, to add to his pile of phrases, to reread, reshuffle the

---

* Le cordon de phrases qui se love dans cette pile et qui me relie directement à ce moment du 1er mai où j'ai
commencé à le tresser, ce cordon de phrases est un fil d'Ariane parce que je suis dans un labyrinthe, parce que
j'écris pour m'y retrouver, toutes ces lignes étant les marques dont je jallone les trajets dejà reconnus, le
labyrinthe de jours à Bleston, incomparablement plus déroutant que le palais de Crète, puisqu'il s'augmente à
mesure que je le parcoure, puisqu'il se déforme à mesure que je l'explore. (p. 187)

information, to try out words and phrases as to their power over the chaos which surrounds him. How far we are from the balance and sanity of James' *Ambassadors* and how far from its synthetic vision! Revel's journal, as he despairingly realizes, is no more than an "exploratory description, the basis for a future interpretation, a future illumination" (p. 275). It remains unfinished. With every sentence, it brings home Revel's incapacity to finish it, his insignificance in the face of the overwhelming task he has taken upon himself.

Even though Butor questions the capacity of the human imagination to impose an order on reality, he deeply shares James' most basic values: the necessity of being awake, the importance of seeing and knowing. Revel's nightly quest for clarity may be a poor substitute for loving Ann and Rose, may cost constant pain and sacrifice, but it is a necessary and heroic stance in a modern world which threatens to overtake us unawares. For Butor, even more than for James, reflection is more crucial than action.

The difficulties Revel encounters make his search all the more necessary, his sacrifice all the more unavoidable. Yet while Strether's sacrifice of an active participation in life is rewarded by knowledge and discrimination, by personal growth and the transcendence of his own limitations, Revel's search results in his dissolution: at the end of the novel, Revel is a phantom. Out of that human debris, out of the fragments of many plots and the abortive efforts to live and to create a human story, there emerges an order after all, but it is no longer a human one.

What begins as Revel's personal diary-memoir, in fact, gradually turns into a portrait of the city and, that being its only possible coherence, it comes to eclipse its author. Revel's realization of this is the most moving passage in the novel:

> ... gradually, through the cracks that my words make, my own face is revealed in its coating of thick grime, my own face being gradually cleansed by my misfortunes and my stubbornness, and yours behind it, Bleston, your face ravaged with inner conflict; and yours will shine through more and more clearly, until nothing can be seen of me but the glitter of eyes and teeth, while yours is consumed at last in an amplified incandescence. (p. 287)*

---

* ... pour me révéler peu à peu, au travers de toutes ces craquelures que sont mes phrases, mon propre visage perdu dans une gangue de suie boueuse, mon propre visage dont mes malheurs et mon acharnement lavent peu à peu le noyau de quartz hyalin, mon propre visage et le tien derrière lui Bleston, le tien miné de guerre intime, le tien qui transparaîtra de plus en plus fortement, au point que l'on ne distinguera plus pour ainsi dire, de moi-même, que le brillement des iris autour des pupilles, et celui des dents autour de la langue, le tien se consumant enfin dans son incandescence amplifiée. (pp. 276-277)

Perhaps Revel's greatest illusion concerns the nature of his writing. Imagining it first as a means to uncover the hidden meaning of his own experience, then as a letter to Ann, he is forced to recognize that it is a document of the city, dedicated to and dominated by Bleston. It is not a human story. The art works and the myths which seemed metaphors of Revel's experience are revealed instead as mediators to the truth of the city: ". . . the Museum tapestries, those great illustrative panels woven of wool and silk, of silver and gold, which have so often provided me with terms of reference for understanding you, Bleston, whose trees have enabled me to discover some of your trees, whose seasons have revealed your seasons" (p. 305)* There is in *Passing Time* no human character who can represent the city as Mme. de Vionnet represents Paris, although Revel, in calling Ann and Rose, Ariadne and Phaedra, would have liked to attribute similar roles to them. Bleston is not defined by its inhabitants, as Paris is; its walls and stones, its rivers and parks, its monuments alone are lasting and vital. Far from being able to affect the city, the people are subdued and shaped by its phenomena. Whereas Paris enhances both Chad and Strether, Bleston diminishes its inhabitants:

> . . . the wind that whipped up accomplice clouds of dust and sent the people scurrying as though in midwinter, sent the meager un-smiling men and women, . . . back to the homes where a precarious peace awaited them, peace painfully acquired at the cost of relent-less efforts, great stubbornness and patience, long attrition, with so much renounced and rejected, so much buried, besmirched and betrayed, so many humiliations endured, so many needs unful-filled, so many vital secrets lost, so much forgotten. (p. 127)*

The city is no longer a feature in a human story, a monster in a human myth. Bleston is its acidic air, its cold wind, its persistent rain. It is, in fact, no more than its unfathomable size, its repetitive streets and interchangeable buildings, its labyrinthine bus system and dirty river, its moving fairs and perpetually grey sky, its unpalatable food and dirty-looking beer. In a sense, Bleston

---

* . . . les tapisseries du Musée, les grandes illustrations de laine, de soie, d'argent et d'or, qui m'ont si souvent servi de termes de référence dans ton déchiffrage, Bleston, dont les arbres m'ont fait découvrir certains de tes arbres, et les saisons voir tes saisons. (p. 295)

** . . . le vent qui levait des armées complices de poussière, et qui chassait, pressés comme au coeur de l'hiver, toutes ces femmes sans hanches, tous ces hommes sans épaules et sans sourire,... qui les chassait vers leurs maisons, médiocres fours où cuit pour eux le pain d'une tranquillité précaire, péniblement acquise à grand acharnement, à grande résistance et patience, à grande usure, à grands renoncements . . . à grands secrets perdus, à grands oublis. (pp. 122-123)

requires a vision as broad and generous as Paris, a vision that would go beyond the hatred of George Burton and Horace Buck, a vision that would be content with the realities of the city and willing to sacrifice a humanly imposed poetry for them. While for Strether the enigma of Paris resembles that of a human being and its enticement is the erotic lure of a mysterious and beautiful woman, Bleston's complexity does not warrant the terms enigma and mystery. Only Revel's hate endows it with human characteristics. In itself, Bleston is merely physically disordered and complex, and therein lies its attraction: it demands to be charted.

A persistent questioner like Revel is forced into a recognition of the city's multiplicity, its concreteness and lack of poetry. Bleston is neither Bellista nor Bell's town. It is not a mythic monster as Revel would have it, but a wall whose crack is yet incapable of destroying it, a new department store which symbolizes its vitality, the flawed New Cathedral. Revel's initial hatred is as blinding as Strether's idealization. The truth of Bleston is morally neutral and the city defends itself against a false humanizing vision; it refuses to be mythicized and mystified. In its speech to him, the city reminds Revel of its power and resilience.

Revel's function is not, as he thinks, to forge an elaborate revenge on George Burton, but to give expression to the city's intricate complexity. The various patterns he follows are not foils but proofs of the city's organic life which Revel, in his many ramblings, re-enacts:

> I went to look once more at the tortoise, which was as huge compared to the living tortoise I had seen the previous Sunday in Pleasance Gardens as was the latter compared to the one I had drawn on my copy of *The Murder of Bleston*, and yet small compared to that tortoise which I had determined to go and look at next day, that monstrous, carnivorous tortoise in the third tapestry of the Museum. (p. 158)*

---

* Je suis allé voir la tortue-luth énorme par rapport à la tortue vivante que j'avais vue le dimanche précédant à Plaisance Gardens, comme celle-ci était énorme par rapport à celle que j'avais dessinée sur l'exemplaire du 'Meurtre de de Bleston' . . . mais petite elle aussi par rapport à cette tortue que j'avais décidée d'aller revoir le lendemain, monstrueuse et carnassière, dans la troisième tapisserie du Musée. (p. 152)

In tracing the relations between these four turtles, Revel is not on the track of some deeper meaning, as he would like, but reveals the city as the living organism that it is. As the instrument of the city's revelation, Revel becomes its Prince; more than "reveil" or "lever," it is his function as "révélateur" that his name announces.

Although they are both observers, Revel participates much more concretely than Strether in the life of the city. Strether's participation remains vicarious and intellectual. Revel becomes involved in the city's very structure. He enacts Bleston's disorder, or its particular kind of order, in his endless ramblings through the city's streets, restaurants and fairs, in his penetration of its multiple layers, in his nightly progress through his labyrinthine journal. Revel's bodily itinerary reveals the city's multiple phenomena. Initially that itinerary tried to order them by relying on certain focal points, the cathedrals, the museum, the fairs and the Chinese restaurants. More and more, these focal points dissolve and each pattern emerges as no more valid than each other one. Arnold Weinstein's valid observation could be used to distinguish Revel from Strether: "It is not a question of imposing a form, but rather, of living it."[13] Revel's persistent suffering attunes him to the city's lament, to its unglamorous truth.

Moreover, Revel participates in the crime that is said to underlie the city; in fact, just as he is "killed" by that crime, the record of the city is born. The cries that recur throughout Revel's stay and to which he attributes so much importance are not false leads; rather, Revel misreads their meaning, as he does with the myths and monuments. Their significance lies in their influence not on the action but on the journal's form, which, in turn, uncovers the form of the city. Thus the crimes, so difficult to acknowledge and confess, are focal points to which he returns repeatedly throughout his journal. The burning of ticket and map, acts so embarrassing, shameful and incomprehensible to Revel, actually provide the impulse for the diary. His more serious crime of revealing Burton's name actually determines the diary's shape, since Revel's frequent re-examinations of this act profoundly upset the meticulous chronology the journal is meant to have. The agony of guilt and confusion that is the result of this mysterious act more and more enables Revel to understand the spirit of the city.

Unlike James' Paris, Bleston is not an individual or unique city. All identity is relational in *Passing Time*; multiplicity and repetition rule: there are two cathedrals, two maps, three railroad stations, three Chinese restaurants, twelve fairs, three copies of Burton's novel, two Bailey daughters and even two young Frenchmen. Personality is fluid; events are foreshadowed, repeated, related. Thus the burning and the betrayal of Burton's name take place twice. Just as within the city nothing exists as a unique phenomenon–everything is but the reverberation of something else – so the city itself echoes the other places which appear in its museum movies, and books. Only a vision which elucidates these relationships and interconnections is a valid one, since it reveals, as well, the city's own lack of uniqueness. As a stranger, Revel is privileged not only in that he is able to view the city objectively, but, free from specific geographical ties, he also personally enacts the interconnection of one city to another. It takes numerous weekly visits to the documentary theatre for Revel to realize that the films provide not an escape from Bleston but a possibility of comparing it to Rome, Athens, Timgad, Petra. The configuration of cities, blessed and damned, which of old formed the subject of the windows of the Old Cathedral and thus elucidated Bleston's relation to the outside world, was destroyed. Another anonymous French artist, another privileged stranger, must reconstruct it:

> At the News Theatre on Monday night, while I was watching that poor documentary about Sicily, the two series of cities and periods portrayed in those two great hieroglyphs of yours, Bleston, were interwoven in my mind's eye, those two series of cities and periods which still live on here, painfully, stifled, mutilated, falsified, pursuing within you, Bleston, within each one of your inhabitants, within each of your street corners, in darkness, their wars and their misunderstandings, those two series of traditions, of translations, interwoven against the blue Sicilian sky behind which I sensed the dawning of a miraculous glow, the red of your inner-most fires. (p. 306)*

Repetition is valued in *Passing Time*. As the New Cathedral is an aesthetically inferior copy of the old, being ugly, crude, unharmonious and yet so vibrant and alive that it symbolizes the

---

* Au Théatre de Nouvelles lundi soir, comme je regardais ce mauvais documentaire sur la Sicile, s'enlaçaient à l'intérieur de ma vision les deux séries de villes et de périodes dont témoignent tes deux grands hiéroglyphes, Bleston, séries de villes et de périodes qui se survivent en toi douloureusement, étouffées, démembrées, falsifiées, qui poursuivent en toi, en chacun de tes habitants, en chacun de tes coins de rues, en pleine obscurité, leurs guerres et leurs méprises, ces deux séries de traditions et traductions devant le bleu de ciel sicilien au coeur duquel je sentais poindre le rouge prodigieux de tes plus intimes braises. (p. 295-96)

present life of the city, so Bleston is an inadequate and distorted
version of Rome or Athens, while yet being vital and permanent.
Revel's comparisons are neither pursued nor synthesized. The
analogies which haunt him are not significant; they are merely there.
His achievement is not a harmonious vision, like Strether's, but
accepting the city for what it is. To reveal the city as an organism in
itself and as a part in a larger organism is Revel's accomplishment. In
a passage which echoes the novel's first paragraph about the
powerless lights, we realize how far Revel has come in his ability to
see:

> But if last week's picture influenced my impression of today's, this
> one in turn transformed the earlier in retrospect: Flavian's amphi-
> theater, the Baths of Caracalla, the Pantheon and the Palatine ruins
> appeared to me through their Athenian echo . . . as the source of
> some gigantic resonance, just as a flame encircled by mirrors is
> multiplied into countless images of itself, casting back its heat and
> increasing the incandescence. (p. 251)*

In this passage Revel realizes the advantage of a multiple vision,
the only vision able to account for the complexity of a city such as
Bleston and for its non-unique inhabitants.

Both *The Ambassadors* and *Passing Time* end in the apparent
personal defeat and renunciation of their protagonists. When all is
counted, however, Strether leaves Europe greatly enriched by an
exhilarating though painful experience. How ironic is his final
statement, that he leaves without having gotten anything for
himself, yet how well it applies to Revel. Strether, the person, is
sacrificed to the intergrity of *The Ambassadors* insofar as his
knowledge excludes the possibility of living. Yet his knowledge,
unlike Revel's, leads to personal growth and expansion. While
Strether's vision of Paris is intensely personal and depends for its
persuasiveness on his own presence, Revel's vision of Bleston is
entirely stripped of individuality. One man's vision no longer
suffices to account for an entire city; herein lies the failure of
Burton: he is too personal, too idiosyncratic. The ordeals imposed
on Revel strip him of personal characteristics and render him

---

* Mais si la séance d'il y a huit jours influait sur ma vision d'hier, celle-ci à son tour a transformé
rétrospectivement la première, parce que l'Amphithéatre Flavien, Les Termes de Caracalla, le Panthéon et les
Ruines du Palatin me sont apparus au travers de leurs écho dans Athènes . . . comme le foyer d'une gigantesque
résonance, telle une flamme qui se multiplie dans une enceinte de miroirs en quantité d'images d'elle-même, dont
la chaleur lui est renvoyée de telle sorte que l'incandescence augmente. (p. 241)

anonymous. While Strether digests Paris, it is Revel who is "had" in *Passing Time*. He is no more than a lens, a vehicle for the city's expression, no longer a polished mirror. Strether leaves Paris as a much richer human being, Revel leaves as a phantom. With each loss, he comes closer to his effacement; reaching it, however, is not a loss but a victory:

> And so I thank you, Bleston, for taking such cruel and blatant re-
> venge on me; . . . I shall still be prince over you since, by acknow-
> ledging my defeat, I have managed to survive (as you secretly wished
> me to) the fate you had in store for me, I have not been engulfed;
> and now, having endured the ordeal of your fury, I have become
> invulnerable, like a ghost; I have won from you this offer of a pact,
> which I accept. (p. 272)*

Paradoxically, Revel's anonymity is part of a larger function. Revel becomes the artist "on whom nothing is lost." Instead of culminating in a satisfying vision, however, his journal is so disordered, his task is so much greater than the possibility of ever fulfilling it, that his personal sacrifice often seems useless: "Now that everything has crumbled about me I have nothing left but this pitiful accumulation of futile phrases, like the ruins of an unfinished building, the partial cause of my downfall, incapable of sheltering me against the torrential, sulphurous rain . . . (p. 262).** In the journal's openness, however, lies Revel's redemption. In the disorder lies the density of a life and the fullness of a city for us to discover and explore. Butor has categorically rejected the identification of art with harmony, order and completion, as he emphasizes in his essay "Babel en creux":

> Any finished, full, closed book is thus a mask, a façade; the true
> book is by necessity itself ruin, decay, discoverer; what the poet
> proposes can only be a set of fragments diverging from one another,
> and revealing in the spaces between them all that they themselves
> could not say.[14]

---

* C'est pourquoi je te remercie de t'être si cruellement, si évidemment vengé de moi, ville de Bleston . . . dont je demeurerai l'un des princes puisque j'ai réussi, en reconnaissant ma défaite, à exaucer ton désir secret de me voir survivre à cette sorte de mort que tu m'avais réservée, puisque je suis devenu maintenant, par ce baptême de ta fureur, invulnérable à la manière des fantômes, puisqye j'ai obtenu de toi cette proposition de pacte que j'accepte. (p. 261)

** Il ne me reste plus dans cet éffondrement que ce dérisoire amoncellement de phrases vaines, semblable aux ruines d'un edifice inachevé, en partie cause de ma perte, incapable de me servir comme refuge contre la torrentielle pluie sulphureuse. (p. 252)

As one individual no longer possesses the power to complete a vision, he relies on others to help him do so. Thus Revel discovers his own potential social usefulness. His redemption lies in his service to a larger community, to the people of Bleston, who often seem to look at him with expectant eyes:

> I stare through the night, . . . the faces of people hurrying homeward muttering or chattering; and when I pass beside them a few scraps of their talk reaches me, and I clutch it like precious ore, although most of the time it is so terribly impenetrable to me, Bleston, that I feel far better able to interpret the sign I read between those two bricks on a cracked wall; that is the message by means of which I can wear down your carapace, Bleston, that slow relentless flame issuing from your own innards, and which gradually will arouse reflections and echoes in the eyes of these passers-by, gaining strength from such resonance. (p. 307)*

The Ambassadors builds up Strether's authority through dialogue and exchange. Strether's speculations are authenticated by the participation of his friends, protected by the participation of the narrator. *Passing Time,* even as it reveals multiplicity and repetition, has a most solitary and isolated prot gonist. The repetition on which the novel is structured only und rscores the loneliness of Revel's quest for awareness. By sitting do n to write, however, Revel engages in a network much more far-reaching than Strether's, one that surpasses the limit of several individuals. Revel becomes a mere pronoun and conforms to Butor's new definition of the individual, "a function occurring in a mental and social space, in a context of dialogue."[15] James' elitism no longer defines culture. Butor's definition of culture rests on its plurality and its multiplicity, he searches for forms which can express this. He admits to being "fascinated by the plural. It is not the singular which is primary for me, it's not the individual, it is the plural, and it is within the plurality that the singular will somehow be condensed."[16] Through his self-effacement, Revel becomes an element in that plurality and relinquishes any pretense to uniqueness. The sacrifice of his individuality is a condition for his ability to envision the immense setting.

---

* . . . je regarde dans la nuit de plus en plus noire . . . ces visages qui se hâtent vers leurs abris en marmonnant ou conversant; et quand je passe auprès d'eux, quelques bribes de leurs paroles m'atteignent que j'accueille comme un minerai précieux, mais qui sont si terriblement opaques la plupart du temps, Bleston, que je me sens bien plus capable d'interpréter le signe qui s'inscrit dans la succession de deux briques sur un mur lézardé, Bleston dont je ronge la carapace par cette écriture, par cette lente flamme acharnée issue de tes propres entrailles, cette flamme qui peu à peu, se reflètera, se réveillera dans leurs yeux, s'affermira par cette résonance. (p. 296)

Both James and Butor consider reflection and knowledge supreme values. In James' novels, reflection is a stance that is chosen over action. In Butor reflection is a necessity; a lack of insight is presented as fatal. The only worthwhile human endeavor is the search for an awareness that can be shared with others. Knowledge is no longer limited to self-exploration; it must be offered to the community.[17]

James is interested in psychological depth and in exploring the human richness made possible by the interaction of insightful people and their human cultures. Butor believes that to survive we need a different kind of knowledge, that we need to understand not only the human, but also the physical, the material, historical, political side of culture; we need to take into account all that defines and determines the human. Revel must understand why the people of Bleston are no more than human shells and must communicate his understanding to them. That learning process demands that he become a phantom like they and, more than that, that he reveal through his own suffering, the costs and pains as well as the benefits of relinquishing the belief in human centrality.

Passing Time is itself as open as Revel's journal. Accustomed to books which are synthesized and patterns which are fulfilled, and suffering from as urgent a need for meaning as Revel, the reader follows all his leads and is as expectant and disappointed as he is. We see beyond Revel only on a few limited occasions: we recognize the black Morris as James' and are quicker at discovering the romances. Basically, however, we re-enact Revel's itinerary through the city in following the labyrinthine order of the novel. We fall for every false lead, continually expect the information to coalesce and are forever frustrated. The reader's false expectations form an intricate part of the novel, as does the reader's education.[18]

There is, at the basis of Butor's work, a structural analogy between text and world: the reader stands in relation to the text, as each individual stands in relation to the world. Herein lies Butor's realism, and, unlike that of his contemporaries, his work is consciously representational: his is not as much a mimetic as an analogical realism.[19] To learn to make sense of the complex structures of Butor's texts is to learn to cope with the plurality and fragmentation of our world. In following, for example, Jacques Revel's itinerary through Bleston's museum as he deciphers the Theseus tapestries, identifying within the eighteen "portes de laines" the place of Theseus in the streets of Athens, his own place in the rooms of the museum, and the relation of those rooms to the streets of Bleston which are visible through the windows, we become conscious of the place of the book in our own room, the relation of that room to the streets of our own city and so on. The boundaries between text and world disappear in the struggle for orientation which is analogous for the reader of *Passing Time* and the inhabitant of Athens or Bleston.

Passing Time itself immerses the reader in the emotional reality of events long before he knows their origin or significance. Like Revel with Theseus, the reader is thus forced to puzzle out identities and actions unaided. Rose and the Burtons, for example, are repeatedly mentioned before we find out who they are and how Revel met them. This device is particularly exploited with Lucien; the description of his arrival in Bleston is delayed until the last pages of the novel and succeeds by months the relation of Lucien's effects on Revel's life. Butor stresses this device as a development of James' point of view technique in his essay on Faulkner's *The Bear*, a development which is in the service of realism:

> The reader always has to be on the inside, that is, he must always be treated as belonging himself to this story which is being revealed. The facts must as much as possible appear to him as they appear to the characters who are inside the work. . . . This deepening of the Jamesian notion of point of view represents a remarkable conquest as far as realism in the novel is concerned.[20]

It is perhaps in its prospective structure, that is, in its anticipation of an extensive involvement, a completion on the part of the reader, that *Passing Time* more than *The Ambassadors* works toward communication and toward a community that is the result of a common quest for knowledge. No synthesis is handed to the reader; there is no "ficelle" who elucidates the novel's mysteries. The international and the epistemological aspects of the novel are identical here, for only understanding can bridge the barrier of culture, can assure our control over our own lives. In experiencing himself the discontinuity of information and participating in the struggle of putting the fragments together, the reader is forced into the acceptance of an uncomfortable truth: the limited capacity and significance of the individual in the midst of a configuration of cultures no longer defined by him. The definition of the new place of the human in this civilization demands our participation.

Thanks to the sacrifice of the novel's central subject, we are able to learn his lesson, to reliquish the myopic structure of self in favor of a new community where the human is but one in a multiplicity of elements. While *Passing Time*, especially in comparison to as strongly an individual novel as *The Ambassadors*, enacts the tremendous pain of losing our uniqueness and individuality, it announces the liberation that follows the loss.

In both *The Ambassadors* and *Passing Time*, the commitment to vision entails a sacrifice of life; the single individual is incapable of combining both. Both Strether and Revel's ultimate loyalty is no longer to themselves but to an order larger and more significant, a vision that transcends individual dimensions. In James, this vision is achieved by and to the benefit of the single individual, while in Butor it arises as a result of his disappearance. Both novels, however, demonstrate the limitations and shortcomings of the single vision in the face of a complex and alien world. Both take us to the limits of the novel form. The novel cannot become the epistemological tool Butor needs: the novel is the account of a human story and with the disappearance of human stories, the novel is no longer appropriate.

The following two chapters explore attempts to expand the novel's focus beyond the single vision to the double vision of *The Golden Bowl* and the multiple vision of *Speculations about Jakob*.

II. INTERACTION

3. *The Golden Bowl:*

"That Strange Accepted Finality of Relation"

A chapter on *The Golden Bowl* in a study devoted to the international aspect of James' work may raise some eyebrows. Traditionally this novel is viewed as poetic and even allegorical; the cultural conflict certainly seems to be subordinated to the moral and psychological one and, more importantly, to formal experimentation and innovation. Not only does *The Golden Bowl* deemphasize the importance of its setting more than most other James novels, but it also has minimized all the superficial international differences on which earlier works had been based. Moreover, it has moved further into the intricacies of the human mind than even *The Ambassadors.* Although James characterizes his late work as a "personal drama," the "dauntless fusions" of *The Golden Bowl* are still fed by the moral differences between American and European culture and propose, through the marriage of its protagonists, a resolution of those differences.

James divides his novel's center of consciousness into two separate minds, each of which is defined through its relation to the other, and thus creates the binary structure that is most perfectly suited to the personal and cultural drama that is played out in his entire work: the conflict between Europe and America. Book I of *The Golden Bowl* is devoted to the reaction of Amerigo, the Italian Prince, from the time which immediately precedes his marriage to the American Maggie Verver, while Book II consists of Maggie's thoughts starting at the moment when she, unconsciously at first, begins to suspect her husband's fidelity. Thus, *The Golden Bowl* is not based on an experiential *donnée;* its only reality lies in the visions and interpretations of its two protagonists. Their competing perspectives, moreover, represent two disparate cultural and moral codes. In the confrontation of Maggie and Amerigo, we have at each point, the confrontation of the new world and the old.

Divided into two points of view, the novel's impulse is toward their interaction, toward the marriage of two people and two cultures. The perspectivistic structure of *The Golden Bowl* makes it a formal statement of division and a formal attempt to resolve that division. Only in such overly structured, excessively symmetrical terms, could the dream of the transcendence of cultural division begin to be put into effect: hence the novel's compositional intricacy.

It is precisely in such formal terms that James speaks of his characters in the novel's preface, stressing another important difference between *The Golden Bowl* and his earlier novels. He considers it not only an ingenious, but also an economic move to have made the involved participants in the drama his centers of consciousness, rather than using the uninvolved observer of his previous works. It is as if, in his image of the great circus arena of art, the author himself were to "rub shoulders" with the participants of the great struggle, thereby providing for the spectators an even greater entertainment. James reflects on the novel's structure in the mercantile terminology that is so prevalent in his writings; he has practised condensation and reduction, has used the fewest possible elements and has yet managed to achieve a great deal. "That was my problem, so to speak, and my *gageure*–to play the small handful of values really for all they were worth."[1] For the purposes of economy, the characters must do double duty:

> . . . the Princess, in fine, in addition to feeling everything she has to, and to playing her part just in that proportion, duplicates, as it were, her value and becomes a compositional resource of the finest, order, as well as a value intrinsic. (*Art*, p. 329)

In "The Jamesian Lie," Leo Bersani expresses shock at this apparent disrespect and exploitation of character. Calling *The Golden Bowl* a model of structuralism, Bersani declares that structural and compositional concerns are the only important ones since not the substance by the relations of the novel's different forms are of primary value.[2] James may reaffirm, however "the moral of the endless interest, endless worth for 'delight' of the compositional contribution" (*Art*, p. 329), and yet be interested in his characters and in the struggle they enact.

The American, *The Europeans* and *Lady Barbarina* are all thematic investigations of the possibility of intermarriage, but all three are failures at resolution. In *The Golden Bowl* the theme of marriage is translated onto a formal level. Through the dual point of view, the novel explores the psychological and moral reality of intermarriage, as well as the differences in outlook that must be overcome. Only in formal terms could the dream of a consensus begin to be put into effect. Yet it can be realized only if the forms of marriage, the novel's dual perspective, are invested with the substance of marriage, with spiritual and sexual communion of its two protagonists. I shall argue that though James poses the problem in formal terms, his attempt to resolve it far transcends the compositional play of the autonomous artist.

Lambert Strether can create an image of Paris and Mme. de Vionnet in his mind and he is able to sustain and refine that image after extensive contact with the actuality of Paris and Mme. de Vionnet. Strether is responsible to the city as well as to the "requirements of his imagination," but, in the confrontation, the imagination is ultimately enriched. As Strether leaves, his vision is spared the final test of an interaction with either Paris, Madame de Vionnet or Maria Gostrey. Maggie and Amerigo, in contrast, are continually responsible and answerable to each other; their visions - disparate as they are - are repeatedly tested against one another. As the two characters face each other at the end of the novel, it is clear that their imaginative visions cannot remain autonomous if the marriage is to go beyond formal alliance to true intimacy. Strether's withdrawal is no longer possible.

In the second part of his preface, James describes his efforts to find illustrations for the novel, i.e., concrete representations of his projected images. This section culminates in two complementary, but not contradictory visions of the artist. Though the small shop in Bloomsbury Street and Portland Place, as well as the novel's other settings, were "of the mind, of the author's projected world" (*Art*, p. 334), James and his companion managed, after long ramblings in London, to find suitable, even wonderful correspondences. To the artist as independent creator, James opposes the image of the artist as one whose business it is "not to 'create' but simply to recognize - recognize, that is, with the last fineness" (*Art*, p. 335), to meet the "prodigious city" halfway. The requirements of successful art, James insists, is that it be an "answer" to what Flaubert calls "the conditions of life" (*Art*, p. 347), that it remain within those conditions, for therein lie its rewards. It is this balance of creating and finding that I see in *The Golden Bowl* as a whole. The transcendence of the single vision of *The Ambassadors* gives *The Golden Bowl* a greater possibility of effecting a community of cultures based on discovery and knowledge.

In its attempt to put the dream of a "sublime consensus" into effect, *The Golden Bowl* represents James' determination to supersede his other international works, to redress all errors, eliminate all imperfections, reconcile all irreconcilables. Its characters are given every possible chance to make it, so free are they of the handicaps that beset the earlier figures. Maggie and Amerigo have Strether's prodigious imagination without his incapacity to live. Can they use their imagination in the service of life?

As reflectors, Maggie and Amerigo are the epitome of refinement and subtlety. They have the added advantage, as we have seen, of being actors as well as reflectors and thus they are even richer and more deeply implicated in the novel's structure. As representatives of their respective cultures, Maggie and the Prince are not typical Americans and Europeans, like Christopher Newman or Isabel Archer, Lord Warburton or Mme. de Vionnet; instead they represent the very finest each of these cultures can produce. In fact, both Maggie and Amerigo have relinquished their personal to their cultural character; they seem to exist solely as the most refined specimens of their race.

Whereas Gilbert Osmond looked like an Italian Prince and could never forgive fate for not having made him a nobleman, Amerigo is a real prince and, in marrying him, Maggie becomes the princess Milly Theale only resembles. Isabel Archer had a "handsome fortune" but Maggie is "fabulously rich," the Ververs' wealth reaches "mythic proportions." In this fairy tale-novel, James has made it a point to make the real match up to the "requirements of the imagination," thereby truly making it possible for his characters to live.

To facilitate the cultural fusion to which the novel aspires, *The Golden Bowl* is set in London. Anglo-Saxon London is foreign to the Prince; he is cut off from his family and his past there. Yet Maggie cannot feel at home in England either; the amusements of the Castledeans are even more foreign to her than to Amerigo, but as a supremely cosmopolitan city (we see in London people of various nationalities, Americans, Jewish shopkeepers, foreign dignitaries at the Embassy ball), London perhaps provides the most suitably neutral ground for the "sublime consensus of the educated," the cosmopolitan society James hopes to create. When one compares the London of *The Golden Bowl* to the Paris of *The Ambassadors*, one is struck by the minor role the setting occupies in *The Golden Bowl*. While the character of Paris and that of Mme. de Vionnet were inextricably linked, that of London has little effect on the uprooted figures of *The Golden Bowl*. It gives them an opportunity to come together and to express themselves, but it does not directly influence them. Charlotte, by the force of her will, should be able to shine in American City as much as she did in Matcham and London. Cultural fusion no longer means the individual's acclimatization to a particular place, as it does in *Lady Barbarina*, for example. It means, rather, a convergence of different visions.

The epitome of polish and civilization, the Prince is presented a a "real galantuomo"; there is nothing about him that is not genuine. To the natural Ververs he opposes the refinement of his history: "I'm like a chicken, at best, chopped up and smothered in sauce; cooked down as *crème de volaille*, with half of the parts left out. Your father's the natural fowl running about the *bassecour*" (p. 4).[3] It is the public history of the Prince that primarily defines him and that attracts Maggie. She freely admits that without his "annals, archives and infamies," without the history which so "sticks out of" him, she would never have thought of him. He is for her a curiosity, a "representative precious object." Maggie, on the other hand, fascinates the Prince because of her innocence and her imagination, what he calls the "American romantic disposition." As deeply suffused with his race as he is, the Prince is tired of its moral ugliness. He considers his marriage a "desire for some new history that should, so far as possible contradict, and even if need be, flatly dishonour, the old" (p. 10). He wants to be infused with a new spirit. Desiring to cultivate his humility and to resemble his namesake and ancestor Amerigo, he goes out to forge his own history. The match is ideal, especially since the Ververs' money will enable the Prince truly to shine (he thinks of it as "exquisite coloring drops" which Maggie scatters into his element), just as the Prince's title and his aristocratic manners will give the Ververs the outward appearance of refinement which is a necessary complement to their money.

And yet, as the Prince recognizes during the first scenes of the novel, their dispositions are alien to each other and their union involves great risks. The Prince really does not understand the

Ververs. Faced with them as the historic Amerigo was faced with a huge unknown continent, he sees a white veil, "a dazzling curtain of light" (p. 14), impossible to interpret.[4] Feeling himself lacking in what he calls "the moral sense," one he supposes particularly strong in the Americans, the Prince does not know what is expected of him by his new family. It is significant that he thinks of himself as an antique embossed coin of unknown value. He is afraid of being put to the test and of having to expose his component parts. It is perhaps the Verver's excessively financial outlook that worries him, as well as the financial character of their marriage. Do they know exactly what they have bought when they bought him, and what do they think they have spent such a great deal of money for?

Not by accident is it the Prince who serves as the center of consciousness of the first book. He is extremely aware of the problems involved in such a marriage; he is curious and interested in American values and desires to be enriched by acquiring them. Amerigo is an explorer, eager to know and learn. Maggie, on the other hand, enters into her marriage in a naïve and unreflective manner. She has not the Prince's ability to distinguish between surface and depth. For her, Amerigo is the beauty of his brilliant exterior, the glory of his history, the fame of his first name. She is not interested in his private self and believes she knows him because she looked up his history in the British Museum. She delights in the decorative quality of his difference and acquires him like an ornament. Unlike her, Amerigo immediately perceives the truth beneath the surface. Only much later does Maggie begin to measure the adjustment her marriage demands of herself. With the realization of the difficulty their difference poses, she becomes at once more inquisitive and more accommodating, "a settler or trader in a new country; in the likeness even of some Indian squaw with a papoose on her back and barbarous beadwork to sell."[5]

The marriage itself is also seen very differently by the four main characters. Maggie, for example, believes that she can continue her intimacy with her father in spite of her marriage. She believes that she need not fulfill the social functions of her role if Amerigo and Charlotte are willing to do it for her. She acts with innocence and naïveté, but also with the consciousness of her wealth and the egotism of someone who has never wanted. The Prince sees the matter quite differently; he is struck by the absurdity of a situation his wife and father-in-law deem normal: "What was supremely grotesque, in fact, was the essential opposition of theories—as if a galantuomo, as *he* at least constitutionally conceived galantuomini, could do anything *but* blush to 'go about' at such a rate with such a person as Mrs. Verver in a state of childlike innocence, the state of our primitive parents before the Fall" (p. 238). His moral code demands adultery of Amerigo as the only possible response to such a situation, just as Maggie's defines such an act as betrayal.

Although in *The Golden Bowl* the potential for a fusion is posed formally, the actual fusion takes place neither on the level of form nor meaning. Just as the two competing perspectives never actually come together within the confines of the novel itself, the success of the experiment remains extremely tenuous. I would like to suggest that the fusion depends on the response of the reader who may combine the two separate sections of the novel and thereby effect the meeting of Amerigo and Maggie's points of view. The novel's ellipses invite the reader to participate in its structure and to fill that structure with meaning; here is the reader's concrete role, implied within the structure of the text.[6]

Most of James' other novels end in renunciation, but *The Golden Bowl* ends in an embrace; each character has returned to his or her rightful partner and the Prince and Princess can finally be together. This seeming closure, resembling the structure of comedy, breaks down as soon as the couple's union is viewed in moral terms; the strange look in the Prince's eyes which makes Maggie turn away in pity and dread certainly raises doubts about the value of their reconciliation.

This open-endedness has exasperated critics who have been forced to terminate their inquiry by admitting the novel's irreducible ambiguity. In juxtaposing the two perspectives of *The Golden Bowl*, the reader finds it impossible to take sides: the Prince's betrayal of Maggie is attenuated by her greed, her selfishness and neglect of him, and Maggie's innocence becomes ominously manipulative as her knowledge grows, and as the single-minded determination to keep her husband makes her relinquish any claim to moral superiority. The gender juxtaposition is equally ambiguous—the women are strong and in control while the men are easily manipulated—and so is the cultural one: the Europeans, products of a history of deceit and artifice and perpetrators of betrayal, ironically emerge as victims, while the natural, innocent and honest Americans emerge as deceptively ingenuous, even violently cruel. If the Prince is defined by the brutality and hypocrisy of his public history, then Maggie is tainted by the commercial spirit with which Adam Verver goes out to collect Europe. The Prince marries for money and the Ververs acquire him like a "morceau de musée." The novel's relationships are brutal and violent under the surface yet there are neither definable heroes nor villains. I would like to suggest, however, that the novel's perspectivism of moral value leads the reader not to ambiguity but to the necessity of making a choice. Far from condemning the reader to what Sallie Sears[7] calls "unrelenting duality" or what Dorothea Krooke[8] deems an insoluble ambiguity, *The Golden Bowl* demands a reading that weighs the evidence, measures the sacrifice involved in sustaining each of the points of view and discriminatingly evaluates the reality of their interaction.

Ambiguity can only be the result of a purely formal reading, like that of a Colonel Assingham who suffers from a "want, alike, of moral and of intellectual reaction" (p. 46). We can read the novel as a frivolous game, posing purely compositional problems or as a serious imaginative participation in a quest for knowledge and definition, looking beyond the geometry of relationships to their pain and pleasure, their triumphs and failures.

The novel's perspectivism becomes truly troubling at the point where its duality breaks down, i.e., with the emergence of Maggie's astounding soars in Book II. The imbalance of *The Golden Bowl* explodes the apparent symmetry of the two perspectives at every level.[9] For the reader, the novel's symmetry would mean openness, freedom of choice and possibly ambiguity; its breakdown results in the text's manipulative imposition of a number of different successive choices.

The Golden Bowl gradually becomes Maggie's novel; it is her education and development that is of central interest. While the Prince merely observes the beginnings of a relationship, Maggie sounds the depths; she alone is given the power that comes with knowledge. While Amerigo's book, half of which is devoted to the thoughts of Adam Verver and the Assinghams, is designed to give background information and merely contains the Prince's reactions to given situations, Maggie's book is composed of the intensity of her thoughts, the growth of her knowledge, the flights of her imagination, the depths of her suffering, the thrill of invention. Maggie's desire to pay all is as greedy as her desire to have all. Precisely when the story becomes problematic Maggie's book begins, and thus the Prince is deprived of an opportunity to display whatever growth he may undergo. Instead of portraying the development of two central consciousnesses, the novel seems designed literally to build up Maggie's authority, to make it possible for *her* to create a marriage and a fusion.

Maggie moves from an unconscious participation in a civilization marked by selfishness and exploitation to a willful and studied adoption of duplicity and manipulation. She does so to preserve appearances and institutions in whose reality she no longer believes. Maggie's growing realization of the cost of maintaining appearances, of the need for lies and duplicity, and of the need to utilize others forms the subject of Book Two. While, in Book One, Maggie appears as the innocent bride, the childish Princess, the devoted daughter, in Book Two she is the "tired actress," and "overworked little trapezist girl" who knows how to perform several feats at once. The frequent images of the stage characterize Maggie's realization of the need to play a role, to play the public part of the Princess which by definition destroys the intrinsic royal nature she possessed. In developing an outward polish distinguishable from her inner self, Maggie comes close to the Prince and the civilization he represents. It is the worst of European and American qualities which brings the two together. Maggie's change, however, and the pain and sacrifice it entails are necessitated by her desire to understand the Prince. Maggie is tainted by her American background but, in acquiring some of the Prince's European values, becomes even more so. Like Lambert Strether, Maggie comes to combine two sets of values, two civilizations. The difference between Maggie and Strether lies in the fact that Maggie is working on her marriage, that her success depends on the response of her husband and is not her work alone. Maggie, unlike Strether, is not free to create a personal vision but must constantly measure that vision against the Prince's.

In a society where all human relationships seem to be marked by the mercantile spirit of Adam Verver and the duplicity of European "civilization," love cannot but follow the same pattern. As

John Bayley points out, love and knowledge are fundamentally linked in *The Golden Bowl.* Charlotte and Amerigo come together as a result of their shared knowledge or, as the Prince himself puts it, of "an exquisite sense of complicity" (p. 238). It is their knowledge of Maggie and Adam's naïveté, of a deeper passion and intimacy that brings Charlotte and Amerigo together. Their intentions are decent but, since their calculations are faulty, their intimacy is based on a false premise. Moreover, good intentions cannot obscure the victimization of their spouses.[10] Charlotte and Amerigo's judgment of the Ververs represents a kind of prison, a cage of ignorance or, as Maggie visualizes it, a "sense of a life tremendously ordered and fixed" (p. 334). Maggie refuses to be the victim of their union, as every union must have its victim, every happiness its price; she recognizes that in order not to be manipulated she must learn to manipulate. More importantly, she refuses to be excluded from their knowledge, and, as she gradually realizes the extent of her exclusion, she treats her insights as the most valuable possession, virtually getting drunk on the sense of her richness. Maggie's growing intimacy with her husband is again based on their shared knowledge, and, this time, on the exclusion of Charlotte who in her ignorance becomes the victim of this new intimacy.[11] Again there is an "exquisite complicity" which goes so far as to affirm Charlotte's stupidity for not having known better, while yet absolutely refusing to enlighten her. Maggie's growing consciousness is charged with a sense of possession as well as manipulation; she is now able to use her knowledge, impart it to others at her wish.

The loss of Maggie's innocence is offset by a tremendous gain; knowledge, even the knowledge of evil she was to be spared from, lifts her to unprecedented heights. She gains the intensity of a highly conscious life which makes her innocent state seem impoverished and somnolent:

> There was a phrase that came back to her from old American years: she was having, by that idiom, the time of her life – she knew it by the perpetual throb of this sense of possession, which was almost too violent either to recognise or to hide. It was as if she had come out—that was her most general consciousness; out of a dark tunnel, a dense wood, or even simply a smoky room, and had thereby, at least, for going on, the advantage of air in her lungs. (p. 434)

Note the double meaning of possession; the exaggerated terms in which knowledge is described suggest that Maggie not only possesses, but is possessed. This kind of knowledge is a form of madness. Even her lowest moment, from a moral point of view, is full of a sense of excitement:

> The sharp, successful, almost primitive wail in it made Charlotte turn, and this movement attested for the Princess the felicity of her deceit. Something in her throbbed as it had throbbed the night she had stood in the drawing room and denied that she had suffered. She was ready to lie again if her companion would but give her the opening. Then she should know she had done all. (p. 512)

The utilization of her knowledge proves even more exhilarating than its possession. She begins by drawing up a plan and by, at first carefully, then more confidently, testing her power over those around her. Sending Charlotte and Amerigo off on another weekend together is a modest test; she wanted them to go to confirm her suspicions, and she makes them do it by banking on their fear of her, a fear which gradually develops into terror: "'And that's how I make them do what I like!' " (p. 371). Fanny's reaction to this report of Maggie's only confirms a sinister impression: "'You're terrible.'" All this seems mild when measured against the rest of her plan, her silent understanding with the Prince that they were both to lie to Charlotte and the subtle but effective manipulation of her father. Fanny's admiration only grows: "You're like nobody else—you're extraordinary" (p. 441).

Maggie's sense of possession, her joy and exhilaration at her knowledge and power are suspect not only in themselves but also in the comparison they afford with Fanny Assingham. In this so carefully structured novel, Fanny, with her rather lame machinations and not quite harmful speculations, represents the underside of Maggie. True, Fanny has no noble motive to excuse her; she decidedly selfish; still, her reactions are very much like Maggie's. She enjoys being in the know, she likes knowing more about everyone than they know about each other, she likes disposing of that precious knowledge at will, and she likes getting people to do what she wants. Fanny also has an idea and a plan; in its intricacy it quite resembles Maggie's. Both are desirous of "satisfying their imaginations," to use the words of Ralph Touchett of *Portrait of a Lady*. Their activities are of the same nature; whether Maggie's high intentions outweigh the mental violence with which she carries them out can only be answered by the novel itself.

The tremendous difference between Maggie and Fanny Assingham, however, lies in the extent of their personal involvement in their manipulations. Fanny fulfills the functions of the traditional Jamesian observer figure; in her conversations with her husband she provides an intelligent and perceptive commentary to the action. The fact, however, that the Assignhams' activity of supposition and speculation is relegated to the background of *The Golden Bowl*, and is very far from providing the central interest, sufficiently underscores the uniqueness of this novel in James' work. The Prince, early on, wonders what Fanny's motive for making his marriage could have been. Her profit, he reasons, could not have been pecuniary, nor had he rewarded her by making love to her. For the reader who has the privilege of Fanny's private conversations with Bob, the mystery is easily solved. Fanny clearly enjoys her power of manipulation and arranges the marriages so as to "satisfy her imagination." This undoubtedly is the meaning of Fanny's equivocal attempt to relieve her worries: "Besides, it's all, at the worst, great fun" (p. 62). Bob, however, misunderstands her meaning and in so doing he gives us a momentary glimpse of the underside of James' vocabulary of consciousness. For Bob "great fun" is the fun of betrayal and adultery; for Fanny it is the intensity of her speculative activity.[12]

For Fanny there are no limits and no real punishment is possible, but Maggie is limited by her own suffering and by her empathy for Charlotte's. Maggie's plan requires a tremendous amount of restraint and self-control and, consequently, a terrible loneliness. Gone is the protectedness of Lambert Strether who, though a middle-aged bachelor, had devoted companions who were always eager to share his worries. Maggie's plan leaves her alone, unable to confide fully in Fanny, and condemns her to resist the strong charms of her husband. Nowhere is her pain more poignant than during the carriage ride where, determined to succeed in her scheme of separating Charlotte and Amerigo, she resists the strength of his grasp. The scene is reminiscent of Gardencourt where Isabel Archer for the first time feels the power of male sexuality and runs off from Caspar Goodwood. The quality of the two scenes is quite dissimilar, however; Goodwood's embrace inspired Isabel with more fear than attraction. For Maggie, on the other hand, the attraction is pure and the sacrifice enormous. It is not, as it was for Strether, a question of relinquishing life for the requirements of her vision, but of creating a vision which will enable her to live:

She should have but to lay her head back on his shoulder with a certain movement to make it definite for him that she didn't resist. To this, as they went, every throb of her consciousness prompted her— every throb, that is, but one, the throb of her deeper need to know where she 'really' was. By the time she had uttered the rest of her idea, therefore, she was still keeping her head and intending to keep it; though she was also staring out of the carriage-window with eyes into which the tears of suffered pain had risen, indistinguishable, perhaps, happily, in the dusk. She was making an effort that horribly hurt her, and, as she couldn't cry out, her eyes swam in her silence. With them, all the same, through the square opening beside her, through the grey panorama of the London night, she achieved the feat of not losing sight of what she wanted; and her lips helped and protected her by being able to be gay. (pp. 327-328)

Her perception of the pain she inflicts on others, on Charlotte especially, disciplines Maggie even more. Unlike Strether, she understands her manipulative role. Maggie's relationship with Charlotte, as that between Isabel and Madame Merle or Kate and Milly Theale, is the most interesting and the most problematic of the novel. Charlotte shares Maggie's initial American innocence; her poverty, however, forces her into a European role of duplicity and exposes her to the acquisitive spirit of the Ververs. Thus Maggie and Charlotte, although schoolmates, are hardly equals. Charlotte, moreover, demonstrates quite pathetically the underside of the "sublime consensus of the educated." Her outward polish and grace cannot conceal her inner alienation. Even though she can imitate the gestures of both societies, she is deeply alienated from both and even though she seems to combine the virtues of both worlds, she is inwardly frightened, awkward, and scared.

Their personal relationship is one of alternating cruelty and sympathy, violence and admiration. Maggie's sympathy is sincere and with it she accepts the responsibility for Charlotte's suffering:

Even the conviction that Charlotte was but awaiting some chance really to test her trouble upon her lover's wife left Maggie's sense meanwhile open as to the sight of gilt wires and bruised wings, the spacious but suspended cage, the home of eternal unrest, of pacings, beatings, shakings, all so vain, into which the baffled consciousness helplessly resolved itself. The cage was the deluded condition, and Maggie, as having known delusion—rather!—understood the nature of cages. (p. 449)

Maggie's sympathy is translated into action when she pleads for her with Amerigo. Her final panegyric of Charlotte to her father must be read, not as hypocrisy, but as sincere admiration for someone whose "talent for life," in the words of *The Wings of the Dove*, has enabled her to raise herself up from the depths of despair, to redefine her role according to new conditions, and to reach the point of believing in her own deception. Though Maggie's sympathy is strong and sincere, it is not powerful enough to induce a gift of insight which would free Charlotte from her cage. Maggie suffers for her but guards her precious possessions—her husband and her knowledge, thereby making sure that Charlotte will remain in her power.

One particular scene in *The Golden Bowl* poignantly defines the extent of Maggie's manipulative power and her intensity, as well as the loneliness such power entails. It takes place at Fawns toward the end of the novel. Verver, Charlotte, Amerigo, and Fanny are playing cards and Maggie, standing outside the window, observes each of them closely. Then she walks along the porch and stands for a while outside the empty drawing room windows. The scene is peculiarly reminiscent of Strether's day in the country and a comparison will again demonstrate the difference between the two novels. Like Strether, Maggie feels particularly in control during this scene and takes pleasure in exercising, imaginatively, her authorial powers. But unlike, Strether, she has real power over her companions:

> They might have seen . . . figures rehearsing some play of which she herself was the author. . . . They might in short have represented any mystery they would; the point being predominantly that the key to the mystery, the key that could wind and unwind it without a snap of the spring, was thee in her pocket. . . . Spacious and splendid, like a stage again awaiting a drama, it (the drawing room) was a scene she might people, by the press of her spring, either with serenities and dignities and decencies, or with terrors and shames and ruins, things as ugly as those formless fragments of her golden bowl she was trying so hard to pick up. (pp. 454-455)

While Strether merely indulges in an imaginative game which ultimately amounts to no more than his own pleasure at the structures of his mind, Maggie's imaginings could at any moment be put into effect with disastrous results; the decorum of the scene is entirely in her hands.

Maggie's loneliness in this particular scene may resemble Strether's, but her responsibility far outweighs his. She remains distant even from her father who, failing to meet her desperate and silent appeal, refuses to share that responsibility with her. In explicitly calling Maggie an artist and in enabling her to realize the imaginative structures she invents (only a few pages later the drawing room is actually peopled and witness to the high drama she foresees), James acknowledges the highly manipulative and exploitative nature of the artistic process, as well as its profound implication in the Prince's Roman heritage, in the society of Adam Verver and the Castledeans.

Where does Maggie gain the power to overcome the resistance of the real that has discredited the imaginative power of the narrator of *The Sacred Fount*, of the publishing scoundrel of *The Aspern Papers*, even of Lambert Strether? A combination of forces work in her favor, as I have already suggested. Her personal involvement, her will to live, and her responsiveness to others distinguish her greatly from those protagonists whose visions remain private and isolated from the world that surrounds them. Maggie's authority is gradually but poignantly built up throughout Book Two, not only for the reader, but also for her husband, for Fanny, and perhaps for her father and Charlotte. While she initially seems confused, puzzled and insecure, her growing knowledge, derived through actual proof in part, but mostly through her own power of divination, gives her such credibility that the reader not only fully accepts the accuracy of her observations, but even accepts for truth those imagined unspoken speeches which initially seem contrived and ridiculous.

Moreover, an intricate pattern of images builds up Maggie's credibility. She is quite often portrayed as a child or a doll; these are images which do more than to underscore her innocence. As James' Maisie demonstrates, the child is perhaps best able to expose the corruptions of the adult world, though, unlike Maisie, Maggie is forced to become implicated in them to do so. Surely the most potent image pattern is the religious one. The Christian vocabulary associated with Maggie enables her to overcome any resistance that may have been left. In the card party scene this is clearly the source of her authorial power:

> They thus tacitly put it upon her to be disposed of, the whole com-
> plexity of their peril, and she promptly saw why: because she was

> there, and there just *as* she was, to lift it off them and take it; to
> charge herself with it as the scapegoat of old, of whom she had once
> seen a terrible picture, had been charged with the sins of the people
> and had gone forth into the desert to sink under his burden and die.
> (p. 453)

Maggie is at best a satanic Christ, and the irony of this image pattern should not be overlooked. She makes everyone pay for her initial victimization. Although she succeeds in preserving appearances, and in saving at least the shell of the institution of marriage, Maggie does not quite manage to ward off "the horror of the thing hideously *behind* . . . (the) badfaced stranger surprised in one of the thick-carpeted corridors of a house of quiet on a Sunday afternoon" (p. 455).[18] Maggie is clearly unique in James' work, combining, as she does, nature and innocence with art, reconciling European and American values and yet insisting on using her knowledge for living. The sinister character of the novel, however, lies in its sequential nature—it is not, as Bersani says, that Maggie is a combination of Isabel and Madame Merle, but that she is an Isabel who develops into a Madame Merle.

After tracing Maggie's growth, the profound imbalance of this novel is keenly apparent. She alone develops, she alone grows and suffers, pays and gains. Throughout the novel, the Prince is reduced to passivity; his father-in-law takes care not only of his material needs, but of his wife as well. His mistress, moreover, makes all the arrangements for their encounters. He is "in a position in which he has nothing in life to do" (p. 195).

Even in the final scene, the Prince's opportunity for *action* is pitifully small. Having engineered the solution to their problem, Maggie is the one who directs his response by implicitly giving him "a bunch of keys or a list of commissions" (p. 442). Instead of allowing Amerigo to express that very private self on which he so insists, she gives a chance only to say yes or no, to follow her instructions or be destroyed. She creates his need for her and she fills it; she builds his cage so that she can be the one who gives him the key.

For the reader, the Prince remains an unknown quantity. Those who try to sustain the novel's duality inevitably come to neglect the Prince as they are pulled into the intricacies of Maggie's more fascinating mind, as they suffer with her, are elated by her power even while being terrified of her. They will conclude that it is

Maggie's novel, that she, like Lambert Strether, single-handedly overcomes the cultural barrier by incorporating American and European attributes, no matter how morally questionable they might be. Amerigo does succeed in cultivating a new humility, one which looks beautiful to Maggie. As his old standards seem meaningless when faced with Maggie, we realize that he has forged a new tradition for himself as well, but the price he pays seems excessive. Amerigo's initial hopefulness gives way to a disillusionment exemplified in observations such as tis one: "Everything's terrible, *cara*–in the heart of man" (p. 535). Such a vision could be a basis for a fusion, but a flawed one, at best.

The metaphor of the golden bowl, that of the crack hidden beneath a beautifully gilded surface, holds for the novel itself, a novel which, in trying to reconcile all differences and effect a perfect fusion, reveals the hunger of a heroine who wants all that Jamesian heroes have never been able to combine: her father and her husband, money and civilization, innocence and knowledge, the imaginative and the real. Maggie overcomes the cultural barrier in a more real way than Strether; she truly incorporates the attributes of each culture and accepts Europe in her imagination and in reality. In so doing she by necessity relinquishes the integrity Strether was able to preserve by leaving Europe.[13] Even more than *The Ambassadors*, because it attempts something so different, *The Golden Bowl* is a celebration of the self, the individual, the single creator fed not only by the human beings, but also by the cultures around him. James, it seems, needs the cultural opposition to create superior individuals who can use it to expand themselves. Instead of in a fusion, the novel seems to culminate in what Sally Sears so aptly calls "the arbitrary reign of consciousness," a celebration of the power of the absorbing single mind.

Such a reading makes the novel's perspectivistic structure a foil for Maggie's own growth at the expense of the Prince, her father and Charlotte. Instead of either letting the reader choose between two points of view or of enacting their fusion, the novel seems to pull us into the intricacies of Maggie's mind and of her vision. I would like to argue that this imbalance provokes, instead, a response, on the part of the reader, that might yet effect the consensus of cultures that Maggie alone cannot create, by the compulsion to restore a balance that has been upset.

Reading, like business, love, marriage, and friendship is, for Henry James, a relationship of exchange. The literary text takes shape in response to the efforts of its readers. James' novels, characterized by ellipsis and ambiguity, suggestiveness and open-endedness, seem to be particularly dependent on the reader's participation. As James will have it in the Preface to *The Golden Bowl*, the more intense the reader's involvement, the greater the rewards of the text which gives out "its finest and most numerous secrets . . . under the closest pressure. . . . [The text owes] the flower of its effect to the act and process of apprehension that so beautifully asks most from it. It then infallibly and not less beautifully, most responds" (*Art*, pp. 346-347). Only as the reader passionately gives of himself, is he rewarded with what James calls "poetry in the largest literary sense."

And yet the specific response to a given Jamesian text is not freely determined by the reader, but directed by James himself. In spite of their apparent openness, these works contain built-in structures that channel the reader's judgment. James speaks of the relationship between author and reader in terms of control:

> In every novel the work is divided between the writer and the reader, but the writer makes the reader very much as he makes his characters. When he makes him ill, that is makes him indifferent, he does not work; the writer does all. When he makes him well, that is makes him interested, the reader does quite half the labour.[14]

Thus the interaction between author and reader creates the same tensions that exist between James' characters: exchange inevitably becomes manipulation, balance gives way to control. Like Isabel Archer, Lambert Strether and Milly Theale, the reader loses all sense of freedom as he becomes aware of the manipulatory structures in which he is caught. Thus the relationship between Maggie and Amerigo involves the reader directly by reflecting that between the author and himself. The discomfort of dissymmetry, however, could be a provocation to provide what is missing: the Prince's point of view, his reaction to Maggie's change, his answer to her final challenge. One reaction to the novel's ellipsis is to see it as an invitation to complete it. This, of course, constitutes the only possibility of reinstating the novel's dual structure and its symmetry, effecting, by an acceptance of Maggie, the marriage of the two protagonists. The implied reader thus has the crucial role of replacing the empty forms of marriage, "that strange accepted finality of relation" (p. 543), with a fusion based on mutual understanding. Thus the reader has the opportunity to become a part of James' envisioned "sublime consensus of the educated" and thereby to give that communion of cultures a chance to be realized. It is in the text's ellipses that the implied reader finds the opportunity to participate in the novel's structure, to do "half the labour."

Maggie does not emerge from the novel unvictimized. Not only does she amply pay for her growth and incur tangible loss, but, by being placed in the foreground, she also single-handedly takes on the burden of the novel's structure. Her role as the author of a complicated scheme isolates and exposes her. James half-deploringly, half-excitedly reveals this hazard of the author's role at the end of the novel's preface. A part of him, but out in the world, his work is an act which "has its way of abiding and showing and testifying" (*Art*, p. 347). Maggie not only seeks to know, but, through her acts, she offers herself to be known as well; as author she reveals to her reader (the Prince) the very brutality of her greed and quite conspicuously lays bare her machinations in all their dubiousness. We have seen that Maggie remains in command throughout and that she gives the Prince only a carefully limited chance to respond. In the last scene, however, Maggie poignantly relinquishes her control and lets the success of her entire plan depend on the Prince's judgment. As she awaits, in terror, his full payment for her efforts, expressing fear for herself and concern for him, she cannot resist offering one last suggestion about Charlotte, "to explain and to finish," thereby setting the tone of their meeting and giving the Prince his cue. Nevertheless, at this point, Amerigo does have the genuine choice of accepting Maggie and returning her passion, thus redeeming her action, or of turning away from "the horror of the thing hideously behind" Maggie's captivating eyes. In identifying with the Prince, it is the reader who must decide whether Amerigo's "I see nothing but *you*" is said out of terror or out of love, whether or not the last embrace announces a true fusion. It is through Maggie's view that we see the Prince's eyes wherein is mirrored an image of herself that makes her turn away in pity and dread. The intensity of this scene, reminiscent of the moment in *The Turn of the Screw* where the governess, looking into Mrs. Grose's eyes, sees herself as the ghost, suggests the grave risks of Maggie's scheme and the tenuousness of its success. In choosing to forgive Maggie, the reader would relieve her of the excessive structural burden the novel imposes on her and give to the embrace its seeming finality. In the last scene, Maggie waits for Amerigo's acceptance just as the author awaits the reader's; the novel's resolution is in the reader's power and depends on his assumption of the Prince's role.

I have already complained of Amerigo's limited maturation in the novel. His vision does not grow and develop as far as the reader can see. The novel's failure to reveal more about the Prince could be due to James' and Maggie's disinterest in the real person behind the polished mask. Maggie's complex development could be said to rob her husband of a chance to express himself in the space of the novel. However, Maggie's lack of curiosity about the Prince might well be a form of respect rather than an appropriation of his space. While the Prince and Charlotte mistakenly freeze Maggie into a narrow image of innocence and naïveté, Maggie grants Amerigo a certain impenetrability. She admits the aura of his name and ancestry, the power of his intense sexuality; she preserves his mystery and his integrity and never ceases to believe in his "incomparable superiority" (p. 420). As author, Maggie is completely exposed. As reader and knower, the Prince can remain unknowable, therefore protected. Not less guilty than Maggie, he can, until the end, hide that guilt behind a polished surface.

If, with the character of Maggie, James comments on the exploitative and manipulative quality of the authorial role, with that of Amerigo, James lays bare the moral dubiousness of the reader's activity. Greed and self-interest define the Prince's appropriation of the Ververs. His narrow vision of them is as confining as Adam Verver's suffocating care of the Prince. By definition, the reader is one set on penetrating, analyzing, revealing, exposing. He manipulates his subjects, puts them to personal use, destroys their integrity. An activity defined by hunger and greed, reading is perhaps even more suspect than Maggie's authorial manipulation because of the reader's protectedness. Although led along, even guided to the point of James' and Maggie's transparent contrivance, the implied reader and the Prince can remain virtually unexposed.

It is their fear of exposure that causes so many of James' protagonists to remain protected observes. Lambert Strether, having absorbed all, chooses to flee the consequences of his knowledge and Milly Theale takes her knowledge to the grave. Maggie does not fear exposure and thus becomes the most successful artist figure in all of James; she develops her art specifically in the service of life. In fact, Maggie is the only Jamesian heroine who bears a child. In Maggie's affirmation of life with all its risks and impurities lies the uniqueness of *The Golden Bowl*. By following her step into life, however, the novel demonstrates the very real dangers implicit in the artistic activity of James' characters, and the protectedness of James' observer figures.

Clearly, the reader's assumption of the Prince's role is a natural consequence of the novel's distribution. Clearly, the Prince's guilt provides a basis for a fusion with the equally flawed Maggie; and the reader could, through a consciousness of his own guilt, become the vehicle of such a fusion. But is it the role of the implied reader to supply a resolution which is not present within the confines of the novel, to provide, as it were, a Book Three of *The Golden Bowl?* There is much in the novel that is not meant to be revealed, and it becomes difficult to determine when an ellipsis constitutes an invitation to complete, and when it does not. The perspectives of Charlotte and Adam Verver, for example, are almost entirely missing from the novel. Should the reader supply those as well, thereby enlarging his sphere of identification even more? Or is he, like everyone else in the novel, compelled to preserve Verver's suggestive mystery? There is not much we can know about Adam and Charlotte. Verver's mystery pervades the novel and provides the opportunity for much guesswork. We know, however, that his is a false mystery. The veil cannot hide Verver's "years of darkness," the questionable sources of his wealth, his shady business deals, his way of reducing people to objects. Neither the repeated suggestion of Verver's ignorance nor his identification with God can succeed in redeeming the novel. Still, the novel seems to invite the reader to preserve the mystery of Adam Verver, to participate in ignorance as well as in knowledge.

The refusal to know, to go beyond the surface, past the seduction of silence and ignorance, is a strong one in this novel, as in James' work generally. There are several possible aesthetic justifications for openendedness and ellipsis. First, mystery is a great deal richer and more suggestive than revelation. The insignificant object manufactured in Woollett, for example, gains importance precisely by not being named. Following a well-known mystery story device, James capitalizes on a guessing game to add spice and interest to the story. Similarly, Maggie could be said to preserve the mystery of the Prince not so much out of respect, as out of selfishness to increase her own interest in him. Second, revelation can be fatal, as it is for Milly Theale; at best it is frightening. Consciousness has more horror than beauty. Strether turns away from the tearful Mme. de Vionnet, just as many Jamesian heroines turn away from the reality of adulthood and sexuality. It is to Maggie's benefit that, unlike Isabel and Maisie, she herself rarely turns away, and that she stages a compelling though horrifying scene for the captivated Prince, thereby making it difficult for him to turn away. After holding back and waiting for so long, Maggie is ready to know the sexual passion that her husband offers. Thirdly, the preservation of mystery can represent respect for the integrity of the individual. It is Maggie who says, "There are things that are sacred—whether they're joys or pains" (p. 131). She dreads the Prince's confession, convinced that "she should be ashamed to listen to the uttered word" (p. 548), and thus Maggie preserves his beauty. Why does James withhold the fusion toward which the novel tends and which would give full value to the dual point of view technique? What might make the Prince's mystery an invitation where Verver's is not? Can the reader supply what the novel only suggests?

The truth is that the success of James' aesthetic depends on the presence of mystery and the power of suggestion. The power of his fiction derives from a sustained ability not to name things. Booklength studies have been written about all that we do not know in *The Golden Bowl*. Only someone as insensitive as Bob Assingham would ask for fact: "But what the deuce did they *do*?" Discrimination and interpretation is the only real way to arrive at knowledge: "I know." "Do you mean that they've *told* you?" "I mean nothing so absurd" (p. 261). The most meaningful communicaton in the novel is mute and depends on interpretation. Only thus can knowledge become an exhilarating possession. Just as Maggie sends the Prince to "find out for yourself," so the text invites the reader to participate directly and personally in the process of knowledge that can unite husband and wife, the knowledge of the brutality of relationships, the power of passion.

Circuitous paragraphs and involuted sentences create a rich novelistic surface that hints as prodigious depths but that only rarely leads the reader to them. David Lodge aptly calls James' language "a treacherous medium of communication, concealing as much as it reveals."[15] The reader is invited to participate in the sophisticated psychological guessing game, such as that between Strether and Maria, or that between the Assinghams; only rarely is he urged to sound the suggested depths. Unique among James' novels in many respects, *The Golden Bowl* goes further in involving the reader in the realities beyond the novelistic surface; it exposes not only the brutal facts of human nature and the decay of a civilization, but also the dubious morality of the artistic process itself. Not only does the author appear as at once more vulnerable and more powerful than in previous works, but the reader is also shown to be an exploiter. If the reader does become the agent of a fusion, it can only be a fusion based on the consciousness of a common flawed state.

In relation to earlier works, *The Golden Bowl* takes a big step toward a collective vision. Both protagonists are given a voice, both are equally flawed. The novel's final mirror scene represents the possibility of a mutual, and perhaps collective, guilt. If the reality of that perception and its consequence, the meeting between Maggie and Amerigo, is withheld, it is to let the reader enact a process of discovery as painful as that of the characters.

Thel's motto from Blake's "Book of Thel" is one source of the title of *The Golden Bowl.* The concern of Blake's poem with the hidden nature of sexuality is well known, but it is the poem's interest in naming things, in defining and shaping what is hidden and unknown that warrants an interpretation of the motto as a representation of the artistic process:

> Does the eagle know what is in the pit?
> Or wilt thou ask the mole?.
> Can Wisdom be put in a silver rod?
> Or Love in a golden bowl?

Thel's motto consists of four questions and therefore invites its reader to respond, depending on that response for completion. The first two questions concern the nature or, more specifically, the content of "the pit." The eagle and the mole provide two disparate perceptions of that hidden quantity.

The second group of questions deals again with the combination of two separate entities, with the marriage of wisdom and love. For the marriage to take place the content of the abyss must be faced and accepted, just as the forms that effect the marriage, the "silver rod" and the "golden bowl," must be filled with the substance of wisdom and love. The artist is one who can see and represent the abyss from the height of the eagle and the lowly perspective of the mole. Able to combine different viewpoints, the artist is the agent of the marriage. Yet with the motto's question form, the artist leaves the resolution open. We know that Thel refuses to expose herself to the realities of "the pit" and is therefore condemned to an eternal and unproductive innocence. She fails to meet the challenge of experience and of adulthood. The artist will fail as well, if he does not combine the viewpoints, if along with creating artifacts such as the silver rod and golden bowl, he does not experience the reality of the pit. If one wants to know life, he cannot remain removed but must live it. One must suffer the pain of revelation, one must, in fact, go beyond the mediation of art.

The novel's dual perspective form has the potential of allowing the reader to participate in the marriage, in the communion of perspectives which together can define the nature of the unknown, the abyss. James' use of this form takes him further than ever toward his dream of a meeting between Europe and America. The artistic process, as he characterizes it in the novel, is deeply implicated in the capitalist-acquisitive system that relates the two cultures and becomes, therefore, the locus of learning about personal and cultural relationships.

I have suggested why the reader cannot hover somewhere between the eagle and the mole, but must participate in their disparate visions and must enact the struggle of those visions, if the novel is to "give out its finest and most numerous secrets." The repeated journey back and forth between the Prince and Princess, the transcendence of the illusion of duality and the resistance to the absorption of the Prince by the novel's structure constitute the essence of the response invited by the novel. This exercise in response demonstrates, perhaps rather painfully, that the process of reading must be situated within the general scheme of human relations. In his adoption of Maggie's perspective and especially of the Prince's, the reader experiences, very concretely and personally, the mutual exploitation which is shown to be the basis not only of their complex relationship, but of all relationships, whether they be personal, cultural, or aesthetic. The realization of James' dream of a cultural fusion is profoundly called into question by the novel's concrete enactment of mutual exploitation.

I hope to have succeeded in going beyond the acceptance of irreducible ambiguity. To do so is to follow the novel's process of knowledge to the point where it makes the step into life. It is a step that Maggie carefully wills into existence and which takes her and her husband to the place earlier described as "that of the fundamental passions" (p. 516). The Prince does not quite understand Maggie's final comment [16] about Charlotte but is willing, in following Maggie to abandon the careful discrimination on which he has so prided himself. I would like to suggest that the place of the "fundamental passions" is beyond language and beyond the confines of artistic structures,[17] although art, as Maggie proves, can lead us there. It is beyond the social decorum that Maggie so carefully preserves and beyond "the taste he [the Prince] had always conformed to" (p. 532). Beyond the gilded surface, deep within the pit, lie the pain and terror that come with the acknowledgement of a common guilt. Yet here is where Maggie and Amerigo can find a love that is, in Maggie's words, "beyond everything."

For James such a step out of language and fiction cannot but be frightening, filled with terror, pity, and dread. There is a difference between choosing not to name things and being unable to name them. Maggie's passion threatens the social forms much more than the Prince's adultery. To follow her is not to forget the tremendous human and moral cost of that passion. It is not surprising that the choice of life should be such a terrible one for the master of renunciation. Nor is it surprising that his affirmation of that passion should be so very tentative. The characters of this novel are as isolated from one another as the eagle and the mole. The role of art is an important one, but the novel insists on its dubious morality as well as on its mediation and indirection. And yet James, even as he holds back himself, does take his reader to the point where the distinction between text and world dissolves, where the fiction steps into life as the reader steps into the fiction to complete it. At this point the novel's dual perspective becomes multiple and communion is made possible.

The Golden Bowl demonstrates the dangers and rewards of the autonomous imagination, as well as showing ways to limit its power by making it responsible and answerable to reality, thereby leading it out of the impasse to which it had taken Lambert Strether. James' formal innovation, the dual narrative perspective, makes this transcendence possible. Uwe Johnson's *Speculations about Jakob*, the subject of the next chapter, not only experiments even more radically with this perspectivistic narrative structure, but does so to respond precisely to the dangers that Jamesian fiction explicates so well, the dangers of the autonomous imagination.

4. *Speculations about Jakob:* "Truthfinding"

In *The Golden Bowl*, the ethics of American capitalist-imperialism, translated onto an aesthetic plane with the character of Maggie Verver, threatens to taint any possibility of human community. Manipulation, dominance and possession become the instruments of knowledge and understanding as well as the agents of Maggie's marriage. And yet, the novel's open-ended biphonic structure sets up the possibility of a type of community through the participation of a third consciousness, that of the implied reader, a reader aware of the threats of manipulation and willing to resist them. If there is a possible community in *The Golden Bowl*, it is extremely tenuous and it takes place outside the confines of the novel. The fictional process is itself too seriously implicated in the power structures that define the cultural interaction. But with the consciousness of the implied reader there also emerges a fourth consciousness, that of the manipulative implied author; the triangle becomes a square and the power struggle remains central.

This politcal consciousness, translated onto a formal level within the novel, links *The Golden Bowl* to Johnson's *Speculations about Jakob*. Johnson begins with the silence with which James ends, with the consciousness of the limits of fiction as an epistemological tool and an instrument of community. Johnson's silence comes out of a feeling of paralysis brought about by the political division of Germany and the linguistic contamination it produces. Johnson's short 1961 text "Berliner Stadtbahn," one of his few quasi=theoretical statements, outlines the dilemma of the writer in the politically defined world of the divided Germany.

"Berliner Stadtbahn" begins with a nucleus of a potentially dramatic situation, one which Johnson intended to incorporate as a vignette into one of his novels, but which he found impossible to write. It was to concern a young East German man who gets off the train in a West Berlin subway stop, crosses the platform and walks toward the street.[1] In view of the political situation of Berlin at that time, this seemingly simple story is full of ambiguities involving the young man's motivations—is he going to the West for a visit, is he moving there, or should one say he is fleeing the East?—his expectations and fears, the reality of the life he leaves behind and of the one to which he can look forward. To talk about the young man's simple outward action is to consider not only motives, desires, and feelings but a complex social and political situation that has invaded all areas of individual existence. In "Berliner Stadtbahn" the initial fictional kernel is overgrown with the writer's doubts, questions, insecurities. Writing any human story in the context of a divided country involves a battle with the clichés of thought and language of two opposite political and ideological systems, what Johnson calls "alternative realities." Doing justice to both without getting trapped by either one seems impossible. The writer feels paralyzed by this dilemma. Not a single area is neutral in the particular context in which Johnson writes; even facts and statistics are loaded.

> He can consider the single universal. He can call the private typical. He can wish to recognize a law, where there appears a mere statistical accumulation. He is in the constant danger of trying to make something true that is merely factual.[2]

The writer's inability to describe either the behavior or the motivation of an individual, or the scene in which he lives, is due in part to the corruption of the language available to him as a tool. The linguistic conventions and structures that arise out of different political systems require an extreme caution on the writer's part if he tries to stay out of their propagandistic influences. Despite the acknowledged difficulties, Johnson's goal remains to find "a language . . . that can get a handle on both regions and can also be trans-regionally understood."[3]

The significance of Johnson's dilemma is not restricted to the particular situation in post-war Germany, however; as the essay clearly demonstrates, most of the factors that paralyze Johnson are merely intensified versions of those that hover over modern literature in general. The general breakdown of the modern writer's capacity to uncover and communicate an external reality makes any third scheme that Johnson might want to oppose to the two politically tainted schemata that usurp his character's story equally partial and suspect. The modern writer is limited in his single point of view and his unreliable personal experience. He cannot generalize on the basis of his own vision. Language itself is contaminated by ideology. In a politically defined world, the form of the word is evaluative and no neutral words external to the ideological system can exist. This Roland Barthes point out in *Writing Degree Zero*:

> In the Stalinist world, in which *definition*, that is to say the separation between Good and Evil, becomes the sole content of all language, there are no more words without values attached to them, so that finally the function of writing is to cut out one stage of a process: there is no more lapse of time between naming and judging, and the closed character of language is perfected, since it is a value which is given as explanation of another value.[4]

Here Barthes speaks of Marxist and Stalinist literature but the problem is naturally aggravated when two separate value systems exist next to and against each other as they do in Germany: "Both Berlin cities call themselves free and each other not free, themselves democratic and each other undemocratic, themselves peaceful, each other aggressive, etc."[5]

For all these reasons, the author's and the reader's position in the literary text is a problematic one and demands constant redefinition; the author's freedom is in need of severe limitation:

> If the author first has to invent and put together his text, how can he then sit on the high chair above the playing field like the umpire in tennis, know all the rules, how can he both know the characters and observe them impeccably, interfere at any time he chooses and even change places with one of his characters and know them as he can hardly ever know himself. The author should admit that he invented what he presents, he should not disguise the fact that his information is partial and precise.[6]

"Erfindung" for Johnson is not the free invention of an independent imaginary realm but the only possibility for a writer whose insight into himself and his world is limited, to gain at least some form of knowledge: "With my writing I would like to find out the truth. With my characters I am trying to reach the actual life."[7] Paradoxically, Johnson has to invent a fictional world to find out the truth about reality. With knowledge as the stated goal of Johnson's writing, the direction of his fictional invention is delimited not by the richness of his imagination but by the astuteness of observation, the accuracy of information, and their responsible rendition.

Johnson's statement is reminiscent of James' credo about the observed life which forms the substance of the artist's creation; the metaphors of the umpire in the great arena describe the author's relation to his work in strikingly similar ways. In contrast to James, however, Johnson allows the artist little freedom to alter and embellish the meager observations he might have been able to gather; piecing the fragments together is his job: "Precision is demanded of him."[8] James claims exactly that privilege that Johnson denies the author: to move at will between his place as arbiter of the great game and in the middle of the arena itself. James' privilege protects, just as Johnson's limitation exposes the author.

In the divided condition of Germany, the reader's role becomes more problematic as well. The reader is called upon to shed his assumptions, taking nothing for granted, and to participate in the arduous search for the truth which alone can preoccupy the conscientious writer. The novelistic form that arises out of the dilemma described in "Berliner Stadtbahn" is a collaborative and self-conscious, often tortuous, effort:

> He can admit this by demonstrating explicity the difficult search
> for the truth, by comparing and relativising his conception of the
> events with his characters, by omitting what he cannot know, by not
> exposing as pure fiction what amounts to a kind of truthfinding.[9]

Johnson's "truthfinding" is quite different from James' reign of an imagination which, at every point, threatens to lose contact with the real. This form to which "Berliner Stadtbahn" itself conforms enables the writer to avoid at least some of the pitfalls the text describes and to approach the goal of honesty. The structure of this short text is symptomatic for Johnson's other works; not a story but the negation of a story emerges. Its final sentence suggests the compensations such a form can offer the reader who is cheated out of the tale whose impossibility it recounts: "I hope nevertheless to have described the difficulties with the subway in such a way that you can imagine it somewhat." Thus the story emerges out of the account of its impossibility and through the imaginative investment of the reader. "Berliner Stadtbahn" gives us the material of a potential fictional situation; if it were to tell us a "story" it would be partial at best, utterly false at worst. Johnson's questions about the possibilities of fiction and his efforts to broaden its capacities are his response to division, his effort to understand it and thus to investigate the possibility of a reunification.

The political situation of Germany—its confrontation of two "alternate realities"—exacerbates the individual's limited capacities of knowledge and the possibility of perception emphasized by James. To write an individual story is also to describe the political, historical, geographical and economic forces that shape behavior and character. To do so, Johnson finds that he must redefine the fictional forms he has inherited: "Of a writer we expect information about the situation, should he describe it with means which it has long surpassed? . . . [He tries] constantly to change the aesthetic instruments with the constant changes of reality."[10] Like Butor, Johnson finds that to be a realist he must be an experimentalist. The solutions he suggests in "Berliner Stadtbahn" do not solve the writer's dilemma but present him with a medium in which it is feasible to continue writing: fiction as "truthfinding," as both a search for truth and the depiction of that search. It is a collaborative process all of whose materials are laid bare; it is unfinished, imperfect, in demand of constant revision.

The central intelligence in James' fiction, in its attempt to exercise control amidst the competing individual realities and to impose, through manipulation and force, one of those realities over the others, demonstrates the moral dangers of authority, the dubiousness of authorship. In Johnson's work, the break-up of fictional authority is a response to political authoritarianism. The authoritarianism of the East German state, the assumption of absolute power by a small number of strong individuals in the name of a supra-individual cause, is an extreme manifestation of the strong individualism which is at the basis of James' aesthetic. The details of Rohlfs' investigation in *Speculations about Jakob* are but a political, an official version of the prying questions, the suppositions and speculations, of the secretive dialogues of the Assinghams, for example, the difference being that here they are *official* facts, backed up by political power:

> The eyes had no scruples and avidly seized upon each detail solely for the sake of finding out (as a lover might pursue a mistress he has never met) yet this was an assignment, and the hirelings the wage slaves . . . forgot what they saw, derived neither benefit nor experience from it for their own lives. Thus, reports and speculations grew out of meetings and neighborliness and telephone conversations and indifferent glances exchange in city conveyances, and took shape on tape recorders and typewriters and in the intimate atmosphere of whispers and were sorted out and bundled and stapled to-

gether and stored . . . for a man who gave a different name to everyone he met, who therefore, even nominally, could not muster anything but a general and public concern for Jakob's well-being.
(p. 23)*[11]

In this passage, it is not only the growth of a story out of small
fragments and suggestions that is reminiscent of James' novels, but
also the lack of real commitment to the subjects of the speculations.
James' observers are motivated by curiosity, Johnson's by an
assignment. Rohlfs' political plots correspond to the manipulative
plots of Maggie and Fanny and by extension to the fictional plots of
the traditional omniscient author that Johnson attacks.

Johnson's aesthetic, the dialectical juxtaposition of multiple
narrative perspectives, is devised in reaction to such a central
controlling power as that of the state and has as its goal the
restoration of the individual's voice. The extensive search for a truth
in which a multiplicity of voices can participate is contrasted to the
imposed control of a power that admits only single answers and
interpretations. Offering an alternative to the fictional structures of
the past, Johnson's novels point out the connection between
fictional and political structures and respond to political
authoritarianism with fictional openness. The fragmentary style
and structure of Johnson's fictions dramatize the division of a
country that was once one, as well as the alienation of the individual
in a system which he can neither fully understand nor identify with.
In their openness and their suggestion of new structural
possibilities, the novels are experiments in reconstruction. They are
formal representations of the perspectivism of value and meaning
that results from the political division of a country, of the modern
world into two camps, East and West. The unbiased inclusion of
many voices is an attempt to develop an idiom that could include
both camps, to create a common ground on which they could meet.
With conjecture and speculation as the cognitive mode, Johnson's
works are formal images of the elusiveness of human motive, of the
individual's growing inability to recognize a proper place within the
warring systems that control his life.

---

* Der Einblick war bedenkenlos und ergriff gierig jede Einzelheit nur um sie zu wissen (wie einer nachlaufen
kann einer unbekannten Geliebten), doch war er beauftraft, und die Bediensteten die Lohndiener . . . vergassen
was sie wahrnahmen und zogen aus dem nicht Vorteil noch Belehrung für das eigene Leben. So aus Begegnungen
und Nachbarschaften und telephonischen Gesprächen und gleichgültigem Blickwechsel in den Fahrzeugen des
städtischen Verkehrs ergaben sich Berichte und Vermutungen, die nahmen Gestalt an in laufenden Tonbändern
und schreibenden Maschinen und in der innigen Atmosphäre des Flüsterns und wurden sortiert und gebündelt
und geheftet und . . . aufbewahrt für einen Mann, der seinen Namen austauschte vor jedem Gegenüber und also
schon dem Namen nach keine andere Teilnahme an Jakobs Ergehen verwalten konnte als eine allgemeine und
öffentliche. (pp. 18-19)

While James' attempted fusion of cultures is a desire for enrichment and enlargement, Johnson's represents the necessity of reuniting that which was severed. Culture, for Johnson, is defined neither by history nor geography, neither by moral nor by intellectual values. It is politics that has severed the country and has divided its cities, its language, objects, and people. For Johnson, then, the question is not to reach a "sublime consensus of the educated," but to survive in a country that has been forcefully divided.

Speculations about Jakob, published in West Germany in 1958, is about the effects of the division: "This situation has altered considerably the life of so many people, and my life as well, often negatively," says Johnson. "And we will die from it—or end up well."[12] When Johnson says that the differences between the two German states are serious enough to kill us, he is not using a figure of speech. The novel deals not with the interaction between two people but with the fragments of one victim of the division—the dead Jakob Abs. The effort to reconstruct his life is at the same time an effort to restore to Germany its common history, its common language and tradition; it is, one could say, an effort to transcend the political differences through the revived consciousness of what is common.

The novel has the form of an investigation; a number of people connected with Jakob's life get the chance to express their thoughts and feelings about him, either through the mediation of a third-person narrator, through direct dialogues or through interior monologues. The novel has two levels: the speculations about Jakob which take place after his death and the reconstructed story that emerges from them. Johnson's approach to his subject is perspectivistic; he illuminates it from as many angles as possible so as to have the best chance of arriving at the truth. Among Johnson's work, *Speculations* uses the technique of multiple perspectives in the fullest way.

The fact of Jakob's death reduces the narrators of his life to conjecture and speculation and is responsible for the inordinate complexity of this story. There are in the novel several emblems for these perceptual hardships: the attempt to distinguish the figure of Jakob through the thick morning fog, the difficulty of reading Rohlf's old map of the Jerichow region in which water, flatland and mountain are all indicated by the same color, the effort of the philologist to reconstruct old speech patterns from fragmentary and incomplete evidence: in each of the cases, conjecture is the only possible cognitive mode.

The novel's reader has to rely on conjecture as well to integrate versions and interpretations, piece together a variety of small independent details, weigh often contradictory evidence with very little guidance. Enmeshed in dialogues and monologues whose speakers remain, until the last scene of the novel, unidentified, the reader, in trying to deduce their identity and their relationships from the context, becomes a participant in the speculations about Jakob rather than the recipient of a story.[13]

Most facts are known; it is their motivations, their psychological background which remain a mystery. This is so because of the complex interrelations between individual actions and the supra-individual context in which that action occurs. Thus, even though the suppositions of Johnson's characters have a firm basis in fact and although concrete detail and minute description form the substance of a great deal of this novel, the individual seeker is exposed to a world where nothing is certain, nothing clearly knowable, no one trustworthy.

Skepticism about the accuracy of observation and conviction of the subjective nature of perception make even observable facts questionable. The numerous mechanical aids to perception, such as photographs, tapes, movies, and official documents, do not alleviate the mystery; they can all be quite misleading. The picture taken in the car by Gesine shocks Jakob because of its failure to represent the people clearly and objectively: "I don't think one ought to ... use a camera that way,' he said. 'Everything looks alike, you understand? As though Rohlfs might just as well be working for *your* secret service?' "*(p. 227). Not only must facts be pieced together from units of perception reported at different times, and objects from their separate facets, but the usefulness of these factual details is increasingly called into question. When Cresspahl gets on the train with two suitcases, does that mean that he is leaving the country? Not necessarily. The narrators gain an increasing conviction that the truth does not lie in the factual realm. It is a conviction that the reader quickly comes to share. We can determine the exact time of every event in the novel, as we can reconstruct the appearance of Cresspahl's house and the layout of the control tower, but that does not bring us closer to Jakob's truth. In spite of the novel's organizational complexity, we can piece together a comprehensible

---

* "Ich glaube es ist nicht richtig ... so zu fotografieren ..." sagte er. "Es sieht aus als wär alles eins, verstehst du: als könnt Rohlfs auch bei Eurem Geheimdienst sein?" (p. 191)

plot, as well, a plot of mystery, detectives, spies, the police, and secret arrests, similar in its nature to the "feature" film in which Gesine is sometimes aware of playing a part. Neither the novel's focus, nor the story of Jakob lie in this adventure-filled plot, however, and the precision of the novel's details culminates in the elusiveness of the whole.

Supposition and speculation are the cognitive mode and the narrative method of James' novels, as well. Here too we are concerned with a truth that is hidden and perhaps unreachable. The same technique is applied quite differently in the two writers, however. The success of James' style depends on a certain amount of concealment, on a rich surface that suggests multiple depths without actually revealing them. There is, then, an aesthetic justification for vagueness and mystery that is absent from Johnson. His ellipses are due to the incapacity to disclose the truth. There is in the intricate conjectures of the Assinghams or those of Strether and Maria an element of game and pleasure, the pleasure of invention that is not weighed down by the attempted fidelity to fact. Without Johnson's factual basis, the speculation of James' characters is often a totally imaginative activity. Whereas in James, mystery is necessary to the success of the story, and the central narrator exercises a certain amount of control over concealment and revelation, mystery has become the condition for the writer who reveals as much as he knows. Mystery is never intentional mystification in Johnson's work.

Not only the congitive but also the linguistic tools have become insufficient, as the old linguistics professor demonstrates in his lecture. In order to speak at all, he must surpass syntactical and lexical rules:

> . . . words were not enough too polished threadbare to express the
> giant maze of proved and assumed facts, tirelessly he'd add to his
> sentences, break them off ruthlessly as soon as they led to some-
> thing new. (p. 211)*

The professor tries to extend the potentials of the language and creates a disorderly pattern that is more and more difficult to follow, yet is better able to render complexity and multiplicity.

---

* . . . die Worte reichten ihm vor lauter Abgeschliffenheit und Dürftigkeit nicht aus für die übermässige Verschränktheit der bewiesenen und der vermutbaren Tatsachen, unermüdlich erweiterte er die begonnenen Sätze and brach sie rücksichtslos ab, wenn sie ihn einmal an einen brauchbaren Nebenansatz gebracht hatten. (p. 177)

Johnson's style, as well as the structure of the novel and its narrative technique, represents a movement away from imposed authorial control toward openness and variety. Johnson's stylistic devices are interesting, not only in themselves, but also as manifestations of his larger aesthetic. For example, the frequently criticized habit of using a row of adjectives to modify each noun is a manifestation of Johnson's general effort at precision and individualization. His punctuation is also quite unusual. He omits commas almost consistently, suggesting perhaps that the several adjectives which modify a noun are not additional to each other but are to be understood as alternatives. The frequently used colon has the function of pointing to that which follows, thus creating a choppy rhythm, separating the different parts of the sentence from one another. The parenthesis, another mark of Johnson's style, permits the inclusion of grammatically unrelated parts within a sentence. All of these syntactic devices are aimed at enlarging the complexity of traditional syntax, so as to render different relationships that traditional syntax is unable to render. The thrust of Johnson's epistemological search is to define the evershifting relationships between private and public, individual and collective, personal and impersonal. The sentence thus reflects the structure of the entire work and of the world that the work represents; relations between syntactic units can indicate relationships between elements of that universe.[14]

Parataxis, the formal juxtaposition of the parts of a sentence indicates, the precise logical relationships between its different parts; in a paratactic sentence there is no subordination. Instead, each unit is autonomous and asserts its individual importance. Again, this syntactic principle can be extended to the novel as a whole. The structure of the entire novel is characterized by the disjunction of separate autonomous elements whose relationships are to a large extent left up to the interpretation of the participating reader.

There is, on every level of the novel, a tension between the subordinate function of various fictional elements and their desire for self-assertion. Initially, the different narrators, as we shall soon see in more detail, are mere vehicles to Jakob's story and define themselves only in relation to Jakob. As their involvement progresses, however, they increasingly assert their own personality to the point where it becomes a distorting filter greatly affecting the evocation of Jakob. Jöche and Jonas, the two characters least

personally tied to Jakob and to each other are the dialogue speakers of the first two chapters, whereas Jonas and Gesine who are in a complex triangle relationship with Jakob speak in the third chapter, and the deeply involved Gesine and Rohlfs virtually fight for Jakob's soul in the fourth chapter.

Such autonomy is granted neither to James' characters not to any of his syntactic or structural units. James' syntax is also additive, as modifier is piled upon modifier, suggestion upon suggestion, layer upon layer. Its different elements stand in a fixed relationship to each other, however. The effect of vagueness is due to the effort at multiple suggestion which sometimes resembles mystification. James' language is less concerned with a correspondence to a certain vision of reality than how much it can suggest, so as to contribute to the richness of the imaginative structure that is being raised like a gilded pagoda. In his admirable essay on the first paragraph of *The Ambassadors*, Ian Watt [16] names as the prevalent characteristics of James' style the delayed specification of referents, his preference for nontransitive verbs, the frequent use of abstract nouns, of elegant variations that avoid using "he," "his," "him," and of many negative constructions, as well as his preference for reported rather than direct speech. James' is an abstract style that situates the action in a mental setting removed from time and space; he passes through the filter of a literary intelligence with aims at the most suggestive expression possible. When Cresspahl analyzes Jonas' manner of using words to complicate reality, he could be speaking about Henry James:

> How reckless he was in his handling of words. Easily, fluently, they poured from his mouth, sometimes Cresspahl had the impression of sorcery: as though someone were constantly drawing nasty cartoons of the world—an accurately calculated world, in spite of all the exaggerations and condensations, with nothing omitted; its truth looked unfamiliar... he sacrificed all customary means of communication with his twisted, triple-meaning insinuations. (pp. 135-137)*

At the close of these reflections Cresspahl expresses a requirement or a wish: ". . . a thing should be crystal-clear and handy. You'd like that, wouldn't you?" (p. 137).** Whether the last sentence is his own

---

* Nun hatte er eine gewissenlose Weise im Umgang mit Worten. Sie gingen ihm leicht und ohne Zögern vom Munde, so dass Cresspahl manchmal einen Anschein von Zauberei wahrnahm: als bringe jemand ohne Aufhören immer neue boshafte Zeichnungen von der Welt zustande, und darin sei bei aller Übertreibung and Gedankenverkürzung doch genau gerechnet worden und nichts unterschlagen; die Richtigkeit sah fremd aus... er gab mit seinen dreideutig verknoteten Wortbezüglichkeiten die herkömmliche Weise von Verständigung auf. (pp. 113-114)

** . . . die Dinge sollten klar sein und handlich. Ja, das möchtest du wohl. (p. 114)

self-deprecating exclamation or the author's ironic reminder that things just are not clear, Johnson takes Cresspahl's requirement seriously. The small components of his story are as straightforward as possible, only their relations are hazy and ambiguous.

Yet James' style is no less a response to complexity than is Johnson's. Watt speaks of the relationship of character and narrator as a relationship which indicates that behind every individual circumstance there ramifies an endless network of general moral, social and historical relations. James' style, Watts says, "can be seen as a supremely civilized effort to relate every event and every moment of life to the full complexity of its circumambient conditions."[17] This is the effort of Butor and Johnson as well; although, through Jacques Revel, Butor also demonstrates its absurdity. Johnson expands on the two voices whose interplay suggests those complex relations in James, by creating a forum in which a multiplicity of voices are heard. Similarly, he allows one individual syntactic unit to assume more than one function.

Lexically, as well, Johnson's style is marked by a concern for directness and precision. Rejecting the worn-out phrases of traditional usage as well as the politically contaminated expressions of the divided country, Johnson dramatizes the tension between automatic unreflected responses that are no longer communicative and the spontaneous individual form of expression that is so hard to achieve. It is to clarify this distinction that Johnson intersperses his text with a number of alien codes such as Russian propaganda slogans, common English idioms, Italian and American advertising slogans, expressions in Pommeranian dialect, popular songs and childern's riddles, as well as echoes of Lutheran German. Most of these are formulae, instinctive responses triggered off by one word or thought, representing the first unreflected reaction to a particular situation. The false sense of community that such forms of "communication" engender is demonstrated by the music in the train compartment: the travelers who listen to popular songs throughout the journey suddenly begin to speak in the first person plural. The unreflective nature of these responses is illustrated by Gesine's talk in her sleep: "Jakob, how broad you've grown!" (p. 168). The famous line from "Little Red Riding Hood" that is an analogue for Gesine's concern with the changes she finds in Jakob, just as the biblical "Es ist meine Seele die liebet Jakob," expresses her love for him. This choice of expressions points to Gesine's distance from her own feelings about whose legitimacy she has doubts.

Different from these automatic forms of expression is the Pommeranian dialect. Standing in sharp contrast to the stilted high German used by Rohlfs and other party officials, this private idiom is the most direct and the most vivid. It can still be communicative because, as an archaic form, it is protected from both political and commercial corruption. Dialect is less vulnerable to distortion than the official language used by media, press and political propaganda. It is a language shared by a limited number of people and excluding all others.

The narrators of Jakob's story interact in different ways within the novel's three narrative media: interior monologue, dialogue, and narration. James used the multiple perspective form to present two different perspectives one after the other; the narrative remains within the mind of each and they interact only in a few ritualized dialogue passages. For this reason they need a mediator, a third who might effect a meeting between them. Johnson, in contrast, attempts to use this form not only to present several points of view but to demonstrate their interaction. It is a vehicle for sorting out individual and supra-individual impulses, private and public motivations. It could be the medium through which the gap between the personal and the collective might be bridged, where disparate perceptual grids might be integrated to bring about a consensus. Such a consensus is the necessary basis for a community that would supersede deeply ingrained differences of outlook and ideology.

The interest and involvement of each narrator demonstrates the danger of authorship, the violation inherent in the process of "truthfinding." As these different perspectives are juxtaposed, we recognize the limiting perceptual grids of each individual, the necessity of collaboration and its difficulty. The conglomeration of viewpoints suggests the possibility of transcending single and superior authorship.

Jakob's story unfolds from the narrations and discussions of Jonas, Jöche, Gesine, Rohlfs and an impersonal narrator; it does not exist independently of these filters. Similarly these main characters are defined primarily through their connection to Jakob, either on the past level of the novel, by their personal relation to him, or on the present level, in their function as narrators of his story, their service to his memory. There is, as I have mentioned, a continuing tension between the subordinate function of these figures and their desire to assert their own individuality. At first, they are no more than anonymous voices whose identity cannot be determined; gradually they become recognizable as their language, their interests and their narrative methods become more and more differentiated. Speculation is never disinterested and the image of Jakob is shaped by the narrators' needs and dreams. The effort of discovering the truth about Jakob is frustrated by the distortions of their own interest in the outcome of the common investigations. Yet only their deep involvement can make Jakob as strongly present as he comes to be. Only the strongly affective quality of the reminiscences can suggest the pain of his loss. Unlike the missing voices in James, those of Adam Verver, Charlotte and even Mme. de Vionnet and Amerigo, Jakob is the focus of the story, the locus for everyone's imaginative investment, the force that brings them together in the effort to understand him. Like the fog in which Jakob and Gesine walk, the narrator's mediation both shields and reveals.

Jonas is a linguist and a humanist. His language is clearly that of an intellectual, "he was talking—to no one in particular, sure of himself, practiced, breezy" (p. 79).* In spite of his careless use of language in his dialogue with others, Jonas' thoughts are filled with his concern for words and his consciousness of their insufficiency in the face of a real person like Jakob. *"If I remember correctly, I immediately began searching for words. Which I discarded again, one after the other, they all described a characteristic, this mn didn't seem to have any"* (p. 59).** Jonas feels that by describing Jakob through words he would rob him of everything that is personal and unique, and Jakob's individuality is of primary importance to Jonas. His criticism of the East German government concerns their lack of respect for the integrity and self-determination of the individual, an attitude exemplified in their distortion of literature and of the past:

> Language lives in the community that speaks it and perishes with it; whereas literature preserves for us one individual's relationship to the world, should one pay exclusive attention to the individual . . . and the linguistic means it used to come to terms with and overcome the world? . . . Whereas, on the other hand, if history is a history of class struggles and literature a tangible illustration of Marxist theories, the benefit is undeniable . . . And if one fine day each word

---

* [er] sprach...sicher geübt respektlos vor sich hin. (p. 66)

** *Wenn ich mich recht erinnere, begann ich sogleich nach Worten zu suchen. Das Nächste war dass ich ein Wort nach dem andern wegwarf, sie meinten sämtlich Eigenschaften, dieser schien keine zu haben.* (p. 49)

that has been written with literary intention finds itself twisted
around and around. . . (p. 81)*

For Jonas, Jakob is still the kind of person who, unlike Jonas
himself, could form the subject of literature. Jonas is determined to
salvage the individual from the manipulation of the Marxist regime
and Jakob is for him the example of autonomy.

As an intellectual, Jonas feels removed from the immediacy of
experience and the directness of response of which Jakob and
Gesine are capable. Jonas' relationship with Cresspahl's cat,
described at great length, is an effort to achieve an intuitive, non-
cerebral form of experience: ". . .but could life be found in a text? he
had the impression it was passing him by" (p. 85).** When he visits
Jakob at his job, he suddenly feels the desire to participate in a
similarly concrete form of work: "These were tangible durable
objects, boxcars, locomotives, coaches; . . . every occurrence in
Jakob's head corresponded to a reality, something really did
happen" (p. 192).*** Jakob is all that Jonas is not, unquestionably
committed to communism and fulfilled by important and necessary
manual labor. For the unselfconscious and reflective Jakob, freedom is no more than the strength of his unquestioning attitude;
the meaning of the state has become second nature for him. For
Jonas he is "the reasonable practical justifiable side of life" (p.
191)."**** How different is Jonas from this image of Jakob, Jonas
whose life is marked by the effort to define freedom, to reflect,
understand, and explain.

As a narrator, Jonas shows a great deal of empathy and intuitive
understanding even while being painfully aware of the limitations
imposed on his ability to perceive the truth about others. That Jonas
is suspicious of the distortions a narrator's imagination can inflict is
apparent in his wonderfully evocative description of Gesine:

---

* Die Sprache lebt mit der Gemeinschaft, von der sie gesprochen wird, und vergeht mit ihr; in der Literatur
aber ist erhalten das Weltverhältnis eines einzelnen Subjekts . . . und welcher sprachlichen Mittel es sich bedient
zur Erfassung und Bewältigung der Welt? . . . Andererseits, hingegen, wenn die Geschichte eine ist von
Klassenkämpfen, die Literatur als anschauliche Illustration zu den Lehren des Marxismus. . . . Und wenn nun
eines Tages jedes in literarischer Absicht hingeschriebene Wort um und um gedreht ist. . . (pp. 67-68)

** . . . war aber das Leben in einem Text? er kam sich vor als versäume er es. (p. 71)

*** Hier handelte es sich um feste dauerhafte Dinge, Wagen, Zugmaschinen, Apparate . . . aber was in Jakobs
Kopf vorfiel und geschah, das hatte eine wirkliche Entsprechung, da fiel in der Tat etwas vor. (p. 161)

**** das vernünftige, verantwortbare, praktische Leben. (p. 160)

> She was in his memory like a feeling of an inexchangeable way of
> looking at one, of climbing stairs, of startled halts: details could
> be dismissed, because the inexchangeability stemmed from all this
> being real in itself, independent from any spectator or listener or
> someone who was, strangely enough, sitting in the Jerichow Raths-
> keller thinking about her. In the end, one could merely express
> one's gladness that such things existed in the world . . . without
> reservations. (p. 144)*

This is one of the few times that Jonas shows complete
confidence in his perceptions. He is so convinced that he has gotten
at the very essence of Gesine in this observation that he does not
hesitate to represent a feeling as a reality that exists independently
of himself as observer. Willing to efface himself in his function as
narrator, Jonas expresses a vision of Gesine unmediated by his own
interests and discovers an intuitive form of understanding that is
based on trust rather than on analysis or narrative. This unique
form of knowledge represents the only kind of certainty in this
novel, because it is a knowledge that respects the individual's
integrity.

Both his aloof intellectualism and his desire not to impose
himself allow Jonas to continue entertaining several different
interpretations of Jakob's death. He is convinced, however, that,
whether his death is accident, suicide, or murder, Jakob could be the
one person able to elude the pressures of the state. As the ideal
communist citizen, Jakob thus continues to justify Jonas' efforts to
reform the system. Thus Jonas simply cannot avoid imposing on
Jakob his own vested interest: the success of a communist ideology
independent of the present regime.

Unlike Jonas who, in spite of his dissatisfaction, remains in the
East and attempts to change it, Gesine leaves out of a compulsion.
The move turns out to be less satisfactory than expected; working for
NATO in a reaction to the East, Gesine is still full of sympathy for
communism and cannot commit herself to the West. The division of
her life into two irreconcilable parts has severe repercussions on
Gesine's state of mind. In her life and work in the West she feels
disillusioned, fragmented and isolated to the point of abandoning

---

* Sie war erinnerlich als das Gefühl einer unverwechselbaren Weise von Augenzuwenden und
Treppensteigen und Erschrecken und Stillstehen: da konnte man von den Einzelheiten absehen, denn das
Unverwechselbare hing daran dass dies alles für sich selbst wirklich war unabhängig von einem Betrachter und
Zuhörer und einem, der sonderbarer Weise im Jerichower Krug sass und sich ihrer erinnerte. Am Ende war nur zu
sagen man sei zufrieden dass es dies gebe in der Welt, es war nichts zu bedenken. (p. 120)

even the hope for companionship, in the East there remain mere childhood memories, not the hope of a future.

Gesine needs Jakob as the symbol of her unspoiled past, as the solution to her present discomfort. Eager to re-establish a link with her own childhood, Gesine is the only one to offer us an insight into Jakob's childhood and youth. Perhaps her desire to emphasize Jakob's wholeness and integrity which makes him so much like her father and so unlike herself makes her vision too rigid. She is loath to admit any changes in him. Their somewhat incestuous relationship can be seen in Gesine's flight back into childhood and away from the conflicts of the divided country. In her concern for Jakob's integrity, Gesine refuses to believe that Jakob ever intended to stay in the West. She despairs at the lack of a place where they could live together so as to reunify their severed lives.

In spite of the importance she has for all the other characters in the novel, Gesine remains a mysterious figure. The nature of her trip to the East—she comes with a gun and a miniature camera—is never elucidated. Her feelings of guilt and responsibility for Jakob's death undoubtedly color her memories of him: "As long as nobody can get up and say: This is how it was and no other way. It's this one's, it's that one's fault. What if it were your fault, Jonas?" (p. 132)* Gesine's frequent use of Lutheran German or of English idiomatic expressions when she speaks of all that is closest to her reveals her unwillingness to face her own feelings. Although she has known Jakob the longest, her relationship to him is the most conflicted and undefined at the time of his death. Her ability to convey the strength of Jakob's personality, his warmth and tenderness, is offset by the interested nature of her reminiscences. Gesine best conveys the impact Jakob could have on others, and, as the person closest to him, she also reveals his ultimate unknowability.

As a representative of the East German state who takes personal responsibility for the regime, Rohlfs is the most dogmatic of all the narrators. Unlike the representatives of the official position in Johnson's other novels, Rohlfs is a complex and full figure with dreams and ideals. He is eager to stress the difference between himself and the policemen he calls "dogcatchers." Rohlf's loyalty to the state is a complicated phenomenon. He will go so far as to relinquish his personality to serve the state. He is initially presented

---

* Ich möchte nur wahrhaben dass keiner sich hinstellen kann und sagen: So war es und nicht anders. Die Schuld hat der und der. Wenn du sie nun hättest Jonas. (p. 110)

as a faceless shadow, a mere instrument of the government investigation: his numerous names attest to a similar willingness to efface himself for his mission.

Insight into Rohlfs' reflections discloses his desperate spiritual dependence on the rightness of the communist regime. Unlike Gesine, who values wholeness to the point of accepting the responsibility for the ugliness of the German past, Rohlfs sacrifices his youth and his parents to the communist present: "the same stubbornness that considered half of his life an error: in order to make the present look right" (p. 145)* His willful rejection of all doubts and questions makes Rohlfs' perspective terribly narrow. He will accept, for example, only one view of the nocturnal landscape around Jerichow, thereby revealing the precarious security of his position:

> The regular shimmering structure of the castle that rises from the forest in the night and draws the onlooker's eyes along the lanes of its park is not architecture or petrified history, but a memorial to exploitation. Whoever is not for us is against us, and unjust with regard to progress. Who is for us: will be the question; and not: how do you like the night with the dark villages between the curves of the soil under the huge cloudy sky (p. 147).**

In this interpretation of the landscape Rohlfs places himself in opposition to his father whose old map he is using. He demonstrates that the communist ideology can only impose itself by displacing all other meanings and interests, whether they be geographical, historical, geological or simply the enjoyment of a beautiful night. it needs to co-opt entirely the mind of the individual.

As a government agent instructed to win the services of Gesine for the East, Rohlfs should have no personal commitment to Jakob's story. As he gains insight into Jakob's life, however, Rohlfs comes to see him as the ideal communist, totally fulfilled by his work and his service to the state. He believes that Jakob shares his strongest convictions. Although he denies this personal affinity, Jakob treats Rohlfs as a friend. Their mutual sympathy turns out to be less powerful than their disparate social positions, however.

*...[der] Eigensinn, der die Hälfte seines Lebens für einen Irrtum ansah: damit das Gegenwärtige das Rechte blieb. (p. 121)

** Der schimmernde ebenmässige Bau des Schlosses, der aufsteigt aus dem nächtlichen Wald und den Blick des Betrachters an sich zieht durch die Alleen des Parks, ist nicht Architektur und stehengebliebene Geschichte sondern ein Denkmal der Ausbeutung. Wer nicht für uns ist ist gegen uns und ungerecht im Sinne des Fortschritts. Es wird gefragt werden wer ist für uns und nicht wie gefällt die die Nacht mit den dunklen Dörfern zwischen den Falten des Bodens unter dem mächtug bewölkten Himmel. (p. 123)

Using Jakob as a test for the rightness of communism, Rohlfs becomes humanly involved with him and with the interpretation of his death. In their conversation, Rohlfs and Gesine virtually for Jakob's soul; Rohlfs has to believe that Jakob hated and condemned the West, that he returned out of conviction and that his death was death was an accident. Thinking of a scene that Gesine mentions from Jakob's trip to the West, Rohlfs vividly imagines Jakob's ardent defense of communism and his condemnation of the West German revival of Nazism. To Gesine's different picture he says, "But I can't listen to you without prejudice or else I mislay Jakob. I can no longer fit him into my memory" (pp. 221-22),* evoking her reproach: "What do you do with facts you don't like? . . . But can't you see that you are belittling reality?" (pp. 222-24). **

In his function as narrator, Rohlfs appears as a compulsive figure reminiscent of Faulkner's Jason or Beckett's Moran. His observations are primarily factual; with all the technical aids available to him, the lives of Jakob, Gesine, and Jonas are totally open to him. He notes down every detail about their lives, but soon realizes that even his knowledge is only minimal. His interior monologues are marked by paranoia and nervousness as well as by selfconsciousness and hastiness. His hate and fear of others dictates his perceptions. Rohlfs' feelings of inferiority are due to his crippled hand and foot, injuries inflicted accidentially by a comrade during the war. His concern for his small daughter who often appears in his thoughts, as well as his touching desire for her respect, reveal the vulnerable side of Rohlfs' personal character.

The power Rohlfs gains from his official status and from the detective apparatus that facilitates his investigation gives him a virtually authorial control over the lives of the other figures. Yet his advantage becomes less and less real. Rohlfs' one-sided interpretations continually clash with others that are at least as valid. In spite of the wealth of information available to him, Rohlfs also experiences the precariousness of all knowledge.

In his goal of influencing other people by convincing them of the rightness of his own vision, Rohlfs resembles Maggie Verver.

---

* Aber ich kann Ihnen nicht zuhören ohne Vorurteil, denn dann gerät Jakob mir in Verust, dann passt er nicht mehr zu meiner Erinnerung." (p. 186)

** "Was machen Sie eigentlich mit solchen Tatsachen, die Ihnen nicht gefallen? . . . Aber sehen Sie denn nicht dass Sie die Wirklichkeit verarmen?" (pp. 187-188)

Like Maggie, he derives his authority from a supra-personal source; Maggie represents her civilization, Rohlfs the communist regime. It is his failure to be totally authoritarian that is Rohlfs' mistake as well as his humane substance. Admitting that "compulsory decisions are no decisions" (p. 229),* he gives his subjects a choice, lets them reflect and compare, waits for them to respond. Thereby Rohlfs relinquishes the advantage his detective apparatus gives him, one he finds useless anyway. He makes himself vulnerable by offering Jakob his friendship: ". . . this is my face, take a look at it, Jakob" (p. 228).** In this offer, he endangers both his own position and Jakob's: ". . . he spoke to him as the State: personally" (p. 129).*** Such a relationship is a contradiction and a failure. Rohlfs rightly suspects that he might have done better with "dogcatcher" methods. His insistence that Jakob embrace communist ideology out of conviction and not out of unreflective necessity endangers Jakob's security and constitutes a plausible cause of his death.

Unlike Maggie, Rohlfs is not aware of taking risks; the strength of his conviction makes him utterly blind: *"I thought there was only one answer. And I expected it from people who don't have my interests at heart. Conversation is an error. 'Perhaps you'd have done better to refrain from this democratic fraternizing' "* (p. 229).**** While Maggie's entire existence depends on the Prince's answer, Rohlfs easily survives a failure that has devasting effects on the lives of Jakob, Jonas, Gesine, and Frau Abs. He is the only one able to walk away: ". . . he thought of tomorrow, that the sun would rise anew, that they'd be somewhere else, nothing but files would be left of today and of the day before" (p. 238).*****

The relation of Jakob's story by such different individuals dramatizes not so much the unreliability of single narrators as the different perceptual grids that delimit our apprehensions. Rohlfs' optic is reductively political, just as Gesine's is lyrically personal and

---

* Erpresste Entscheidungen sind keine. (p. 192)

** . . . so sehe ich aus, sieh es dir an Jakob. (p. 192)

*** . . . da redete er mit ihm als Staatsmacht: persönlich. (p. 107)

**** *Ich habe gedacht es gibt nur eine Antwort. Und habe sie erwartet von Leuten, die es nicht absehen auf meine Sache. Gespräch ist ein Fehler. "Hätten Sie doch lieber verzichtet auf diese demokratischen Brüderlichkeiten."* (pp. 192-193)

***** . . . [er] dachte . . . an den folgenden Tag und dass dann wieder die Sonne aufgehen wurde und dass sie die Zeit auch verbringen würden an einem anderen Ort und dass von Heute und Gestern nur Aktennotizen übrigsein würden. (p. 201)

Jonas' narrowly intellectual: "Cresspahl would say: most of them were probably there, but each saw a different house burn down. And houses never look alike anyway" (p. 53).* The question that is raised here is what we see when we see and what influence our personal and ideological outlook has on our perceptions.

More than Rohlfs, the narrator is privileged in having an overview and in being able to supplement substantially the dialogues and monologues of the other narrators. He introduces, for example, the accounts of Jonas' secretary and Jakob's assistant. Moreover, he has the function of providing the voices of those characters who lack the verbal ability of Rohlfs, Jonas and Gesine and who prefer silence, Cresspahl and Jakob especially. Although a conversation between Cresspahl and Jonas is announced in the last chapter, its content is never revealed. Cresspahl remains a closed and silent figure, representing a certain type of integrity that Johnson opposes to the intellectualism of Jonas or the garrulity of Rohlfs. As Peter Demetz says, Johnson's "narrative cards are stacked against quick thinkers and articulate intellectuals who do not work with their hands but merely with paper and words: and Johnson's explicit sympathies are with the inarticulate craftsman who putters around with old furniture [Cresspahl]; the near-silent dispatcher who cherishes his systematic work."[18] Such figures can be brought to the fictional surface only through the mediation of a narrator able to make his vision present without compromising his natural reticence and silence.

In spite of the material available to him, the narrator does not reach the truth about Jakob more easily than the other characters. Although he is able to assess evidence from various sources and to provide a consensus and although he is not weighed down by a personal involvement with Jakob, on many occasions he is forced to resort to conjecture in his interpretation of the facts, providing that narration cannot help but be interpretive. When he relates the occasion on which Jakob gives Cresspahl Gesine's gun, he is unable to choose between two possible versions and so presents both. The reader must decide which is the more truthful. Thus the narrator conforms to the requirements of "Berliner Stadtbahn"; he admits the limits of his knowledge.

---

* Cresspahl würde sagen: anwesend seien wohl die mehreren gewesen, aber da habe jeder ein anderes Haus brennen sehen. Häuser seien sich ohnehin nicht gleich. (p. 44)

The narrator's tone is polemical; he addresses the reader as a partner in a dialogue and invites him to participate in the speculations about Jakob and even to become personally involved in the story: "But Jakob always cut straight across the tracks" (p. 7); "But if someone should happen to ask you" (p. 12); "And she didn't look as though she had been crying; that's a point we do want to make" (p. 240).* The impartial reader is perhaps in the best position to attempt a clear vision of Jakob's life and his mysterious death. While the novel's characters see each other only from the outside and are unable, even through great efforts at empathy, to penetrate each other's thoughts, the reader is privileged to their interior monologues in addition to external observations, and so has a greater overview even than Rohlfs. The difficulties are great nevertheless. Rather than gaining a clear insight into the person Jakob, as we do with Lambert Strether or Maggie Verver, we experience in a very real way the difficulties of the process Johnson calls "truthfinding." In its language and structure, the novel acts out the ambiguity and complexity faced by the actual "readers" of Jakob and the reader's experience parallels their.

Jakob's story violates all our preconceptions about fiction. Rather than unfolding, it demands to be painfully recomposed out of disjointed fragments. It thwarts our need for order and plot and forces us to deal with fragmentation and disjunction. An agent of "truthfinding," the reader must recognize and attempt to avoid its inherent exploitative impulse.

The complex structure of third-person narration, interior monologue, and dialogue presents serious problems of orientation for the reader. While monologues are indicated by italics and dialogues by hyphens, the respective speakers are hardly ever identified.** Not only must the reader learn to identify the different speakers as he becomes more familiar with them, but he must also keep track of the sudden transitions from one mode to another, transitions which often involve changes in time from the scene of the dialogues after Jakob's death to the remembered weeks leading up to it presented in the other two modes. While it is often possible to identify the speakers of the monologues from the context, the dialogue scenes are not set up until the fifth chapter. Jöche and

---

* "Aber Jakob ist immer quer über die Gleise gegangen" (p. 5); "Aber wenn einer Sie mal fragen sollte" (p. 9); "Und sie sah nicht aus wie eine, die geweint hat; das wollen wir doch mal sagen" (p. 202).

** The English translator has supplied the speakers' names in the italic passages; they are not given in the original text.

Jonas, for example, speak from page 7 (p. 5) on, but are not introduced as characters on the inner level of the story until pages 46 (p. 38) and 57 (p. 48), respectively. The scene of their conversation on page 7 (p. 5) is not described until page 237 (p. 200). The reader, then, not only joins the other narrators in their speculations about Jakob, but is forced to speculate about every scene presented to him. Sometimes it is impossible to determine the source of a comment or a thought, since the three modes are often mixed:

> *And Jakob was holding his hand out to her from the other side of the brook so she wouldn't skid on the smooth slimy gnarled logs and she said, so, on her toes bent forward for balance and, no, Jakob said. Even if they had seen something, it couldn't be told. (p.150)**

These sentences are part of an interior monologue of Jonas. From his narration it is unclear whether it was Gesine or Jakob who said no. Moreover, as Jonas is telling a story that was reported to him, it is unclear whether the last sentence of the quote is a reflection of his own effort to retell their experiences, or whether it is a comment made by Gesine when she told Jonas of the scene.

Through the immersion into almost entirely anonymous thoughts and reminiscences, the reader experiences a great emotive immediacy. He gets the emotion before being able to situate it intellectually. Becoming involved with Jakob and experiencing the depth of his loss through all the mediating narrators, the reader feels compelled to penetrate his mystery. The affective power of Johnson's style and the elusive absence of Jakob himself substitutes for the suspense of traditional narrative.

The structural principle of the novel and its syntactical property, the conglomeration of unconnected fragments, attributes to the reader the important role of arranging and compiling. The material resists the reader's impulses, however; it resists what Johnson calls his "curiosity for stories."** It is in *The Third Book about Achim* that the tension between the writer's and the reader's impulse to shape a life into a unified and harmonious form and the resistance of that life to such manipulation is most vividly

---

* *Und Jakob auf dem andern Ufer hielt ihr die Hand entgegen dass sie nicht ausrutschen sollte auf dem schmierig glatten knorrigen Baumstamm und sie sagte so auf den Zehenspitzen vorwärtsgebeugt im Gleichgewicht nein Jakob sagte. Selbst wenn da etwas in Sicht gekommen wäre liesse es sich nicht erzählen.* (pp. 125-126)

** Neugier nach Geschichten.

dramatized. In *Jakob* the "feature" Gesine speaks of, the romantic love story, stands in contrast to the shapeless fragments of Jakob's story. Jakob is protected from the assault and manipulation of his "readers" not only by the fact of his death but also by his inherent mystery, elusiveness, silence. His entire mode of being is non-verbal and opaque. We know what he means to his friends and how they see him, we know what he looked like and how he lived, but we never find out what he felt and why he dies. His love for a mechanical job, the efficiency with which he lets the Russian military train pass through are factors which are hard to reconcile with the positive picture the narrators draw of him. The essence of Jakob's character, his deepest feelings about the East, the West, about Sabine and Gesine are forever unknowable. Ironically, his integrity lies in his mystery.

The other characters' usurpation of Jakob's life and character for individual purposes, their greed to know, violate his privacy and constitute a comment on the moral ambiguity of the reader's position.

The interior monologues are similar to James' method, in that they demonstrate the great difference between the various out-looks—in the two accounts of Jonas' and Gesine's first meeting, for example—and the isolation of the helpless single mind faced with a complex reality. The narrator's passages combine different viewpoints and provide the scene for arguments. Even though he is uninvolved, he is a filter and can provide only the chance for a meeting, and a mediated one at that. The dialogues are the most original of Johnson's experiments. Here people get together to search for the truth about Jakob, to confront and challenge each other's opinions and join in remembering and imagining different scences. When Rohlfs and Gesine imagine Jonas' arrival at the control tower, they literally piece the incident together in a wonderful example of communal storytelling. Those two most contrary of the characters establish a relation of mutual sympathy in their conversations about Jakob, even if they cannot ultimately develop a common vision.

In these dialogues it is the dead Jakob who becomes the potential vehicle for a meeting of his different friends. He is continually being used for their individual needs. People's appraisal of each other is subject to a self-interest and greed that resembles that of Jamesian characters. Jakob becomes their puppet, as they are each other's. The literary act, the process of narration as well as

reading, is revealed as tainted by self-interest. The desire to know is greedy and can have destructive effects; Rohlfs' direct questions to Frau Abs are an example, but are they so different from Jonas' "avid excitement" as he watches Jakob on the train?

The artistic process becomes doubly guilty of violating the individual's integrity in its connection to the social and political institutions of East and West Germany, institutions which demand the submission of the individual to the community. Interest in the mysterious Jakob is charged with a nostalgia that the characters as well as the reader feel for the "central" individual, the "central" intelligence celebrated in the work of Henry James, now lost, absorbed by the community. The elusive Jakob defies this absorption, but is unable to survive.

Convinced that had he lived several years earlier, he would have learned how to kill Jews too, Joche denies the individual's power to delineate his supposedly unique personality:

> But this—let's call it: personal uniqueness needs its opportunities, shows up only in exterior things; in what you do and not in how you feel. And the possibilities to do are only those that you find in the light of the world, what the know-betters, your educators, offer you. (p. 77)*

Although this novel focuses on the constraints imposed by the East German state, it dramatizes the fact that any social system demands the conformity of its inhabitants. The hotel clerk in the West German city puts, in a sense, as much pressure on Jakob to behave according to set standards as Rohlfs does. Moreover, in any society the individual's actions are so intimately tied up with those of others that the chance for self-expression is severely limited. Jakob is convinced that the shame of the German past is incompatible with the present German pride and he refuses to participate in it, though he may not personally have contributed to the ugly past. Gesine's job as an interpreter is the emblem of lack of self-expression in our world; the words she says are not her own: "I do nothing but talk from morning to night, just think if I had to answer for all those words" (p. 30).** The individual must fit his

---

* Diese wir können ja sagen:, persönliche Eigenart braucht aber Gelegenheiten, wird ja nur in Äusserlichkeiten sichtbar; in dem was du tust und nicht in dem wie du dich fühlst. Und Möglichkeiten zu tun gibt es nur was du vorfindest im Licht der Welt und was die Besserwisser: deine Erzieher dir anbieten. (pp. 64-65)

** Ich rede von morgens bis abends, bedenk mal wenn ich das alles verantworten sollte. (p. 24)

meaning into impersonal shapes whose meaning is inflexible, not only incapable of expressing uniqueness, but also controlled by prevailing ideologies.

The characters of the novel are caught between two crucial political events which determine their lives but over which they have no control: the Hungarian Revolution, on the one hand, the Suez Crisis, on the other. Jakob's refusal to stop the Russian military train to Hungary is his resigned and cynical comment on the individual's impotence in the face of political events. It is one of the most powerful scenes in the novel and one of the most pessimistic. Jakob dismisses Jonas' suggestion of personal resistance as "playing stupid just for the fun of it." The only form of protest Gesine can envision against the British bombing of Egypt is to leave her job at NATO. Jonas' scientific response to political events is judged equally weak and insufficient.

The supra-personal power, the cultural force that in James was still defined by the individual, in Butor by other than human factors, is circumscribed by the political reality in Johnson's world. His book investigates the individual's freedom in the context of a given ideological system. More than just the general social and political factors named above, however, Johnson examines the specific position of the individual in the East German state. According to its own propaganda, the communist state belongs to the people and represents the personal needs and desires of each. In return for total subjugation, the limited existence of each citizen is glorified in the service to a greater goal: " 'Can a man waste himself on a purpose?'. . 'Yes,' Herr Rohlfs said gruffly" (p. 124).* Those who have done so, like Herr Rohlfs, transfer their own greed and self-interest to the state which thereby becomes like an allpowerful individual. The identity of every individual no longer depends totally on the rightness of the state; the individual has ceased to be responsible for itself. The state's destructive power is even greater than that of a single Maggie Verver. It coopts the lives and minds of its citizens, robs them of their power to think and speak. Rohlfs is not satisfied with Jakob's unquestioning devotion; he wants more. Jonas' description of the march is reminiscent of Revel's depiction of the effects of the Bleston wind on its inhabitants; here is the government instead of the city which molds people after a faceless pattern. Cresspahl alone is able to lead a public life defined by his

---

* "Soll einer sich selbst versäumen über einem Zweck," . . . "Ja," sagte Herr Rohlfs grob. (p. 103)

own private essence; he remains in the remote Mecklenburg village as an artisan, continuing his previous existence, unafraid of even the powerful functionaries of the East German regime. Cresspahl, like the cat, embodies what we sense as the reality of freedom from all ideological systems. Cresspahl is connected to the wind and the sea, to Jerichow and *Plattdeutsch*, to his manual work, to the old Germany that so wonderfully rises out of the old map and that represents the setting for Gesine's dreams of freedom and fulfillment. It is a past which Rohlfs and the new regime must reject, but which persists not only in the names of the villages whose suffix *hagen* harks back to forests that disappeared thousands of years before, but also in the dreams and memories of Johnson's characters. Gesine and Jakob's own childhood merges with the undivided childhood of the country. As they dream of flying kites on the beautiful mountains around Jerichow, they express a desire that in its simplicity defines all that is missing in both East and West Germany: *"I'd like to be up there on those clouds"* (p. 231)"*

It is clear that characters with such dreams are not the cripples of Beckett nor the crushed and impotent human beings of Butor; neither, however, are they the all-powerful individuals of James. Although the story of Johnson's characters is so deeply connected to the forces that govern their lives that it is no longer a psychological story, and although he dramatizes the fact that the traditional analysis of character can no longer lead to the perception of his essence, he does allow for a kind of insight that pierces through the protective barrier of the individual without violation and bridges the gap between these lonely beings. Only one form of perception grants the individual's integrity. He assumes the effacement of the perceiver's personal interest and is exemplified in Jonas' reminiscence of Gesine, quoted above, or in Cresspahl's evocation of Jakob, the most suggestive of the whole novel:

> The thought of Jakob made Cresspahl smile, he felt so present. Jakob never froze into an image of departure, he stayed in one's memory as a reality of smiles and answers and fun and life as a whole: like a gesture. (p. 135)**

---

* . . . *ich möchte auf die Wolken. (p. 194)*

** Als Cresspahl sich an Jakob erinnerte, lächelte er vor lauter Gegenwärtigkeit, denn Jakob erstarrte nicht in den Bildern des Abschieds sondern blieb im Gedächtnis als soeine Wirklichkeit von Lächeln und Antworten und Spass und Leben überhaupt: wie eine Gebärde. (p. 112)

These epiphanic moments of insight are very rare in the novel but they form perhaps the basis for a new form of community which would replace the alienating societies in which we live now, the basis for a reunification on an individual and supra-individual level. Non-intellectual and non-narrative experiences of recognition, they suggest a new form of reading, as well, one free from greed and exploitation.

These fleeting moments of contact between Jonas and Gesine, between Cresspahl and Jakob are tenuous, brief, yet they still point to the possibility of overcoming the self-interest of authority and of preserving, in the process of knowing and reading, the integrity of the object of one's quest. For Cresspahl, Jakob is a gesture, an expression that would only be impoverished if analyzed. He wants to remember him, not possess him. For Rohlfs, Jakob is the dove on the roof, someone to be captured, understood, controlled. It is clearly Cresspahl's knowledge that Johnson values and that even Rohlfs would have liked to experience: "That Jakob would have understood. Not with words, in a brief casual silence, just looking at each other" (p. 240).* In its qualifications about both language and "truthfinding" in general and in its elevation of a non-verbal, non-narrative epistemology, Johnson's novel questions profoundly its own premises as a novel. Horst Kruger's description of the emotional background of *Two Views* applies to all of Johnson's works: "This book emerges from the depths of a woundedness that has not healed . . . the toothgrinding protest of a wounded silent man." Johnson speaks because he has no choice.

Jakob resists any form of reading; he resists the exploitative interests of Rohlfs and Jonas, the loving violation of Gesine. The novel's epistemological failure is at the same time the triumph of an unassailable individual integrity. Johnson offers his reader an insight into the moral dubiousness of an activity that, in capitalizing on the lives of others in the effort to uncover all their mystery, is related to the activities of the authoritarian state. To see only plots, whether literary or political, is an act of violation. It is not redeemed by the thirst for knowledge or the cause of communism. James also found the fictional process morally reprehensible, but he redeemed it, at least in part, by the exhilaration of knowledge and power that makes the reader into the potential vehicle of a cultural fusion. In

---

* Dass er mit Jakob darüber sich hätte verständigen konnen. Wortlos, in einem kurzen unauffälligen Schweigen und Blickwechseln. (p. 202)

Jakob, the reader must learn to accept his own humility in the face of a largely unknowable reality.

Each of the novel's characters emerges as an individual struggling against violation and absorption by the system; Jakob, Cresspahl, and the cat, however, escape all the grids; they are impenetrable and inviolable. What the reader learns here is to overcome an appetite for that Other that is enticing and attractive because it is foreign and mysterious. Through his difficulties, through his inability to penetrate some figures, he learns how to approach his object without endangering that mystery and integrity that made it initially attractive. Learning this is a lesson in humility. Jakob himself demonstrates the insurmountable difficulties of that lesson. He may escape the observers' various grids but is unable to escape death. In his life, he may attempt to maintain the greatest possible integrity, but ultimately he cannot escape the assault of the state and also survive.

III. EXPANSION

5.　*Mobile*: "An Orgy of Surprises and Shivers"

　　The four works analyzed in previous chapters are self-conscious novels which test the moral and aesthetic validity of the narrative act. For various reasons and in different ways, James, Butor, and Johnson question the potentialities of narrative as an instrument of knowledge about the outside world and as a form of communication between author and reader. While laying bare the shortcomings of narrative, these three experimental writers attempt to overcome them, to preserve, in some way, the representational and epistemological power of narrative fiction. Both James and Johnson reveal the moral dubiousness of the fictional process, its potentially exploitative and manipulative nature and its implication in oppressive social systems, such as the capitalist-imperialist doctrines of Adam Verver or the authoritarian communism of Herr Rohlfs. James' novels bring out the subtle compensations to be derived from this flawed activity and, far from abandoning authority and authorship, they concentrate on the exhilarating rewards it can afford in its most refined forms. Johnson's novels, on the other hand, emphasize dissatisfactions with narrative and begin to suggest alternatives to it. The exploitation and violation inherent in all "truthfinding" render it incapable of reaching the most fundamental human truths. As it demonstrates this fact, *Speculations about Jakob* borders on self-destruction. Instead of removing the tyranny of a single authorship, Johnson's experiment with multiple narrators emphasize even more the imprisoning perceptual grids that entrap each narrator; the novel ultimately fails to lead to a broader, a collective form of truth. Jakob and Cresspahl, who escape these separate perceptual grids, simply elude the novel. The only moments where genuine empathy and perhaps communication take place are those which begin to suggest an alternative to reading and knowing–Jonas' intuitive acceptance of Gesine and Cresspahl's empathetic identification with Jakob–are distinctly non-narrative forms of human contact. Provisional and tentative as they are, these redemptive moments posit a non-fictional form of knowledge and communication.

　　Butor's interests strongly differ from both James and Johnson; the moral dimension of his epistemological activity concerns him less than its impotency in the face of an increasingly multiple and complex reality. In his essay, "The Novel as Research," Butor states the modern writer's dilemma:

> . . . different forms of narrative correspond to different realities. Now, it is clear that the world in which we live is being transformed with great rapidity. Traditional narrative techniques are incapable of integrating all the new relations thus created. There results a perpetual uneasiness; it is impossible for our consciousness to organize all the information which assails it, because it lacks adequate tools.
>
> The search for new novelistic forms with a greater power of integration thus plays a triple role in relation to our consciousness of reality: unmasking, exploration, and adaptation.[1]

Butor believes that art must *both* uncover the hidden structures of our complex world and create linguistic structures that correspond to that complexity. Naturally these two functions are related: Revel's diary parallels the form of Bleston and thereby aids its reader to penetrate and live the truth of the city. Yet this parallelism takes shape at the expense of Jacques Revel. As he traces the relations between the turtle at Plaisance Gardens, at the museum, on the volume of *The Murder of Bleston*, and on the tapestry, as he renders vibrant and living the patterns of the city, Revel sacrifices those of his own life. The point of view of the single individual is too narrow to account for the complexity of modern life; individual mediation is as inaccurate for Butor as it is blinding for Johnson. Revel's experience reveals that the only way a person can discover an extrapersonal reality is to relinquish all personal needs and desires. The stories of Jacques Revel, Léon Delmont and Pierre Vernier are the accounts of such individual diminution. As readers of an unchartable world, these characters lose their human centrality. The only compensation is the "future book" that will illuminate a communal rather than a personal experience. Of Pierre Vernier, the protagonist of *Degrees*, Butor says:

> This human sacrifice is necessary within the novel. As long as he accepts to be this victim, he can succeed. As long as he admits that this distant music is denied him but that his death will make it possible for others, he is entirely forgiven.[2]

In his reference to the God who uses Moses to lead his people into the Holy Land, but forbids him to enter himself, Butor risks sounding like the Jamesian preface about the author who sits in the stands while his characters fight in the arena. Yet Butor himself is the victim of a medium that has found its culmination in the individual biography and that no longer accounts for the complexity of our life. Instead of continuing to chart the defeat of nameless and powerless individual figures, as do Robbe-Grillet, Sarraute and Beckett, instead of continuing to dramatize the novel's failure to point out the interdependence of individual and culture, Butor attempts to transcend the singularity of the novel form. The story of the individual is no longer interesting. Having become a mere element of the novel's structure, the individual character is no longer a part of its substance. To chart the place of the human in culture, Butor seeks to develop "instruments with which to grasp the movement of the groups of which we are a part."[3] In so doing, he does not depart radically from Balzac and the other nineteenth-century novelists he studies and admires:

> Oh no, the great novelists of the eighteenth, nineteenth, and twentieth centuries fascinate me. I read them, study them, and teach courses about them. They brought about considerable transformations in their time. We must continue in the same vein, transforming that which precedes us. I don't believe in innovation for its own sake. I don't just try to do something because it looks new. It is by doing things other than my predecessors did that I do the same thing they did. It is precisely by trying to do what they were doing that I am forced to do otherwise, because of the difficulties I encounter, you see.[4]

He speaks of these difficulties in relation to his first trip to the United States in 1960:

> I was first in the United States at Bryn Mawr College, they asked me to write a piece for the Bryn Mawr *Alumnae Bulletin*. I wrote something I have never anthologized since. It is called 'Première vue de Philadelphie,' and is very much in the style of the first *Génie du lieu*. The longer I stayed, the more I realized that it just did not hold, that I had to find something different. This realization produced *Mobile* and subsequent books.[5]

In the texts of the early sixties, Butor abandons what he perceives as the novel's myopic structures of individual character and plot. *Mobile, Description de San Marco, Réseau Aérien* and *6 810 000 litres d'eau par seconde* experiment instead with mobile, multiple, and collective forms. Here, groups and their interaction replace individuals and their intrigues as the units of reference. The defeat of an individual intent on maintaining a position of centrality is replaced by the celebration of decentralization and plurality. Instead of the confrontation of character with setting, we have displacement of the character by the setting.

Butor's first non-narrative work and perhaps his most interesting and challenging one is *Mobile*. Although announced and anticipated in a number of his essays, *Mobile* is much more than an illustration of Butor's theoretical system, much more than one element in his elaborate poetic program. I have chosen *Mobile* for analysis in this chapter because I feel it is the post-fictional book of Butor's that works best. This is due to a particularly felicitous coalescence of the subject of America and the form of book Butor had been planning to write. What better locus for the celebration of variety and multiplicity, for the experimentation with plurality and expansion than America, the very seat of cultural multiplicity? In his earlier works Butor had demonstrated that there is no such thing as a single well-defined culture; America, however, is more of a composite than Paris, Bleston or Rome. What better method than Butor's for the exploration of a country that originated amid clashes between Europeans and Indians, grew by the amalgamation of the French, the English, the Dutch, and the Japanese, and that continues to suppress evergrowing tensions between blacks and whites? It is here that the dream of a cultural unity that respects difference can be tested; the potential is there. Butor's plural method, moreover, can successfully cover the spectrum between the extremes of melting pot and struggle.

On a personal as well as a cultural level, the American experience demands an expansion and a transmutation. As Butor says, "America certainly seems to dissolve individuality."[6] The immigrant leaves the old social structures which defined his identity; he is suspended, open, ready to be reabsorbed into a new and different culture, one that he himself must help to define because it also is open. It is that moment of freedom and rebirth that constitutes the basis of both Butor's multiple vision and of the American potential:

> If we have the possibility to become Americans without ceasing to
> be Europeans, if we have the possibility to undergo this phenom-
> enon of dissolution, even while preserving our old structures, then
> we find ourselves with the possibility to re-invent ourselves on a
> superior level.

> There is in all of America, in the whole notion of the 'new world, there is an extraordinary kind of risk; there is a kind of crisis of humanity which emerges not only for the people who are there, but also naturally for all those who are elsewhere.
>
> If we are capable of appropriating this moment of crisis, then we are really capable of inventing a superior kind of individuality, we are capable of leading a different life.[7]

Just as Revel discovers that his journal could become a useful tool to the community and offers it to them as such, so Butor writes *Mobile* as a guidebook and a revelation, a record and a prophecy.

In spite of the successful convergence of a fascinating theme and a revolutionary method, *Mobile* immediately met with negative responses of a reading public that deemed it unreadable.[8] Even today, almost twenty years and innumerable studies later, it is still described as no more than an intriguing experiment. In his excellent essay, "Littérature et discontinu," Roland Barthes has aptly identified the shock value of *Mobile*:

> What *Mobile* injured is the very idea of the Book.... The [traditional] Book is an object which *develops, makes links, spins,* and *flows.* ... The metaphors which describe the Book are the fabric that is woven, the water that flows, the flour that is ground, the road that is followed, the curtain which reveals, etc. ... to write is to flow words into this great continuous category that is narrative.[9]

The innovations of *Mobile* are that it is neither a linear story, nor the account of a personal journey by an individual to or through the United States. It is, instead and as the subtitle indicates, a study for the representation of the United States. While "étude" points to the unfinished and provisional character of *Mobile*, "représentation" must be read in both the sense of "representation" and its additional French meaning of "staging."

And yet, Barthes notwithstanding, *Mobile* is both continuous and discontinuous, both personal and impersonal, both temporal and spatial. It lures us into a story only to interrupt it, it begins to draw a character only to abandon it.

Perhaps the nature of this unusual book might best be assessed by means of the structural models, all indigenous to America, set up as keys within the text itself. *Mobile* is dedicated to the contemporary American artist Jackson Pollock. Pollock's "action painting" uses paint and color as a storehouse of pent-up forces to be released by the artist. Similarly dynamic, *Mobile* relies heavily on the conscious use of the materials of the book. Composed of three kinds of print, capital, roman and italic, of five different margins, and numerous blank spaces, the page becomes a visually vibrant design.

The use of different typescripts, several margins and a alphabetical order is derived from what Butor considers the most widely read American book, the sales catalogue. A name in capital letters attracts the reader's attention; surrounding it are the description of the "item" and of other related "items." Thus a few characteristic elements form the "seal" of every state; blacks are mentioned in connection with the Southern states, the sea in connection with all Atlantic or Pacific ones. Parts of the book even imitate the catalogue's sales language and the back cover of *Mobile*, an excerpt from a "Freedomland" brochure, "sells" Butor's books as "an orgy of surprises and shivers." The advertising jargon underscores the country's consumerism which becomes an important theme in the book. Even the most private aspects of life are phrased in the language of advertising copy: "Smile! . . . Keep smiling! . . . See how our President smiles!" (pp. 70-83).*

The text itself identifies the typically American patchwork quilt as one of its structural models: *"This mobile is composed somewhat like a quilt"* (p. 28).** The traditional quilt is the product of the collective effort of the anonymous members of a quilting bee. It is composed of discrete units of cloth assembled so as to form an aesthetically pleasing pattern based on the principle of repetition of certain colors, shapes, and motifs. It may or may not be representational. Similarly, repetition, and juxtaposition of compositional units are the basis of the structure of *Mobile*.

> There are passages in *Mobile* where I take American monuments, American natural sights, etc., and where I apply to this a list of colors which is American also, but which is originally applied to other objects. The typographical arrangement and the fact that each of these lists has a very strong specificity of vocabulary permits them to slide in relation to one another.[11]

---

* Souriez! . . . Souriez encore! . . . Regardez Mr. Nixon comme il sourit! (pp. 73-88)

** *Ce Mobile est composé un peu comme un quilt.* (p. 29)

The stylized and non-mimetic quality of the quilts, their repetition and regularity are the source of their therapeutic power: *The quilt was made by a wounded, discharged Union soldier toward the end of the Civil War in order to soothe his shattered nerves.* (pp. 176-177)* In contrast to these quilts, *Mobile* does not allow its reader to lose himself in aesthetic patterns, but invites him to endow them with human meaning.

The project of *Mobile* began as a travelogue until this subjective and impressionistic form emerged as insufficient. Still, Butor uses travel descriptions and geography books as models. *Le Sud-Ouest American* by Dodge and Zim, quoted in the first pages of *Mobile*, sets a certain form for the book as a whole.

> . . . little things—sights, sounds and smells—often create the most
> lasting impressions. Here are some:
> - strings of scarlet chili drying against adobe walls,
> - golden aspens mantling a mountain's shoulders,
> - lithe relaxation of Navajos outside a trading post. (p. 9) **

These impressionistic and static *tableaux* are the models of many italic sections of subsequent chapters: *"The sea at night. The desert at night"* (p. 14).***

The book's title suggests perhaps the most important structural model, Calder's mobiles. Like a quilt, a mobile is composed of a number of separate units, assembled so that each moves in relation to all others while the viewer moves around the entire struture. They are like organic structures in that they are responsive to their environment. Their movement is to some extent determined by the composition, yet within that restriction it is free, subject to its environment, unpredictable. The same tension between chance and design characterizes *Mobile*. The reader's role in Butor's book resembles that of the Calder viewer.

---

* *Cette courtepointe fut executée par un vétéran de la Guerre de Sécession, dont les nerfs avaient été ébranlés par ses expériences militaires. De retour, il entreprit cet ouvrage pour se guérir.* (p. 184)

** *. . . ce sont souvent de petites choses vues, entendues, senties, qui créent les impréssions les plus durables. En voici quelques exemples:*
- des lacets de chili écarlate, séchant contre les murs de terre,
- un manteau de trembles dorés couvrants les flancs d'une montagne,
- souple relaxation des Navajos relaxant à la porte d'une épicerie. (p. 9)

*** *La mer la nuit. Le désert la nuit.* (p. 14)

Besides Calder, the title also evokes Mobile, Alabama, the town with which the book begins and Mobil gasoline, of course. In addition to movable, the word *mobile* in French also mean motive and *Mobile* demands to be read, in my opinion, as an account of the motives that led up to the American present, and as a motive for action in its own right, as a challenge and a provocation. Like Butor's early novels, *Mobile* is the account of a possible awakening, a *prise de conscience*. In the absence of a protagonist, the reader himself becomes the agent of this awareness.

The difficulties of this text, I would suggest, lie not in its nonlinear composition: we have become used to reading paradigmatic texts; the interruption of narrative flow by lists and catalogues has been a convention since Homer, through Rabelais and Joyce. We have also learned how to deal with disrupted chronology since Flaubert and Proust; we no longer expect a story to unfold and flow smoothly as Barthes suggests. The airplane vision of 50 states in 48 hours, as well as the progression of the journey, based not on geographical but on alphabetical contiguity, seen appropriate for this subject. Once the principles of composition become apparent to the reader, he learns to deal with his disorientation. Admittedly, *Mobile* is not an easy book to follow, but it has neither the allusiveness of Joyce, the playfulness of Nabokov, the psychological complexity of James, nor the elusiveness of Johnson. It is not a puzzle; Butor's language is lucid and his sources are transparent. As he abandons even the pretense of a story line, we are not tempted to piece one together, as we are in *Speculations about Jakob*. Choosing between a variety of different "trajets de lecture" certainly poses difficulties for the reader, but the real frustrations of *Mobile* lie in its failure to be concerned with the fate of individuals, in its elimination of a central subject. *Mobile* is a journey without a traveler, a search with no seeker, a labyrinth with no Theseus.

In fact, many readers of *Mobile* have tried to introduce a central character into the text. Georges Charbonnier expresses his frustration in his interview with Butor:

> Thanks to you I am very well informed about the American soul, but I would like to recognize the soul of a particular American just like I recognize the color of a particular ice cream. . . . I'm trying

to identify the method by which I could locate an individual and I
realize that an individual is a possibility; there's only one American
left, and it's me.

Butor's reply is not surprising: "No you're not the only one,
because by the very fact that you declare yourself an American, you
declare yourself an American among others." Charbonnier is
uncomfortable with the effects of *Mobile* on his identity: "I, an
individual, am pushed toward a collectivity and I'm pushed to feel
within a group . . . and that's not at all pleasant."[12]

The reader remains the only individual consciousness within
the work, the only one who can attempt to combine the fragments
into a meaningful pattern.[13] By participating in the book's expansive
and inclusive structures, the reader learns to function within a new
world. Reading is no longer a process of identification with
character; nor is it a process of projecting oneself into the place of a
missing traveler or an implied seeker. The text consistently defies
such humanization. Instead, reading is a process of orientation in a
world of fragments: animate and inanimate, past and present,
important and trivial. As we follow the book's intricate patterns, we
accept our position as one of many, empathizing with collective acts
and truths, even with collective dreams; we chart our own course
alongside *Mobile's* Benjamin Franklin and Thomas Jefferson, the
Winnebago Indian Albert Hensley and Susannah Martin, burned as
a witch in 1692 in Salem. As we orient ourselves amidst a multiplicity
of individual and collective dreams, fears and desires, we are forced
to acknowledge our responsibility in the collective crimes that are at
the base of American culture, and by extension, of all Western
culture: the genocide of the American Indian and the enslavement
of the Black African. Butor says: "*Mobile* is a plural work . . . it is
within the plural that the singular will be condensed."[14] In
displacing the individual from the center of his work and thus
avoiding the sacrifice of the individual self that charactertizes his
novels, Butor announces a new collective identity, a collective form
of knowledge, a collective aesthetic.

In the four novels examined in previous chapters, the
epistemological quest took place on the level of character, first
single, then multiple, and only by extension on the level of the text
as a whole. The reader's involvement parallels that of Strether or
Revel, the Prince and the Princess, Jakob's friends. The
epistemological structure of these works rests on the principle of

identification between reader and character. *Mobile*, in contrast, displaces the epistemological activity which is still its principal thrust, from the level of the character to that of the reader; the foreign country to be discovered, the mystery to be resolved, is not as much the American continent as its analogue, Butor's text.

In a reading of the book, I would like to assess the possibilities as well as the rewards of responding to the challenge of *Mobile*. If, as readers, we allow our individuality to dissolve, how do we reach Butor's proposed "superior individuality" and what exactly does it consist of? Is Butor's plural dream as utopian as James' is elitist or can his book, as he suggests, genuinely serve as a guidebook, a dictionary, a catalogue of our world? Is Butor's collective vision enough to compensate for the loss of individuality? To test the success of Butor's experiment, I propose to take two kinds of journeys through the book, a syntagmatic journey through one chapter that will follow the book's rhythm and progression, and a paradigmatic one that will isolate and analyze its structural principles and contradictory impulses.

Although the structure of *Mobile* is non-linear, although each page forms a visual tableau, and although many of the book's smaller units are static, it is difficult to discuss one isolated chapter. The attempt to do so only underscores the interdependence of these units and the book's overall syntagmatic progression, a progression which mitigates against the book's alphabeticl organization. The chapter about New Hampshire occupies an important spot in the text and it is for this reason, as well as for its representative nature, that I chose it. In the 48-hour journey that begins at 3:00 a.m. Eastern Standard Time and ends at midnight, Mountain Time (2:00 a.m. E.S.T.), it occupies the beginning of the second day. This is a turning point according to the pattern of withdrawal, initiation and return outlined by Dean McWilliams in *Michel Butor: The Writer as Janus*.[15] In most Butor narratives the crucial descent and revelation occurs during the hours of darkness and Butor also ends his narratives during the night, so as to force the reader to continue the journey back to light on his own. New Hampshire heralds the sudden emergence of daylight (the preceding chapter was Nevada, Pacific Time), and provides relief from the uneasy dreams of the second night. It foreshadows the third day, the moment of potential rebirth for whose appearance the reader alone is responsible.

Some of the themes and motifs in this chapter occur throughout the entire book, others are particular to New Hampshire itself. Commenting on most of the items in the chapter, I shall use Butor's margins for their convenient reference to the book, as well as to gain an insight into their function. My linear journey through the chapter will be interrupted by general observations and it will be subject to the repetitions within the chapter itself.

Characteristically, the chapter begins with the highway welcome sign "Welcome to New Hampshire," visible only during the daylight hours of the book, and with the announcement of the time. On the furtherest left margin of the page appears the name of a town in New Hampshire, "LEE."

A "calligramme" in the shape of a bird in flight follows; it consists of the names of five bird species. Containing no verbs, these poems derive their movement from their shape rather than from any grammatical structure. Elements of most states' "seal," these bird poems occur in almost every chapter.

The act of naming is perhaps *Mobile's* most important act; the entire book is based on names of states or towns. Most American places and people are evoked by their name alone, here, for example: "Lake Winnepesaukee" and "Hello Jerry!" For Proust's Marcel the signpost in the railway station with the name of a town came to represent the quality of an entire town. Butor, in contrast, uses the names for their sound or their frequency and does not attribute any power to them as signifiers. Naming is, however, an active attempt to understand and to appropriate a new place.

> After passing the boarder to the South, we find ourselves in a town called "LEE," this time in Massachusetts. Thus each chapter is organized around the names of several towns which have homonyms in neighbouring states and in states which are adjacent in the alphabet. "I wanted to apply to the United States a verbal pattern which would be based on frequencies.... I classified and organized these names in such a way that there should be on each page, the greatest number of possible meetings."[15] LEE, Mass., is indented, as is each successively evoked state. Only the original state occupies the left column. We see then, that the alphabetical order of *Mobile* quickly breaks down. Although each chapter is

primarily devoted to one state, each echo of another state is picked up and pursued so that the original state becomes a "crossroads" which reveals complex interrelationships between the different states of the Union, just as Bleston became the meeting place for Athens, Rome, Timgad and Petra. The five margins thus create a feeling of spatial depth within each page, making the reader act out the depth of the country itself.

The transcripts of the Salem witch trial of Susannah Martin are quoted throughout the New England states as a part of their "seal." In his concern to revive some forgotten scenes from the American past, Butor concentrates on those that concern the interaction of the various groups which compose this country. "Witches" are social outcasts like Indians or blacks and the attitude toward Susannah Martin is a good example of the imperialist bigotry that Butor feels characterizes the interaction of groups within the United States. Butor never comments on these quotations directly; their selection and juxtaposition, however, demand the reader's judgment, or, at least, an acknowledgement of this bigotry. For example, in this chapter, an excerpt from the trial is often followed by an excerpt for Trappist jellies. This montage structure, a frequent organizational device in the book, constitutes a commentary on religion, its prejudice as well as its relation to commercialism.

Another part of the seal of New Hampshire, the ocean, is evoked in recurring short poems that imitate its ebb and flow rhythm. In this first such poem the cleansing power of the sea is mentioned for the first time.

"HANOVER, N.H." The text in capital and roman letters that Butor calls the outer shell of the cells that constitute the book (the organic metaphor is significant) contain mainly objective geographical information such as the names of towns, lakes and mountains. The inner core, usually in italics, contains subjective material, such as quotations from other writers, poetic representations of the sea, birds and fish, urban poems, dreams, etc.

Another bird poem is identical in form to the first. There is no progression among these. Linked by their identical typographical shape, their recurrence has the effect of repetition and movement.

While the Esso station links New Hampshire to the rest of the country, the two lakes identify its uniqueness.

"HANOVER, MASS." Again, we proceed to a neighboring state by the homonym, "Hanover."

The second poem to the sea presents an occasion to examine the phenonmenon of thematic progression in *Mobile* as a whole. Although, like the bird poems, the sea poems have identical typographical arrangements, they do not merely repeat by they follow a thematic progression: in this second poem the mood changes indicative to subjunctive, and a first person speaker is introduced:

The sea,
    washes,
rinses,
    rewashes,
rinses,
    *delivers. (p. 163)**

The sea,
    let the sea waste me,
let the sea purify me,
    let the sea take me away,
let the sea bring me back,
    *let the sea change me (pp. 163-164)***

In the following sea poem the tone gains in intensity, as does the cleansing power of the ocean.

---

* *La mer.*
  lave.
rince.
  relave.
rince.
  délivre. (p. 170)

** *La mer.*
  que la mer me lave.
que la mer me purifie.
  que la mer m'emporte.
que la mer me retourne.
  que la mer me change. (p. 171)

> *The sea,*
>> *let the sea cleanse me,*
>
> *of all this mud,*
>> *of all this grease,*
>
> *of all this soot,*
>> *of all this sugar.* (p. 166)*

The last line must be read ironically; it refers to the Trappist jellies that are advertised in the preceding paragraph. Such surprises and ironies are frequently the result of these montage effects. The incremental rhythm of the text's thematic progressions becomes even more apparent if we follow the sea poems further. A source of the dirt, New York is revealed in the next one, as modern civilization in the form of an overabudance of objects is opposed to the purity of nature; this takes place in Connecticut.

> The sea,
>> dirty papers,
>
> cirgarette butts,
>> paper plates,
>
> old sandals,
>> bottle tops. (p. 168)**

The intensity of tone reaches a climax in the following poem:

> *The sea,*
>> *the sea's great washing,*
>
> *let the sea strike me,*
>> *let the sea enter me,*
>
> *let the sea save me,*
>> *let the sea open my eyes.* (p. 169)***

---

* *La mer,*
  que la mer me débarrasse
de toute cette boue,
  de toute cette graisse,
de toute cette suie,
  de tout ce sucre. (p. 173)

** *La mer,*
  papiers sales,
mégots,
  assiettes de carton,
sandales dépareillées,
  bouchons de tubes. (p. 175)

*** *La mer.*
  la grande lessive de la mer.
que la mer me frappe.
  que la mer me pénètre.
que la mer me guérisse.
  que la mer m'ouvre les yeux. (p. 177)

Almost a prayer, this appeal reaches the intensity of the visionary experience of Rimbaud's drunken boat. It underscores the central thrust of *Mobile*, the movement toward awakening and awareness. Just as the dirt of Bleston concealed the truth of the city, its past and its special kind of beauty, so here grease, dirt and mud must be washed away before the eyes can be opened. Butor's book celebrates the restorative power of nature over a degraded civilization. The anonymous voice of these poems appears only as a direct object, a passive figure who waits to be purified by the sea. Is the reader meant to appropriate this role and this wish? Clearly a much more active role is demanded of the reader who is asked to follow the progression of these poems, a progression interrupted by numerous other themes in the chapter, all of which must be connected and evaluated. (Take, for example, the connection between the sea and the witch trials.) The appeal and power of the sea poems, however, is intensified by this perculiar structure of interruption, repetition and subtle progression.

Considering the ebb and flow motion of the sea, it is not suprising that the subsequent sea poems return to a purely descriptive and impersonal form.

> *The sea,*
> *islands,*
> *channels,*
> *narrows,*
> *straits,*
> *reefs.* (p. 171) *

Later still, the sea poems in a collage-like structure with the bird poems; the themes of *Mobile* never quite remain separate.

---

* *La mer.*
îles.
chenaux.
goulets,
dètroits,
récifs. (p. 178)

The sea,
  ebb,
Trudeau's terns,
  gull-billed terns,
detour,
  flow,
    gold-winged warblers,
roar,
  Cape May warbler,
hairy woodpeckers,
  spatter. (p. 173)*

Interestingly, each separate poem maintains its distinctive figural arrangement in this collage; interaction is not penetration.

Returning to the second sea poem on 163, 164 (p. 171), we encounter another excerpt from the trial transcripts and another advertisement of Trappist jellies.

"BERLIN" The voice of a hastry traveler, "still another hour," again links this chapter with the book as a whole and this state with the rest of the U.S. Speed is an important theme of *Mobile*. We repeatedly encounter anonymous travelers in cars of varied make and color who pass each other above the speed limit, waving hello and counting the time it will take them to reach their unspecified destinations.

"BERLIN, MASS." again provides the transition.

Many of the objects that appear in *Mobile* are described in culinary terms: consumption is identified as the favorite American pastime. By randomly applying list of colors to objects ranging from jellies to underwear, ice cream flavors and cars he achieves surrealistic juxtapositions, "magnetic, poetic fields."[17] The effect of using the same words to describe flavor and color ("a gleaming almond Nash" or "a strawberry Cadillac"), is an unusual form of synesthesia that underscores American

----

* *La mer,*
  montée,
sternes de Trudeau,
  sternes bec de mouette,
détour,
  retombée,
    fauvettes à ailes d'or,
grondement,
  fauvette du cap May,
piverts poilus,
  éclaboussement. (pp. 180-181)

consumption. The emphasis on color also has an equalizing influence on various objects, ranging from cars to jellies, all described and identified by means of the same color scale.

A mixture of themes occurs again on page 167 (p. 174), as a quotation from the Montgomery Ward catalogue advertising a "paint by numbers" kit alternates with a list of underpants that come in sets of seven—a different color for every day:

- white for Sunday
    - The Last Supper, with the Sermon on the Mount.
- yellow for Monday
    - Autumn landscape, with the End of the Day.*

Consumerism invades all aspects of American life and art, like religion, is by no means exempt. Moreover, all areas of individual commitment and creativity are cheapened by mass production. The emphasis on imitation, appearance, and surface reveals the extent of this degradation: "a three-carat imperialite, 'the artificial stone that looks like a diamond.' " ** People, places, objects, natural and historical phenomena all become elements of a sales catalogue, or mere aspects of a state seal. All are on the same level in the book's structure:

Salmon Mountain, – Newfound Lake, Canaan Street Lake, – a man's ring . . . a Sandran floor covering, "You've seen it on television, you've seen it in the newspaper. Now have it in your home."***

This device of fragmentation creates separate incomplete units that are then reassembled according to the laws of juxtaposition, repetition and progression. Not only are the larger quotations, such as the Benjamin Franklin letter or the Martin trial transcripts broken up into short sections and disributed throughout the chapters that deal with the states to which these documents pertain, but even the shorter units, such as the enumeration of Trappist jelly flavors, are interrupted by other similar lists or interspersed with geographical information. Some lists, the Howard Johnson ice cream flavors, for example, are distributed over the entire book.

---

* - blanc pour dimanche
    - la Cène, avec le Sermon sur la Montagne,
- jaune pour lundi,
    - Paysage d'Automne avec la Fin du Jour. (pp. 174-175)

** Une impérialite de trois carats, 'la pierre précieuse artificielle que l'on prend pour un diamant.' (p. 175)

*** Le mont du Saumon, – les lacs Neuf et de la Rue-de-Canaan, – ou une bague pour homme . . . ou un revêtement de sol "Sandran," vous l'avez vu à la télé. . . . (pp. 175-76)

Besides equalizing the different semantic units, the disjointed quality of the text prevents the reader from immersing himself in the material. Roudaut defines the special quality of the reading experience:

> The visual arrangement of words on the page makes reading the book impossible at first; our desire to plunge into a sentence, to lose ourselves in its contours, to let the author think for us is constantly frustrated.[18]

As not even a list progresses consecutively, the text succeeds in counteracting the inattention of reading.

Birds appear in two different forms in *Mobile*, in the "caligrammes" of bird names and in descriptions of Audubon plates: "A nest of robins, on a branch of chestnut oak; the female holds a red berry in her beak" (p. 170).* Both of these forms are stylized and remote, calling attention to the mediation which, according to Butor, characterizes America's relation to natural reality. The beauty and vitality of the American landscape is degraded in cheap Sears Roebuck wall decorations. Bringing the expanse of the Grand Tetons into your living room, making them part of your wall, a washable plastic, — what better way to master something foreign and possibly threatening? Similarly, the greatest catastrophes of American history and the most impressive sights of the continent are made innocuous in the Freedomland amusement park, just as the vitality of Indian life serves as amusement to tourists on the reservations.

Butor's insistence on some of these particularly crass forms of mediation, especially Freedomland and Clifton's cafeteria, represents his judgment on a peculiarly American way of dealing with anything foreign. Nature and our history are violated as they are transposed into the medium of entertainment. The only aspect of America that seems to defy such degradation is the sea and thus we can perhaps explain its power to cleanse, a power that reaches far beyond its shores:

---

* Un nid de rouges –gorges sur une branche de chêne châtaigner, à feuilles plissées; la femelle tient dans son bec une baie rouge cerise. (p. 177)

The sea,
    we're so far from the sea,
we've never seen the sea,
        except in pictures,
    someday I'll take you to the sea,
            but I know it'll be too late. (p. 280)**

Besides the elements I have discussed and which are repeated and assembled as I have indicated, a few other themes appear in this chapter: a description of a quilt from the Shelburne Museum (Vermont); an excerpt from the biolography of the Indian Handsome Lake (N.Y.); an excerpt from the Freedomland prospectus (N.Y.); and continuing lists of aspects of New York City; radio stations, restaurants, foreign inhabitants, ships in N.Y. harbor.

"LEBANON, N.H.," provides the transition to "LEBANON, N.J.," and the next chapter.

The preceding journey through one chapter has raised some question about the book that must now be discussed individually in a paradigmatic journey through the book. We have encountered a few contradictory aspects of *Mobile*: a concentration on surface and superficiality as well as a concern with depth, a spatial structure as well as an important temporal progression, a strongly controlled design as well as an impulse toward chance and openness, an individual authorial voice, as well as a multiplicity of voices, both personal and impersonal. I would like to suggest that these oppositions are not mere tensions, but that they are contradictory impulses, which, because they violate our habits of reading, present the reader with difficult and sometimes personal choices and decisions. Butor's work teaches us that a book can be no more than a fragment, that it could not possibly be conclusive, but we also learn, through his works, how to make the choices that might close some of the gaps. *Mobile* gives us more than the fragments of modern American culture; it gives us a means by which to assemble them. In this section I shall try to illustrate the particular kind of reader response demanded by this text. Butor has also demonstrated the impossibility of speaking in single units; I find it difficult to separate these sets of oppositions for the purpose of discussion. I

** *La mer,*
    nous sommes si loin de la mer,
    nous n'avons jamais vu la mer,
        que par images,   *er,*
    un jour je t'amènerai jusqu'à la mer.
        mais je sais qu'il sera trop tard. (p. 292)

shall raise them one by one, without trying to disguise the various points of overlap; this will make my chapter somewhat like *Où* where each chapter overlaps at every point with several others. The following pages might be read, then, not as a consecutive argument but as a series of approaches to *Mobile*.

Surface/Depth/Presence

The fragmentation of material in the book and the intricate arrangement of these disjointed elements could be said to make *Mobile* another Freedomland, another superficial assemblage of different aspects of the country. There are no individual characters in the book; the human element appears alongside places and objects. The dreams of Southern whites, the statements of Thomas Jefferson and the Sears catalogue all assume the same level of reality and importance, just as in Freedomland the New Orleans Mardi Gras and the San Francisco earthquake appear side by side. Both Freedomland and *Mobile* are models and enactments of American life. Butor's particular use of American sights and documents could seem as manipulative as Freedomland, and the success of *Mobile* must be measured against that of the amusement park. Is this what Lucien Goldmann calls "réification" and is Butor creating a literary universe in which the human must relinquish its central position, "this world of objects, in which the human has lost all essential reality both as an individual and as a community?"[19]

In a sense this statement does describe *Mobile*; there is neither psychological depth nor human interiority in the book. Yet there is perhaps another kind of depth here, one different from psychological exploration. Certainly this universe is not reminiscent of Robbe-Grillet's "surfaces without mystery, without depth."[20] Barthes has remarked that Butor's approach to America is an unusual one for a European; instead of marveling at its novelty and youth, he searches for its history. The documents he includes in the book are only rarely encountered here in the United State; few of us read Jefferson or Franklin, fewer even know much about the Chicago World Exhibition or the Indian peyotl cult. There are parts of our history that we simply ignore and to which this text calls our attention. By showing us that these important aspects of our history are as much a part of our daily lives as car makes and ice cream flavors, the book offers us a chance to appropriate them, to look into the past, to know ourselves as a people, to develop a consciousness of ourselves as a group. Seeing ourselves as a group is a condition of survival. Doing so depends on the acknowledgment of the crimes that are in the background of our present life: *"Now since every city*

*in the United States was founded on some recent murder laboriously
but energetically forgotten, Lincoln's murder managed to give this
obscure primordial murder a stunning representation* (p. 130).*
Forgetting and suppressing the truth is fatal and *Mobile* succeeds in
raising to the surface not only the past which we have forgotten but
dreams of our collective psyche which we would never admit: *"I'm
dreaming of buffalo, herds of horses, Indians of the plains, Latter
Day Saints and their trek across the states to new lands. . . . . But I'll
tell them, even my wife, I'll tell them that I'm dreaming of having
money."* (p. 151)**

In addition to restoring our history, Butor calls attention to a
daily spectacle of objects—cars, ice cream flavors, carpets, paintings,
underwear—to which we have become accustomed to the point of
ignoring it. The book sharpens perceptions dulled by the
multiplicity of modern American life.

In *Mobile* all that has been suppressed emerges on the book's
surface not as *superficiality*, but as *presence*. The impulse toward
forgetting is a strong one and the reader must fight it just as Revel
and Delmont fought against apathy and complacency. The book's
disjointed form is one device that forces the reader into awareness.
The equality of elements on the book's surface underscored by the
alphabetical order is, ironically, another. It is only the reader's
human dimension that makes the crucial difference between
superficiality and presence. If *Mobile* succeeds in distinguishing
itself from Freedomland it is because of the response it demands
from the audience: awareness, discrimination, self-consciousness
and valuation rather than the passive attitude of entertainment
consumption.

The text's fragmentation and equalization of elements also
suggests a way to combat the hierarchy and centralization that
characterizes all of Western civilization, according to Butor:

> Formerly, the Western civilizations imagined that the world was
> organized around a center, and since Rome, that center has always
> been a city. . . . One of the things that interests me so much about the
> United States is its nomadic side. People move much more easily.
> Not only are communications easier, but there is a kind of life in the
> car; people bring their houses with them. . . . There are dreams of
> imperial cities in the United States as well. New York, the Empire
> City, and then Washington, the dream of a Roman City. How pro-

---

* *Or comme chaque ville des Etats — Unis était fondée sur quelque meurtre récent difficilement mais
énergétiquement oublié, l'assassinat de Lincoln réussit à donner à ce meutre originaire obscur une représentation
éclatante.* (pp. 135-36)

** *Je rêve de bisons, de troupeaux de chevaux, des Indiens de la prairie, des Saints du Dernier Jour, et de leur
marche à travers les Etats, des nouvelles terres. . . . Mais je leur dirai, même à ma femme je dirai que je rêve d'avoir
de l'argent.* (p. 157)

digious! They even needed a Frenchman for that. In addition to a capitol, they needed an obelisk which was the most Egyptian of obelisks since ancient Egypt. It is not only the obelisk of the city Washington, but also of the man Washington, of a deified man.... There are fascinating phenomena of centralization to study in the United States, but there is also all the rest, all this great movement, this great nomadic life=very instructive for the French to study.[21]

Butor's project of decentralization involves not only a spatial, political and aesthetic reorganization, but also a personal transmutation, a redefinition of surface and depth:

We still have an imperialist conception of the self, whereas we could well see ourselves as elements in a pattern in which others are just as important as we are. . . .

We lose only illusions. There are still things we don't say to others, that we don't tell ourselves, and that creates depth. But depth is not only interior, it is exterior as well. The others also have depth.[22]

Mobile, like *The Golden Bowl* or *Speculations about Jakob*, is a formal response to a certain dilemma; yet to approach it through form alone is to ignore the emotional and moral involvement that makes all the difference. Butor uses the most negative aspects of America, endless repetition, superficiality, disjunction, toward a positive end, by getting the reader to notice the sameness and to rebel against it.[23]

It is precisely *Mobile's* openness and its provocative structure that distinguish it from the amusement park:

Yes, sometimes there are things that needle, things that are deliberately provocative and that cause the reader who circulates within the book as he would in Freedomland to become aware of what Freedomland is. That is the reason why this book leaves no one indifferent: the reactions to it are very violent.[24]

It is not enough to say that the structure of *Mobile* is analogous to that of the United States, or that the structure of Revel's journal imitates that of Bleston. An individual's response to the structures that rule his life might be to produce his own autonomous verbal constructs that either rival with the external ones or correspond to them. What Butor dramatizes is not only this parallelism but also the emotional process of response that defines it. Someone creates the correspondences and it is that human process of creation that is vital and important. In the novels, we empathize with the characters' anguish; in a work like *Mobile* the victimization of a single character is avoided as the experience of learning and awareness is shared, as it becomes a communal experience. By taking on a share of it, by acknowledging the presence of the past, by battling with ancient impulses and habits, we as readers give the book a different depth.

Story/Tableau/Spectacle

In the analysis of the New Hampshire chapter I took several different reading routes through the text. I read several pages in a row, I read all the sea poems in a row and skipped everything else, I discussed the material presented in the furthest left margin. I could have read only italics, only one margin, yet all of these are still sequential readings progressing in time from left to right, in spite of the omissions.[25] The temporal dimension of *Mobile* is both compositional and historical. The book tells, if not a story, then a composite history of America. Instead of a chronological documentary account we get a recreation of the emotional quality of the country's development. History emerges as a steady invasion of a strange and invincible continent.

> *Driven out, fleeing, they left Pennsylvania for Ohio.*
>   *Best wishes!*
> *They left Ohio for Indiana,*
>   *Don't forget us!* (p. 98-99)*

It is the account of the destruction of Indian culture, the annihilation of nature during the nineteenth century, the increasing hatred between blacks and whites. We experience the burgeoning of a nation and the crimes and struggles that underlie its present state. It is a struggle we cannot suppress; our history is carved into the land, and time and space are one:

> *In 1855, the Indian chief Seattle, who gave his name to the largest city in Washington, formerly called New York, declared to the European negotiators: 'Every bit of this land is sacred. . . . Every hill, valley or plain, every woods has been sanctified by some glorious or horrible event in the past. Even the rocks that seem mute and dead when they bake in the sun, tremble with extraordinary events linked to the life of my people. . . . When the children of your children will suppose themselves alone in the fields, the shops, on the roads or in the silent forests, they will not be alone at all. . . . At night, when all sound has died away in the streets of your villages, and when you think they are empty, they*

Chassés, fuyant, ils ont traversé la Pennsylvanie pour entrer dans l'Ohio.
   Bon courage!
Ils ont traversé l'Ohio pour entrer dans l'Indiana.
   Ne nous oubliez pas! (pp. 102-103)

will swarm with the host of those who once lived there, faithful to
that sublime site. The white man will never be alone.' (pp. 219-220).*

Besides this historical growth of the American continent, and
the smaller units of progression that emerged in the New Hampshire
chapter, there is a temporal structure to the book as a whole: the 48
hours of its progression. Significant changes take place during this
time sequence, even though it is continuously interrupted by
geographical as well as temporal jumps, caused by the crossing of the
three time zones. The first night is a "pitch dark" night
characterized by rather superficial dreams, "He was dreaming he
was tall." During the second night, as I have already pointed out, we
reach the greatest depth of the collective American unconscious as
the most terrifying fears and the most hidden desires emerge. *"I
catch sight of one looking at me through the window, and his eyes
gleam so brightly that my sheets burn. . . . I tell him: 'I love you, I love
you, I've never loved anyone but you.' Tears fall from his eyes. That
mouth presses against my mouth, and I am devoured by flames. That
horrible mouth. . . . I'll tell my father to kill you. . . . There's nothing.
Sleep"* (pp. 143-145).** Marked by this uneasiness, the second night
constitutes a turning point in the book. The following day becomes a
time of desired purification and the last night is no longer cursed
but celebrated by a prophetic voice that is very different from the
frightened voice of the second night? *"O night! . . . O cooling
shadows! . . . Future America! . . . After so many upheavals, convulsions, murders"* (pp. 303-304).*** It is a "clear night."

Several critics have commented on the utopian and indigenous
quality of the names at the end of the Book (Elkhorn, Buffalo,
Eden), as opposed to the nostalgic European names in the beginning
(Cordoue, Florence, El Dorado). Caught up in the powerful
rhythmical progression of the book created by all these factors, the
reader is ready to respond to the call to revolution that runs through
the last chapters: *"O upside-down America! . . . Will stone be left on
stone? . . . How long we've been waiting for you, America! . . . How
long we've been waiting for your reversal! . . . How we spy on you at*

En 1855, le chef Indien Seattle, qui donna son nom à la plus importante cité du Washington, déclara au négociateurs européens: 'Toutes parcelles de ce sol sont sacrées . . . Toute colline, vallée, autrefois nommé New York, ou plaine, tout bois a été sanctifié par quelque évènement glorieux ou horrible d'autrefois . . . Quand les enfants de vos enfants s'imagineront seuls dans les champs, les boutiques, sur les routes, ou dans les forêts en silence, ils ne le seront nullement. . . .La, nuit lorsque tout bruit aura cessé dans les rues de vos villages, et que vous les croirez dèsertes, elles grouilleront de la foule de ceux qui ont vècu là autrefois, fidèles à ce sublime lieu. Jamais l'homme blanc n'y sera seul! (pp. 229-30)

** *J'en aperçois un qui me regarde à travers la vitre, et ses yeux brûlent si fort que mes draps me brûlent. . . . Je lui dis: 'Je t'aime, je t'aime, je n'ai jamais aimé que toi. . . . Cette bouche s'appuie sur ma bouche et je suis toute devorée de flammes. Cette bouche horrible. . . . Je dirai à mon père de te tuer. . . . Il n'y a rien. Dors. (pp. 149-151)*

*** *O nuit! . . . O rafraichissants ténèbres! . . . Amérique future! . . . Après tant de bouleversements, de convulsions, de meurtres." (pp. 316-317)*

night!" (pp. 314-315).* After centuries of confidence, our admiration and fear of the mysterious and invincible new continent emerge: *"Terra incognita!"* (p. 331), and the desired awakening takes place.

This is not to say that the reader is deceived by the optimistically prophetic nature of such exclamations, having just relived a number of the most shameful moments of American history. The reader realizes that hope for the future depends on an awareness of these past crimes and on the acceptance of responsibility for them. The text's last word is "Buffalo" and the extinction of the passenger pigeons described on the last page, subsumes the guilt of the past and the implicit hope of a renewed future. Redemption depends on the awareness of the past and therefore on the historical temporal sense produced by the text. The book merely suggests future redemption as a possibility for those who are willing to remember.

I have already described the spatial aspects of the book that impede its narrative flow. As Roudaut says:

> Two meanings are superimposed: that of the page where everything is discontinuous and that of the duration of our reading during which we recompose these fragments. The reader is called upon to reconstitute the book, just as daily he organizes reality.[26]

Roudaut does not mean that the reader is called upon to impose a false continuity on the text, but that we must learn to find our way in the fragmentary, disjointed form of the book. The search for orientation in the pages of *Mobile* is Revel's search in Bleston and the newcomer's search in the United States, illustrating what I have called the text's analogical realism.

Each page of the book is a *tableau*. Semantic fragments are arranged in visual patterns. Some of these fragments are in themselves static—the name of a town or a lake, the description of an Audubon print—others are in themselves mobile—the bird poems move visually, the sea poems enact the movement of the ocean, the interior monologues in italics dramatize the movement of the mind. The overall progression of the text, however, is continually interrupted just as the appreciation of each *tableau* is impeded by the pull of the text's progression. My own reading of *Mobile* oscillates between the recuperation of its inherent structure and progression and a recognition of the text's heterogeneity and multiplicity, its fragmentation and openness. I try to read *Mobile* as someone who grew up reading telephone books or sales catelogues,

---

* *O Amérique renversée! . . . Restera-t-il sur pierre? . . . Comme nous t'attendons, Amérique! . . . Comme nous attendons ton retournement! . . . Comme nous t'épions dans, la nuit!* (pp. 327-329)

but I cannot get around the fact that I grew up reading stories. Out of the tension of *tableau* and story, movement and stasis, emerges what the book's subtitle announces, a spectacle. The tension brings all textual elements onto the surface or stage and demands the reader's participation in their meaningful interaction. The reader must respond evaluatively to the single juxtapositions, as well as respond to the rhythm of the progressions. As the reader becomes a part of the text, *Mobile* becomes a communal artistic experience, demanding the assumption of a communal personality, and the achievement of a communal insight. Rather than annihilating or overcoming difference and struggle, *Mobile* aims at understanding it through collective participation.

Design/Chance/Openness

> *Only the supreme gods could create perfection, and . . . man would be presumptuous to try to produce faultless works. In order to avoid punishment for her audacity in attempting to imitate the divinity, the woman who created a quilt deliberately destroyed the symmetry of her pattern, thus warding off bad luck.* (p. 174)*

> *That glimpse, like all dread glimpses of truth, flashed out from an accidental piecing together of separated things—in this case an old newspaper item and the notes of a dead professor. I hope that no one else will accomplish this piecing out.* (p. 152)**

If symmetry and design seem so dangerous and undesirable as these passages suggest, and if Butor believes that every true work of art must remain unfinished, why does he structure *Mobile* so carefully and deliberately? A structured system that follows definite rules, the book shows an impulse toward closure. Although it includes a great deal, it aims not so much at encyclopaedic breadth, as it is based on careful selection and stringent requirements. Each element is meaningful not in itself, but in relation to many others; it is for its place in the alphabet, its sound or frequency that a name is chosen. The effects of most juxtapositions are studied. To read Butor's descriptions of the work that went into the composition, is to be struck and perhaps even disappointed by its automatism and lack of spontaneity.[24]

---

* *Seuls les dieux suprèmes peuvent créer la perfection, et . . . l'homme serait présomptueux d'essayer de produire des oeuvres sans défaut. Afin d'éviter la punition de son audace en prétendant d'imiter la divinité, celle qui composait autrefois un quilt détruisait parfois délibérement la symétrie de son dessin, détournant ainsi le malheur.* (p. 181)

** Comme tous les aperçus d'une redoutable vérité, cette vision résulte du rapprochement d'éléments séparés: en l'occurence d'un vieil article de journal et des notes d'un vieux savant. J'espère que personne n'achèvera cette synthèse. (p. 263)

Interestingly, this carefully controlled structure does not undermine the book's openness. Butor once said that he wants his books to be spaces for the reader to explore, somewhat like cities or cathedrals, but, as Mary Lydon reminds us, cathedrals and cities are very carefully planned structures. *Mobile's* openness is precisely a result of such planning and guidance, the reader's "trajets de lecture" are not unlimited, his journey is never random. The reader's involvement is made possible, precisely by the text's limits. An unstructured work would be chaotic and would preclude any possibility of response. Butor explains that studied guidance alone ensures the interest and involvement of the reader: "If I am confronted with a broken circle, my eye automatically repairs it. The 'open' work, the fragment in its maturity, implies on the one hand an inner architecture developing with great rigour, on the other, its interruption which, to be fully forceful, must also be rigorously designed."[27]

Butor remains the author of his book; he presents us his vision of the United States, his own idiosyncratic interpretation of American history. His voice, although supplemented by many others, is clearly audible. Still, the openness of *Mobile* is genuine; the text is no more than a study for the representation of the United States. There are a number of effects that the author cannot and does not control. In that, *Mobile* resembles a collage and its aesthetic is surrealistic. By means of fragmentation and repetition, each sematic unit is juxtaposed to as many others as possible, and therefore is meaningful in a new way each time. These frequent "rencontres" dramatize the multiplicity of our lives. By placing some of these elements in continually new contexts the book revitalises clichés and questions preconceptions. The suprise and sometimes shock created by some juxtapositions cannot be fully preplanned, for it depends on the reader's response and involvement. The reader alone can exploit the resonances of these unusual groupings. Their meaning is not in the text but is an event that takes place between the text and the reader. Since the connections the reader is invited to make are based on value judgments, as the book unfolds, they contribute to a very special sort of moral education, one planned by the pupil more than by the teacher. Revel experiences a similar kind of education in Bleston, a discovery of the values that underlie the culture and the assumption of a stance in relation to them.

Pages 89 and 90 (p. 93) will serve as an example. We begin with an advertisement for Chapel Lake Indian Ceremonials: *"Enjoy the* *most thrilling one-night vacation and camera's delight. . . ."** A description of an Audubon print follows, then a name "WATERLOO, Jefferson," and excerpts from the peyotl visions of the Winnebago Indian John Rave: *"The first night's vision was terrifying: a huge snake that came toward me, threatening."*** We are outraged at the degradation of Indian culture in Chapel Lake, especially if we compare the tone of John Rave and that of the prospectus; we rebel against the use of such visions and ritual for the purpose of public entertainment. The static bird family on a dead tree stump represents the lifelessness of Indian culture in our time, the co-optation of every aspect of native American life for the purpose of entertainment. "Waterloo" has become a cliché for failure and defeat. The name "Jefferson" represents this typically European attitude; the Thomas Jefferson that emerges in *Mobile* is racist and bigoted, he desires to live in America as a European, enjoying the amenities of culture rather than the novelty of the continent. His name here, referring to Jefferson County, connects this passage with other parts of the book. This is only one page; most of them are full of these surprises, as the same documents are iuxtaposed in other combinations. The shock is brought out by the reader's involvement.

Mobile as a whole is structured on the dynamism inherent in the juxtaposition of two national viewpoints. It is a French book, with French names, a French alphabetical order, a French color scheme. All English quotations are estranged as they are translated into French. The historical sense it imposes on the United States is typically non-American. Such juxtaposition brings with it the expansion beyond the single self, the single nation, the single point of view.

Single/Multiple/Collective

Even while espousing multiplicity as the only form of vision and discourse that can do justice to our plural world, Butor brings out some of its shortcomings in the book itself. As we have seen, *Mobile* could be charged with being another Freedomland. Moreover, the practice of *Mobile* is ironically reflected in the brochure from

---

* *"Jouissez du plus grand délice photographique . . . "*

** *"La vision de la première nuit fut térrifiante: un grand serpent qui s'approchait, menaçant."*

Clifton's Cafeteria; by Butor's admission, the ugliest place he has
seen in the United States:

> *Must we only enjoy art in an art gallery, politics in the voting booth,*
> *religion in the church, books in a library, education in a school,*
> *music in the concert hall, business in our offices? Since each of these*
> *is a part of life, why not so organize our daily existence as to express*
> *all these interests in our common daily tasks?* (p. 230)*

These statements sound remarkably close to some of Butor's
essays. They change their meaning however in the context of
Clifton's Cafeteria; inevitably religion is cheapened by the
association with cafeterias and gift shops. The emphasis on plurality
involves the loss of the particular. As America is criticized for not
differentiating between different aspects of its past, for packaging
all of its values in sales catelogues, so *Mobile* could answer to the
charge of not discriminating between aspects of the world it
represents. In its concentration on groups, *Mobile* ignores the
American individual. The book's structure is marked by this search
for the average, for frequency, and repetition. While Johnson
attempts throughout his books to preserve the integrity and the
autonomy of the individual, Butor is interested in the relation of
similar elements.

> MILFORD, on the Delaware, the New Jersey border.
> MILFORD, on the Delaware, on the Pennsylvania border (p. 78).**

In the book, people are not full individuals, but either anonymous
voices that express average or typical American dreams ("I dream of
San Francisco"), or isolated limbs ("A shoulder, an arm, a wrist,
streaming black"). Adjectives are chosen not for their descriptive
power but for the rhythm; interchangeable, they equalize the
objects they should define and individualize: *"Teals with green
wings . . . green sandals . . . soot-colored terns . . . soot-covered
sandals . . . snowy egrets . . . snowy sandals."**

---

* "*Devons-nous practiquer l'art seulement dans un musée, la politique dans l'isoloir, la religion dans l'église
les livres dans une bibliothèque, l'éducation dans une école, la musique dans la salle de concert, les affaires dans
nos bureaux? Puisque chacune de ces choses fait partie de notre vie, pourquoi ne pas organiser notre existence
quotidienne de telle sorte qu'elle exprime tous ces intérêts dans nos tâches communes de chaque jour?*" (p. 241)

** "MILFORD, sur le Delaware, frontière du New Jersey, . . . MILFORD, sur le Delaware, frontière de la
Pennsylvanie . . . " (p. 81)

* "*Sarcelles à ailes vertes . . . sandales vertes . . . sternes couleur de suie . . . sandales couleur de suie . . . aigrettes
neigeuses . . . sandales neigeuses.*"

And yet, as Butor suggests, *Mobile* leads us to redefine our notions of the particular, by exploding the duality of particularity/generality. He shows us instead a network of particulars:

> I would say that these structures do produce the particular: that is how the particular comes to be. The particular American lives in Hanover, Indiana, buys his curtains at Sears, and dreams at night after turning off his television set. Besides this crowd there are small individualities that appear and this individualization is reinforced by the historical individuals (certain Indians, Jefferson, Carnegie, etc.). But for instance, the way in which Jefferson appears destroys him as an individual. We see very well that, in fact, it is not he who speaks, but it is the rest of America which speaks through him. But he could not avoid saying certain things which appear monstrous to us today. Jefferson's individuality, his talent, Monticello, are reversed in some way. The same thing happens to him as to all the others.[28]

As readers of novels, we have difficulty with a book that describes a collective rather than an individual fate; we value the particular, we value human interiority, psychological depth and complexity as it is revealed in James' novels. There individuals loom large, invincible, all powerful; here they appear only as fragments or as attributes of the land, no more important than birds or cars. Butor's vision of America seems general and superficial, as it is incapable of accounting for nuances and individual differences. We may rebel against what seems like the reduction and objectification of our very dreams and could dismiss the book as inaccurate and unsubtle. The book's repetitive and regular patterns, arranged in alphabetical order, are signs of loss for those who expect to follow the development of fictional characters. To appreciate the novelty of *Mobile*, is to transcend the standards of individualism.

In its efforts to overcome such blindness and to move toward plurality and decentralization, the text of *Mobile* profoundly calls into question our notions of authorship; it makes explicit what theorists like Barthes find true of all literary works: that instead of being the original creation of a single author, they are mere recreations, points in a vast cultural and linguistic network. For Barthes, every text is a "tissue of quotations drawn from the innumerable centers of culture."[29] In *Mobile*, the intertextual relationships are explicitly identified by quotation marks and the naming of sources. The inclusion of other voices, ranging from Andrew Carnegie to the Montgomery Ward catalogue, responds to

Butor's attempt to transcend the singularity of authorship, the limited single vision of the individual "author." It represents the movement toward a new omniscience that would be not merely one enriched perspective, but a composite vision of many perspectives. Butor's efforts at expansion and inclusiveness, unlike those of Barthes' "scriptor," are made in the service of a representational art. Butor's text is not a tissue of signifiers, but an instrument of knowledge about an extratextual reality.

Butor's realism is not a naive positivistic copy of a simple and pre-existent reality; his text is the stage for various aspects of American mythology. It represents not the American continent, but the means by which that continent has been apprehended and represented by others. "The book's true subject is reality as it is spoken and as it is forgotten."[30] According to Butor, it is impossible to perceive external reality directly: "It's to a large extent by means of books, notably novels that we know the universe . . . what we see with our eyes plays a small part in relation to what we hear about, and quickly the words we hear with our ears are small in number in relation to those which we read."[31] When quoting other texts, therefore, far from enclosing himself in a hermetic, mental universe, the writer pushes outward toward reality in the only way possible: through others who have preceded him. He is involved in the unending pursuit of an accurate vision which can be reached only by assessing and correcting previous visions:

> The library gives us the world, but it gives us a false world; from time to time fissures occur, reality rebels against the books by means of our eyes, by means of words or of certain books, an exterior gesture to us and gives us the feeling of being locked up; the library becomes a prison.
>
> By adding new books, we try to redistribute the entire surface so that windows will appear.[32]

Butor attempts to break out of the library-prison by acknowledging both implicitly and explicitly his debt to previous writers. By giving them a voice in his book, he hopes to assemble a more accurate model of reality than the work of a single author could ever be. Intertextuality permits the author to examine and correct the myths of other authors, to examine the way by which the country represents itself.

Thus Chateaubriand is implicitly present in *Mobile* and Butor corrects the earlier writer's dream of a rejuvenation of the old world by means of the new. Many American writings, few of them literary, become part of the composite reality the book enacts. The fragmentation and juxtaposition of these texts places each one of them in a new light. If it brings some forgotten texts to our attention, it also sharpens or alters our vision of many well-known figures. For example, Thomas Jefferson, the author of the Declaration of Independence, ironically emerges as a profound believer in the inequality of race purely on the basis of quotations from his *Notes on the State of Virginia.* Commentators of Jefferson usually dismiss some of the content of the *Notes* and redeem Jefferson on the basis of his personal treatment of his own slaves. Butor is not unfair to Jefferson, however, he merely quotes his well-thought-out and articulate arguments, which are doubly frightening because of their eloquence. Revealing the racism of one of our most celebrated leaders is part of Butor's program of awakening. The juxtaposition of Andrew Carnegie's *Gospel of Wealth* and Benjamin Franklin's *Information to Those who would Remove to America* reveals the schizophrenia of a country that daily lives the tension between European values of nobility and aristocracy and the new, typically American notions of classlessness and the work ethic. Butor, in his turn, expects others to follow him to correct his vision. It is in this sense too that his book is open to the future, that it anticipates its revision and completion by others.

To understand the vast and complex American universe demands an individual transmutation that collaboration can help to bring about: "The act of collaborating with another, whether dead or alive, is a means by which to develop a new personality. It is perfectly comparable to the creation of a fictional character."[33] As readers, we enter into a similar kind of collaborative relationship with the various voices of the text. The absence, in *Mobile,* of one central subject, enables us to see the individual self as an arena where various cultural forces interact, and thus better to survive in a decentered universe. Yet as we read *Mobile,* we continue to search for individuality and depth. The text functions within a dialectic. Butor himself, despite his attempt to transcend the singularity of authorship, remains a strong presence in the text, felt not through his voice, but through the process of selection and collection for which he is clearly responsible. The vision of America that emerges in *Mobile* is a biased and personal one, polemical, didactic and provocative in its criticism. On the other hand, the text of *Mobile* clearly escapes the individual control of its author. Its component parts, whether they be sales brochures or Benjamin Franklin adages, are often so familiar as to have the property of "found" objects; they have become a part of the culture in an impersonal sense. In the dialectic between the nostalgia for the singularity of character and author and the celebration of a plurality of historical figures, ice-cream flavors, cars birds, oceans, items in the Sears catalogue, quotations from the Trappist jelly brochures, and even human limbs, there does emerge a collective identity and epistemology in which the reader participates and which moves toward a communal awareness.

The reader is not the expiatory victim who takes the place of the missing character, as critics have suggested. Instead, the reader participates in the creation of a "superior individuality" by being drawn into the text at every point, and becoming more than one of the numerous voices that constitute it, the agent of their interaction. To become a part of his new multiple form of being, however, the reader must accept a communal guilt, and, although not a victim, must expiate.

Europe/America
Invasion/Expansion

A book about the United States by a French writer and attuned to the interests of both the American and the European reader, *Mobile* reenacts the European settler's invasion of America that is still present on every level of our life. The struggle between the old world and the new is a part of our history; it is reflected in the names of our cities and the content of our dreams.

Several different forms of invasion are examined in the book. We re-experience the original settlers' fear of the enormous strange continent, their nostalgic regret for Europe, their desire to assimilate the new country by imposing on it the values of the old. Their inability to understand the novelty is reflected in their choice of names; their paucity reveals the insufficiency of European viewpoints when faced with the richness and dynamism of the new continent:

> *Meanwhile, until this triumphal return took place, why not recon-*
> *stitute a new Europe, effacing as much as possible this continent*
> *that received but alarmed us?*

                              New

                                              France,

                    New   *England*
          Nova
                    Scotia,
          New
                    Brunswick   (p. 95)**

Incapable of inventing new codes that might correspond to the new
world, the European settlers continued to function with their old
frame of reference. Louis Sullivan's "Autobiography of an Idea"
rebels against this destructively nostalgic trend in American
architecture:

> *Thus Architecture died in the land of the free and the home of the*
> *brave–in a land declaring its fervid democracy, its inventiveness, its*
> *resourcefulness, its unique daring, enterprise and progress. Thus*
> *did the virus of a culture, snobbish and alien to the land, perform*
> *its work of disintegration; and thus ever works the pallid academic*
> *mind, denying the real, exulting the fictitious and the false; that*
> *never lifts a hand in aid because it cannot; that turns its back upon*
> *man because that is its tradition; a culture lost in ghostly*
> *mésalliance with abstractions, when what the world needs is*
> *courage, common sense and human sympathy, and a moral standard*
> *that is pain, valid and livable (p. 87)***

The destructive shadow of Europe appears above all in
Washington, the center of white American culture and the exact
center–spatial and chronological–of the book. This empty center
houses the soul and power of the white American. Butor writes
about the "European Americans" in the same tone that they
themselves use for describing the Indians. It is here, in Washington,

---

* *En attendant ce triomphal retour, ne fallait—il point reconstituer autour de soi une nouvelle Europe,*
effacer le plus possible de son esprit ce continent qui nous accueillait mais nous effrayait?

                              Nouvelle
                                              France,
                    Nouvelle
                                  Angleterre,
          Nouvelle
                    Ecosse,
          Nouveau
                    Brunswick   (p. 99)

** *Ainsi mourut l'architecture dans le pays qui était celui de la liberté et du courage, — dans un pays qui*
proclamait sa fervente démocratie, son invention, ses ressources, son unique audace. Ainsi le virus d'une culture
snob et importée réussit-il son oeuvre de désintegration; ainsi travaille toujours le blème esprit académique, niant
le réel, exaltant les fictions; qui jamais ne vous aide, bien incapable; tourne le dos à l'humain, c'est sa tradition; une
culture perdue dans une spectrale mésalliance avec des abstractions, quand le monde a besoin de courage, de bon
sens, d'humanité et d'une moralité simple, sûre et vivable. (p. 90)

that the communal forgetting takes place, that Washington, Jefferson and Lincoln are being worshipped without being known. These figures, carved into Mount Rushmore, symbolize the attitude of the European settlers toward the novelty of America; their effort to assimilate it and render it harmless. Their response was ignorance and pretension rather than openness and curiosity: *"They did not try to know this country, they had no desire to settle here. They were content with temporary habitations. They wanted only to survive and grow rich in order to be able to return."* (p. 95)* Thus they fail to fulfill the dream of a new Babel, a culturally multiple, and therefore truly plural civilization. They fail to exploit the potential of America.

Whether Europeans or Americans, we must acknowledge our violation so as to be allowed to move toward a new future: "For this book, the United States plays the role of an optical instrument, a magnifying glass by which to study a certain number of aspects of Western civilization in general."[34] Europeans are equally guilty. "It is actually the European who by the act of killing the Indians became American."[35] *Mobile* gives us the opportunity to do what one of its voices desires: "If only it were possible to start everything over from the beginning, if only the frontier were still open and we could escape this new Europe and found new cities in a different way." (p. 151)**

We can begin by admitting our crime and by facing the true novelty of America. *Mobile* presents a copy of that novelty; in its revolutionary form, it becomes in itself a sort of "new world" to explore. Accepting it and learning to read it offers us the possibility of participating in a new form of multiple authorship and perhaps of recovering, together with the author and his predecessors, a breadth of vision, an omniscience that the novel has had to relinquish long ago. Then perhaps we can begin to apply that vision to our lives.

The collective aesthetic instituted and celebrated in *Mobile* undergoes significant changes in Butor's more recent texts. After continuing experiments with the form of the "spatial poem" in *Réseau Aérien*, *Description de San Marco*, and *6 810 00 litres d'eau*

---

* *Ils ne cherchaient point à le connaître ce pays, ils ne désiraient point s'y installer. Ils se contentaient d'habitations provisoires. Ils ne désiraient que survivre et s'enrichir pour pouvoir retourner.* (p. 98)

** *Si seulement il était possible de tout reprendre dès le début, si seulement la frontière était encore ouverte et que l'on pût fuire cette nouvelle Europe, et instituer autrement de nouvelles villes.* (p. 157)

par seconde, the individual self returns as the author himself, Michel Butor, in *Où*, *Intervalle*, the three volumes of *Matière de rêves* that have appeared so far, and *Boomerang*. Butor's work does not return to earlier concerns, however, but undergoes a logical development. The "I" of *Où* traces not an introspective but an expansive movement; after the acceptance of the collective in *Mobile*, it was necessary to gauge the process of change involved in such an acceptance. Yet the return to the individual seeker and to the epistemological quest brings with it feelings of frustration and insufficiency, the inability to see and to describe.

The result is, nevertheless, a profound challenge to our notion of selfhood, by means of a fluid and flexible form of identity which dissolves all boundaries between Self and Other. The metamorphoses of *Matière de rêves* enact, on a personal level, the multiplicity celebrated in *Mobile*. The expansion taking place here is almost limitless. It is no longer a question of enriching the single vision so that it can include otherness, nor of collecting a number of individual visions, even less of demonstrating the stereotypes within which each individual functions. It involves, rather, a dissolution and explosion in which the self loses its physical and psychological boundaries in a mystical and dreamlike fusion with the world. Can the human body, can the human psyche survive such expansion, we might ask. And, by extension, can the literary text survive such explosion?

6. *Anniversaries:* "Invention which Becomes a Kind of Truth"

Uwe Johnson's most recent and yet unfinished novel, *Anniversaries,*[1] reveals many of its central concerns within the opening pages. It begins with an evocation of the sea[2] which consists of a painstakingly detailed description of the waves, their color, movement and direction. It is a neutral description, devoid of any particular emotional thrust or poetic tone. A simile that describes the small pocket of air formed by the break of the wave as a secret, made and destroyed, first hints at an authorial presence fascinated by the sea's mystery. It is its power, however, that this description brings out most forcefully, the sheer physical power that causes children to topple over, that pulls swimmers further and further out. The sea, with its unceasing ebb and flow motion, suggests permanence. And yet, this motion varies according to the particular environment and, although the sea has the potency to link such disparate entities as America and Europe, it cannot overcome differences dictated by the individual locality. Thus the present description (later localized on the New Jersey coast) is interrupted by a preterite evocation of the Baltic Sea where, under similar weather conditions, both the waves and their names are different.

The second paragraph of the novel's descriptive beginning concerns the small resort village in New Jersey that welcomes neither Blacks nor Jews. The mention of prejudice brings the as yet neutral and objective narrative into the thoughts of an anonymous "she" who establishes a link with the Northern German seaside village of Jerichow in 1933 and wonders, cannot remember, whether Jews were admitted there. The narrator does not identify this figure but reports about her external circumstances, and especially about her neighbors' inability to fix her identity: they call her "Mrs Cresspahl" even though her mail is addressed to a "Miss C.," and probably view her as an Irish Catholic no different from them.

The short verse in dialect that names the protagonist, Gesine Cresspahl, is in itself cryptic and hardly facilitates her identification. Subsequent descriptions of weather and landscape culminate in further associations between New Jersey and

Mecklenburg, between the noise of the waves and the sound of war movies. The rapid alternation of places and time levels, the anonymity of the mind that makes these jumps without clarifying the connections, and the mention of unidentified people and plans disorient even further a reader who tries to situate himself within as specific a context as possible. The confusion of tenses, present and preterite, reinforces the sense of a shifting point of view; whereas through most of the passage the present is used to refer to the day in New Jersey and the past for Germany in the '30's and '40's, we also find such lines as "The sky has been bright for a long time" (p. 3).* The mixture of impressionistic description and dry report style is equally disquieting. The mind who provides the locus for the narration in this chapter is, on the one hand, trying to relive a remote childhood state and is actively engaged in the process of reminiscence; on the other hand, however, Gesine seems an almost passive recipient of multiple and perhaps meaningful interrelations between countries and time periods.

In spite of the confusions, the novel might, in this first chapter, seem to be a modern story about the inner life of one character, reported in an interesting combination of stream of consciousness, "narrated monologue," and third-person narration. Yet several factors begin to hint at the expansion beyond the limits of psychological fiction that characterizes *Anniversaries*. Two alien voices intrude in italics, one in Mecklenburg dialect, the other in English. They form a counterpoint to the subjective interior monologue passages. So does a paragraph of news reportage about the Israeli war and the New Haven riots. Gesine's letter to the city of Rande, written in the first person and not set off by quotation marks, introduces yet another shift in perspective. Moreover, Gesine's musings are characterized by a surprising lack of introspection or self-analysis. While the first chapter of *The Ambassadors* concerns Strether's ambivalent feelings toward Waymarsh and Europe, these pages concern the physical scene and social matters, the number of Jews or Blacks, for example. Gesine's memories are explicitly factual and seem to aim at as exact a reconstruction of past events as possible; dates, for example, play a major role. Gesine herself is identified in her social, more than her private role. She is a Miss or Mrs. Cresspahl, a "former resident of Jerichow and at one time a regular visitor of Rande" (p. 4)**, and an employee who must appear at her bank job on time.

---

* Der Himmel ist lange hell gewesen. (p. 8)
** Ehemalige Bürgerin von Jerichow und ehemals regelmässige Besucherin von Rande. (p. 8)

The novel's subtitle, "From the Life of Gesine Cresspahl,"* as well as the author's description of the book as a "biography of a person"[3] indeed indicate that this is the story of Gesine Cresspahl. Yet we are struck by the multiplicity and multifacetedness of that life, but its range and scope. Not only does her story reach from the 1930's to the 1960's – the story of her parents and grandparents even predates her birth in 1933–, but it reaches from Mecklenburg, to Richmond, England, to New York, from the Baltic to the English Channel and to the Atlantic. All of these factors must be included in the depiction of her life. The narration of one day allows for the detailed description of a small New Jersey village and for evocations of train journeys in 1941 and 1952. It seems to demand a discussion of the Israeli-Jordanian front and the New Haven riots. Gesine herself almost disappears behind the range of multiple evocations with their complex interconnections. Thus the inner life of Gesine is not the sole focus of the novel. Neither separate nor unified, the individual life becomes a "crossroads" that occasions the panoramic depiction of a world and a half-century. As Johnson says:

> You see, I just don't think that in modern industrial society there
> are clearly demarcated, impermeable environments left. One thing
> connects to and depends on the other.[4]

These connections and interrelations become the focus of the story, as they did in *Passing Time*. Here, however, they do not eclipse the individual protagonist; on the contrary, Gesine's detailed reconstruction of her ancestors' actions and motives creates a sense of depth and continuity which estabilishes Gesine firmly as an individual with a multi-layered history. As Johnson puts it, the novel's basis is "the individual consciousness of one person which contains all this."[5] Note here the representation of consciousness as a container, repudiated by Butor, reminiscent of James. Still, *Anniversaries* is not the account of Gesine's consciousness of New York as *The Ambassadors* is the account of Strether's consciousness of Paris.

Gesine can concentrate neither on one moment or one place; her life provides the meeting ground for most of the century's important events and she seems condemned to live that meeting, on one level or another, during every day of her life. The most striking revelation of the novel's first few pages is the multiplicity of places and time levels to which we refer in the course of a day and the small role of the present in relation to the past in our lives. The exploration of the past does more than to explain the present; it assumes a centrality of its own, competing, at every point, with the

---

* "Aus dem Leben von Gesine Cresspahl"; the translation does not convey the title's second meaning: "About Life by Gesine Cresspahl."

description of Gesine's comparatively uneventful present existence. While *The Ambassadors* focuses on the psychological intricacies of the present moment, *Anniversaries* creates a different kind of depth, both spatial and temporal, which transcends the psychology of the single protagonist. The realization of these multiple interdependencies within the individual life enables Johnson to render, through the biography of one person, the history of our century as well as the portrait of Jerichow and New York. The difference between *Anniversaries* and *Mobile* lies in the importance the individual subject retains in *Anniversaries* even though the novel supersedes the single vision through very similar techniques: chronological arrangement which is interrupted by recurring spatial motifs, fragmentation, juxtaposition, different kinds of print.

Johnson carefully selects (or constructs) his characters. This multiplicity can be rendered not only because Gesine's life has been deeply affected by the crucial historical events of the times, because she has been subjected to the Nazi regime, the Second World War, the division of East and West, the confrontation of Europe and America, but also because, unlike Revel's, Gesine's life is directed toward those events, rather than toward her own self. Her experiences in wartime and post-war Germany, both East and West, have taught her precisely what we learn as readers of *Mobile*, to accept fragmentation, disjunction and alienation simply as conditions of life. Her quest is not, like Revel's, to find her own central place in the chaotic multiplicity, to understand her responses and roles, but rather to live responsibly, by understanding and charting the events that shape the lives of her parents, her own life, and that of her daughter. She starts out doing what Revel finally does in spite of himself.

Critics have noted a much greater ease and confidence in this novel than in *Jakob* and the other early novels; Johnson's questions about fiction as a mode of cognition seem less tortured; a story and a continuity are easier to find. Johnson says himself that "difficulties of the presentation of the narrative are no longer represented, no longer mentioned."[6] I would like to argue that the change is due not to an abandonment of those questions, but to a different outlook on the part of Gesine, to the experiment with different solutions to the same problems:

> I did not want to write a novel about New York, but to concern my-
> self with a person and her story, and story, or history was the catch-

word for the second level of the novel; I wanted to show the
formation of this person. [*Interview*]

In this statement Johnson defines the dual, spatial and temporal,
impulse of his novel. In spite of its pronounced emphasis on time,
rather than space, *Anniversaries* does emerge as an intriguing
panorama of urban life in New York. The diachronic narrative is
interspersed with chapters about different aspects of the city: its
subways and buses, its telephone service, its different noises, its
crime and its bugs. These synchronic *tableaux* give the book a richly
textured surface that enacts the surface of urban life and renders the
most common sights interesting, almost exotic.

More immediately related to Gesine than these general aspects
are the city's varied inhabitants, whether German, Polish, or Czech
immigrants, whether Wasps who live in Connecticut, or Blacks who
run the elevators, whether bank presidents, neighborhood store
owners, or school children. Additional elements of the city--drugs,
crimes, inhabitants killed in Vietnam, fires Mayor Lindsay--intrude
by means of the newspaper that Gesine reads daily and from which
daily quotations appear in the text.

The paper itself relates Gesine to the city, and the city to the
world. The daily segments from the *New York Times* ground
Gesine's individual story in a broader context; they introduce a
public voice that relates the political and social background against
which her daily life is situated: "As if it alone provided proof of the day"
(p. 10)*. Even though these quotations are selected by Gesine and
reflect her personal interests, and although they are somewhat
estranged by their translation into German, they enlarge the scope
of the novel by taking the reader to areas of New York Gesine could
not but encounter vicariously, and by taking us daily to Germany,
Israel, Vietnam and Czechoslovakia. The present level of the novel
(1967-1968), then concerns not only Gesine's daily activities but the
public events of the year, as well as the varied aspects of urban life.
The *New York Times* introduces not only breadth but authority,
claiming, as it does, to include "all the news that's fit to print."
Gesine's wavering relationship to the *Times*, her questions about the
paper's supposed and perhaps actual omniscience and impartiality,
and her characterization of the *Times* as tough and experienced old
aunt provide some of the most complex passages of the novel. It is

---

* Als sei nur mit ihr der Tag zu beweisen. (p. 15)

the *Times*, after all, that circumscribes Gesine's apprehension and judgement of all the events that influence her life but which she cannot experience directly.

Space and time merge in *Anniversaries*: "Where were you–A few years ago" (p. 84)*. The novel's present level takes place within one year (August 20, 1967 to August 19, 1968) in New York. Departures to the past are, at the same time, journeys to Germany. It is through its relation to the present moment that the past emerges; memories are triggered by association or by the connection of dates, or they emerge in Gesine's conscious effort to reconstruct chronologically the 1930's and 40's in Jerichow. The book's title, then, refers to the connection between present and past, to the anniversary that is made present through its observance. In the repeated juxtapositions of past and present, connections emerge that are not always transparent. Thus we relate the antisemitism of the 1930's with racism in the 60's, or news about Vietnam with stories about concentration camps. The extent and seriousness of such comparisons are difficult to determine because, as in *Speculations about Jakob*, the separate elements within the novel's montage structure assert their proper individuality above their place in the configuration as a whole. Yet it is the discovery of such connections that constitutes the major thrust of *Anniversaries*. Thus, the book is a history in the private as well as the public sense: we must remember that the German word "Geschichte" refers both to "story" and "history."

The history of Gesine and her epoch is, as the other meaning of the book's subtitle indicates, narrated by Gesine herself. As the rendition of her life becomes a daily event for Gesine, she makes explicit the importance of the past in all our lives. While in the book's first pages, Gesine was the passive meeting ground of different time levels, she subsequently becomes the agent of remembrance and relationship, so as to uncover the meaning of such connections as her mind made by the sea. Similarly to *Mobile*, the book emphasizes the necessity of an informed remembrance, of keeping the past in the foreground so that we might learn from it. Awareness is the only possible stance in this complex world: *"It's what I've been left with: to find out about things. At least to live with my eyes open"* (p. 142)**, Gesine says as she literally devotes almost all her free time to this quest for awareness.

---

* Wo warst du.—Vor ein paar Jahren. (p. 120)

** *Es ist was mir übriggeblieben ist: Bescheid zu lernen. Wenigstens mit Kenntnis zu leben.* (p. 209)

The title "*Anniversaries*" points not only to the past, but also to the future. The repetition of events in our memory will continue into the future. Only if we ward off forgetting, if we make a conscious effort to preserve and to understand the past, can we ensure that that repetition will be meaningful, because then it will be conscious and understood.

It is Gesine's daughter, Marie, who presents the impulse for her mother's narration; it is she who represents the future. It is for Marie that Gesine tapes the record of her past, preserving her turbulent life for posterity. To Marie, the motives and behavior of her ancestors have the didactic value of models and possibilities and the excitement of fiction: "But what she wants to know is not the past, not even her own. For her these are a presentation of possibilities from which she believes herself immune, and in another sense stories. (I haven't actually asked her.) This is how we spend some of our evenings" (p. 103).*

Although the novel's spatial impulse consistently undercuts it, the pattern of repetition and continuity is as important here as in *Mobile* and it takes on an even more positive role. While repetition means the degradation and destruction of individiduality in *Mobile*, it builds the individual identity here. The numerous rituals in the protagonists' lives--Saturday on the South Ferry, purchase of the paper in the morning--present a kind of learning that occurs by returning and re-experiencing. Thus, repetition becomes progression. Herein, as well, lies the value of recovering the past; an individual is defined by past, family and circumstances, and if he is to understand himself, he must examine previous generations. But Marie finds such a collective identity difficult to accept:

> I often think it's terrible the way you can believe that all those
> people in Jerichow made you what you are; that today you're what
> you are because they were what they were! (p. 363)**

Although the experience of reading *Anniversaries* is not quite as discontinuous as reading *Mobile*, it also demands the recomposition of disjointed elements. There are three different kinds of print:

---

* Aber was sie wissen will ist nicht Vergangenheit, nicht einmal ihre. Für sie ist es eine Vorführung von Möglichkeiten, gegen die sie sich gefeit glaubt, und in einem anderen Sinn, Geschichten. So verbringen wir einige Abende. (p. 144)

** ... oft finde ich schrecklich, wie du glauben kannst, sass alle diese Leute in Jerichow dich gemacht haben; dass du heute bist wie du bist, weil sie waren wie sie waren! (p. 562)

although these divisions are not always consistent: roman is generally used for narration; italic for interior monologue and imaginary dialogues with anonymous voices that, chorus-like, comment on the narration; a different kind of roman print is used for Cresspahl's voice at the end of Volume 2. Jumps from *New York Times* quotations, to a letter Gesine might have received, to her own narration or that of the external narrator are difficult to follow and to identify. Yet it is still the alternation between the present and the past level of the novel that is the most demanding. As in *Mobile*, each chronological progression is continually interrupted by another one. Thus we follow the perfectly chronological account of the year 1967-68 as well as the less ordered and less complete rendition of the years 1930 to (presumably) 1967.

Gesine's present life consists of a tedious and uninteresting routine. The people with whom she comes into contact, the diminished victims of war and emigration, of a harried and difficult urban existence, are, with some exceptions, quite colorless. Gesine's relationship with D.E. has settled into a calm, though tender routine: even if it ever results in marriage, it will never be passionate. The one suspenseful "plot" on this level of the novel, the kidnapping of Karsch by the Mafia, smacks of contrivance and therefore serves as a reflector on the less exciting personal events. The panoramic chapters on aspects of New York life are the most interesting sections on this present level of the novel. As Erich Würderich says, Gesine's "life in New York hardly provides the stuff of a novel."[7]

In contrast, the story of the Cresspahls and Papenbrocks in Jerichow is full of suspense, adventure, mystery and danger. The reader cannot help but find it more engaging than the account of Gesine's job or Marie's school problems. One wonders, however, if this strongly felt qualitative difference between the two time levels is inherent in the two periods themselves or whether at least part of the difference is imposed on the narrated reality by the selective process of memory and by the activity of narration in which narrator and reader collaborate in mythicizing their material. Moreover, we find in the choices and motivations of Cresspahl and Lisbeth a psychological and political drama much more compelling to readers of the psychological novel than even the best of the New York sketches, the description of Sam's coffee shop, of life on Broadway, or of a conversation with the bank president de Rosny. What distinguishes *Anniversaries* from the psychological novel and even from the James novels in this study is the tight interrelationship of psychological and political motives: it is impossible to determine whether the failure of Cresspahl's marriage is due to psychological imcompatibility or to the onslaught of the war and Nazism, whether Cresspahl ends up working for British intelligence because of his hatred of Nazism or his desire to avenge the death of his wife.

After the first passive moments, Gesine takes almost full responsibility for uncovering and relating the events of her past. Her method resembles that of the narrators in *Jakob*: in her desire to establish the facts of the past, Gesine is forced to speculate and guess, often even to posit hypothetical occurences, so as to flesh out her skeletal information, to create out of fragments of hearsay and memory a story that is both plausible and close to the truth. Here again, the narrative is colored by Gesine's needs, wishes and desires, her unconditional admiration for her father, for example, or her strong aversion to all she knows about her mother.

Yet, here again, multiple viewpoints are at work, challenging Gesine's view and pointing to the relativistic and perspectivistic nature of all narration. Gesine's consciousness might contain all of the story's materials, but it is only one of a number of consciousnesses in the novel. It shifts and organizes but it does not dominate.

The role of the external narrator is important:

> *Who's telling this story, Gesine?*
> *We both are. Surely that's obvious, Johnson* (p. 169)*

His job is to put her preverbal thoughts and her oral narration into writing, to supplement and to organize the material, to do all that her job and lack of time prevent her from taking care of. As this narrator's role is more limited than in *The Ambassadors*, Gesine enjoys support but is less protected, more exposed. Johnson calls this a "naturalistic point of view": "I tell as much as the character can know, not what she couldn't know."[8] Whatever information surpasses Gesine's direct experience, and much in the novel does, must be read, invented, guessed by her.

It is Gesine's daughter Marie, however, who, besides Gesine, has the major role in the narrative process. Their dialogues, ranging

---

* *Wer erzählt hier eigentlich, Gesine?*
  Wir beide. Das hörst du doch, Johnson. (p. 256)

from games to arguments, become experiences of communal storytelling, similar to those of *Speculations about Jakob*. Marie's challenges and questions provide the necessary impetus for Gesine as narrator and they take the process of remembrance from a subjective to a communicative and therefore useful realm: "Her questions sharpen my imagination" (p. 103).* They lead Gesine not only to tell, but to explain and to justify the past, to relate it to present and future.

Such an activity depends on a great deal of conjecture, speculation, and even invention. As in *Speculations about Jakob*, the truth that is the object of the book's search concerns, to a large degree, people who are dead, periods that are remote. The story itself is a complex one with important political and personal implications. Memory is fragmentary, information full of gaps, yet it is a full picture that Gesine and Marie seek to construct:

> If only memory could contain the past in the receptacles we use to
> sort the elements of present reality! . . . At a nudge, prompted by
> even partial congruence, by the random and the absurd, it will
> volunteer facts, figures, foreign speech, unrelated gestures; offer it
> a smell combining tar, rot, and fresh sea breeze, the faint whiff from
> Gustafsson's famous fish salad, and ask for the contents of the void
> that was once reality, life-awareness, action: it will refuse to supply
> them. (p. 47)**

Their job is not simply to reconstruct specific events, but to organize and integrate a multiplicity of half-remembered episodes and people, to build a life. Many of their decisions are subjective and personal. They fill in gaps, speculate about motives, try to iron out contradictions. They come to acknowledge the fallibility of memory, the necessity of invention: "You have to invent it even if it's correct."*** They recognize the impulse of memory toward falsification and exploitation, the dubiousness of its truth:

---

* Ihre Fragen machen meine Vorstellungen genauer. (p. 143)

** Dass das Gedächtnis das Vergangene doch fassen könnte in die Formen mit denen wir die Wirklichkeit einteilen! . . . aus dem blauen Absurden liefert es freiwillig Fakten, Zahlen, Fremdsprache, abgetrennte Gesten; halte ihm hin eine teerigen fauligen, dennoch windfrischen Geruch. . . . unde bitte um Inhalt für die Leere, die einmal Wirklichkeit, Lebensgefuhl, Handlung war: es wird die Ausfullung verweigern. (pp. 63-64).

*** Selbst wenn es stimmt, du erfindest es doch! (p. 584)

> I know no more than I need about your father. And I don't trust
> what I know because it hasn't always been there in my memory, and
> then without warning it turns up as a recollection. Maybe my
> memory creates a sentence such as Jakob said or maybe said, might
> have said. Once the sentence is complete and there, memory builds
> the others around it, even the voices of quite different people. That
> scares me. All of a sudden my mind is carrying on a conversation
> about a conversation at which I wasn't even present, and the only
> true thing about it is the memory of his intonation, the way Jakob
> spoke. (pp. 255-256)*

Two kinds of remembrance emerge in the novel: Gesine's narrated
memories and the intuited, non-verbal leaps to the past that she
achieves only at rare moments. Whereas she trusts this latter form of
remembrance, she fears narration because it presents, at every
point, the risk of inaccuracy and falsehood. Nevertheless, memory
has become a vital and necessary part of their lives. Enmeshed in it as
they are, they accept its dangers and risks.

It is herein that the difference between *Speculations about
Jakob* and *Anniversaries* lies. The former novel reveals a profound
suspiciousness of fiction; its narrative shies away from plot and
refuses to tell the stories that are suggested throughout. We never
find out why Gesine comes back to the East with a gun and a
miniature camera, for example. Here all such stories are told; Gesine
accepts the fact that we cannot help apprehending our life through
the mode of fiction and, although she fights its falsification at every
turn, she is ready to accept the subjectivity of all truth:

> 'What you don't know in your story you fill up with other stuff, and
> I believe it anyway,' she says.
> 'I never promised to tell the truth.'
> 'Of course not. Only your truth.'
> 'The way I imagine'. . . . 'Whatever you imagine of your past must in
> the end be reality.' (pp. 436-437)**

It is Marie, the skeptical listener, who is overly suspicious of
contrivance, chance, or anything that looks like a well-made plot,

---

* Von deinem Vater weiss ich nur das Notwendigste. Und ich trau dem nicht was ich weiss, weil es sich nicht
immer in meinem Gedächtnis gezeigt hat, dann unverhofft als Einfall auftritt. Vielleicht macht das Gedächtnis
aus sich so einen Satz, den Jakob gesagt hat oder vielleicht gesagt hat, oder gesagt haben kann. Ist der Satz einmal
fertig und vorhanden, baut das Gedächtnis die andern um ihn herum, sogar die Stimmen von ganz andern
Leuten. Davor habe ich Angst. Mit einem Mal führe ich in Gedanken ein Gespräch über ein Gespräch, bei dem ich
gar nicht dabei war und Wahreit ist daran nur die Erinnerung an seine Intonation, wie Jakob sprach. (p. 387)

** " 'Was dir fehlt beim Erzählen, füllst du aus mit anderem, und ich glaube es doch: sagte sie.'
'Nie habe ich die Wahrheit gesprochen.'
'Gewiss nicht. Nur deine Wahrheit.'
'Wie ich sie mir denke.' . . .
'Was du dir denkst an deiner Vergangenheit, wirklich ist es doch auch' (pp. 670-671).' "

while at the same time she shares a typical reader's "curiosity for stories": "That's one coincidence too many for me . . . . I don't like it when everything falls into place like this."* Their conversations thus form a dialectical approach to narrative in which each choice and version are carefully questioned and examined: the result is not "the truth" but merely one among possible versions. As narrators, they do what Johnson demands in "Berliner Stadbahn"; they reveal the limits of their knowledge.

In admitting invention as a viable supplement to a necessarily limited body of direct information, Gesine concurs with Johnson's statements in "Berliner Stadtbahn" and elsewhere. Johnson distinguishes between "Dichtung" in the German sense of pure fantasy, and "Erfindung" in its sense of finding, as a means toward knowledge. Thus, he speaks of "an invention which is truth, becomes a kind of truth." Gesine admits using images from Marie's childhood to describe her own, or images from Vietnam to evoke World War II. She has no choice, as her memory is flawed and her information sketchy. Even actual research, such as a weather report from 1930, a letter from Rande, or the "omniscient" *New York Times* itself, are revealed as partial at best and dubious at worst. Gesine admits that some things are unknowable and that most people, even those who are closest, are inviolable, hopelessly opaque. Even her own father and mother will in many respects remain incomprehensible. She therefore tries to approach them in as many possible ways as she can think of: she tells several versions of some events, asks Marie's help to interpret others, uses the less conscious states of fever and dreams to get closer to her story. Her narrative is limited only by the needs of her story and the response of her audience. It is a model for narrative because of the degree of involvement and commitment of both teller and listener. No wonder, then, that remembrance and narration actually begin to take on a more important role in the lives of Gesine and Marie than their everyday life.

The narrative process in which Gesine and Marie are engaged reveals increased capacities of fiction as an instrument of knowledge about a complex social and political reality, especially when compared to *Speculations about Jakob*. The paradox which characterizes their activity actually describes the novel as a whole: the necessity to invent a fictional context, to supplement and amend it with factual research so as to get at the real truth about a period which neither report nor invention alone can describe. The

---

* Es ist mir ein Zufall zuviel. . . . Ich mag es nicht wenn etwas so genau zusammenfällt. (p. 833)

acceptance of this paradox, uncomfortable as it may be, makes this novel less tortured than *Speculations about Jakob*.

I have pointed to three areas in which *Anniversaries* goes beyond the level of the single moment and the single individual. Presenting a panorama of New York and a vivid evocation of Jerichow, and alternating between these two settings, it situates the individual in a broad spatial configuration. It also defines the history of the protagonist and attempts the integration of different time levels in that individual's life. Thirdly, *Anniversaries* is not only a diary, but also a dialogue, and that on many levels. The interplay of voices, Gesine's, Marie's, the external narrator's, the quotations from the *Times* and the intrusion of anonymous voices in italics brings Gesine's life into a public realm and illuminates it from a number of shifting perspectives. Narration becomes the means of knowledge, the agent of continuity and progression.

As in *Speculations about Jakob*, the single individual remains of central concern; yet the attempt to salvage out of the public arena an individual essence is more and more difficult. The individual must be defined not as an isolated entity, but as the product of social and political forces. Due to her Marxist upbringing, Gesine is always conscious of the events that shape the individual's life and of the stance that the individual can take in response to these events:

> And since Gesine had a Marxist upbringing, she doesn't only think about whether her grandfather was a nice man; no, she wonders first what role did he play during the Kapputsch of 1920 and then that's certainly a legitimate question. [*Interview*]

Gesine's daily reading of the *New York Times* reflects her political upbringing and brings the public events that influence her life into the foreground of the novel. Her response to all public events is not political action but awareness, an awareness that will uncover the external forces that make her what she is:

> This woman Gesine Cresspahl has been wooed by several social structures and they have tried to mold her for their purposes, even to exploit her. This person is therefore for me a part of our century or an example. [*Interview*]

The assault on the individual's integrity by various systems is a theme that runs through most of Johnson's work. In a sense,

Anniversaries is the search for a place where the individual might be able to exist untainted and integral, to develop to her fullest potential, as Lambert Strether was able to do in Paris. While Strether, however, could return to America, enriched but untainted by what he has observed, the Johnson character is not easily able to sacrifice her involvement in the world or to divorce herself from those aspects of society that threaten her integrity. Much more than an observer, the Johnson character is very much *in* the world; involvement is necessary on every level of existence.

Gesine's decision to leave West Germany is taken in direct protest against the NATO actions in the Suez crisis; she finds in *Speculations about Jakob* already that both Germanies demand too much of a compromise from her. On America, she attempts to impose her personal and very rigid standards of justice and equality. The racism and prejudice she encounters nearly precipitate her return to Europe. If she stays, she does so fully conscious of the country's shortcomings and as a compromise for the good of her daughter. The hope of the novel is the development of a new and more human socialism in Czechoslovakia and Gesine actively works for the Dubczek regime. Yet we know that the novel is due to end on August 19, 1968, the day of the Russian invasion.

In spite of continual assaults, Gesine miraculously manages to maintain a very precarious, a very tenuous form of individual freedom throughout the novel. "For you, there still are some real things: death, rain, the ocean",* D.E. tells her. Part of her vitality can, ironically, be attributed to New York which, in Johnson's novel, is not as much a degrading as a liberating environment. New York is not the locus for reunification that it could be; it is a city of strangers, only the semblance of a home: "It is an illusion, and feels like home" (p. 95).** Its inhabitants all yearn to return home where the bread tastes right, where manners are familiar. The immigrants of the Upper West Side are caricatures of James' cosmopolitan society; they traveled out of necessity, not out of choice, and if Mrs. Ferwalter knows five languages, there is not one she speaks correctly.

Ironically, though, the anonymity of New York is a blessing of sorts, as its sustains the individual's independence and freedom. New York is not only buildings and subways, it is the river Gesine

---

* "Für dich gibt es immer noch wirkliche Sachen: den Tod, den Regen, die See." (p. 817)

** Es ist eine Täuschung und fühlt sich an wie Heimat. (p. 134)

sees from her window, the trees on Riverside Drive, the bay she visits weekly on her excursions to Staten Island. Her freedom is affirmed, as well, in her decision not to marry D.E. while yet being involved in a close relationship with him. Her freedom is threatened by her involvement in the bank plans to loan money to Czechoslovakia out of purely imperialist motives, and yet she finds such involvements unavoidable. Gesine's is a freedom based on compromise. The great dreams of *Speculations about Jakob* have become attenuated, and the search for the "moral Switzerland" is undertaken with cynicism.

Gesine's solution depends to a large extent on her status as a foreigner and, for this reason, it is a very unique solution. As the cynical comment about the moral Switzerland indicates, the ideal country does not exist. Neither is it possible to move to a country that does not demand moral involvement and responsibility; a moral vacuum does not exist. The exclamation "in such a country!" runs through the book: "What kind of place is it where you live of your own free will? In a country where blacks are murdered." Gesine's status as a foreigner enables her if not to remain aloof and relinquish responsibility, then to escape some of the guilt: "It's got nothing to do with us, we're guests here, we're not to blame" (p. 66).** The integrity she thus maintains is threatened daily by those who will hold her responsible: "Explain this to us, Mrs. Cresspahl. That's also where you're from, isn't it? Explain to us all about the Germans."*** Gesine resists this confusion of the person with the national origin, as she calls it, and insists on a personal identity that she tries to achieve precisely by responding daily to external assaults.

Gesine's struggle resembles that of Strether and Maggie Verver in that it represents a desire to assert her individuality over the constraining stereotype molds imposed by a "national identity." After a novel like *Speculations about Jakob*, these molds seem not inhibiting to the individual's personal growth, but terrifying in their invasion of every aspect of individual life, their prevention of any development of individuality. Gesine strives not for an identity that would subsume several cultures, but for one that leaves her as free from national definition as her involvement in German and American life will allow: not for a multi-cultural but an extra-cultural identity, not for self-assertion but for self-preservation.

---

* In was für einem Land lebst du aus freien Stücken? In einem Land, in dem Neger umgebracht werden. (p. 962)
** Es geht uns nicht an, wir sind hier Gäste, wir sind nicht schuldig. (p. 90)
*** Erklären Sie uns das, Mrs. Cresspahl. Sie sind doch auch von da her. Erklären sie uns dies mit den Deutschen. (p. 1263)

Cresspahl, however, demonstrates the tremendous dangers inherent in the foreigner's position, dangers Marie is much quicker to recognize than her mother. Neither in England, nor in Germany, was Cresspahl forced to confront his own responsibility for the events of the 1930's; he was, after all, a foreigner in both places, protected by his inner distance. Cresspahl's ultimate integrity in *Speculations about Jakob* becomes highly suspect when seen in the light of the information of *Anniversaries*. Withdrawal is the solution of Lambert Strether as well, and, as we have seen, it has its very serious costs.

Gesine's own "solution" is based not on a withdrawal from social action or involvement but on the desire to be free from any specific national allegiance. Her work for Czechoslovakia is the last chance she will give the success of communism and it will be her third disappointment. This last hope is measured against the continued co-optation of the country or one system by another that the book enacts: the invasion of Europe by the Germans, of Germany by the Russians and English, of Vietnam by America, of America by Europe and Europe by America. Gesine's solution, or what I have chosen to call a solution in spite of its tentative nature, is the daily struggle against co-optation. It is a living compromise, examined and reinvented daily and sustained through the novel. It is based on daily choices ranging from the school to which she will send her daughter to whether she will get an American passport. It outlines a possibility of survival, fully conscious of its precariousness as well as of its restriction to those who have money and belong to the middle class. It is not elitist, although it is unique. It is a model only because of the critical outlook, the discrimination it demands, and because of the responsibility it insists on assuming.

Most critical commentators of Johnson deplore the development of his work from an experimental fictional medium to the more traditional and less exciting form of the almost straightforward simple story of *Two Views* and the generational chronicle of *Anniversaries* that still seem to believe that an entire society can be captured through fiction. As we have seen, Johnson has not abandoned, but has redefined his questions about fiction and language in "Berliner Stadtbahn," *Speculations about Jakob*, and *The Third Book about Achim*. Thematically *Anniversaries* constitutes not only a continuity with the earlier experimental novels but broadens their political, historical, and social context. *Anniversaries* presents the history of Europe and the cause for the division that has become our condition. More than lamenting the division of Germany, it moves on to discuss the division of Western civilization that is the result of World War II and that determines our life as well as our fiction.

Both *Speculations about Jakob* and *The Third Book about Achim* border on self-destruction by implicating all forms of "truthfinding" in political corruption and the exploitation of the individual. The fictional process is paralyzed by the political definitions all language and form acquire in a divided yet still connected Germany, i.e. one whose wall is still open. After these first two novels, Johnson had the choice of silence, or of the continuing search for a fictional medium that might be able to overcome the pitfalls he outlined earlier. While Butor transcends fiction as insufficient, Johnson attempts to redefine it, because, as *Anniversaries* illustrates, it helps us learn about ourselves and our world; it helps us to survive.

The form of *Anniversaries* is mixed and open, made possible by the expansion beyond the two Germanies. I would like to suggest that it is precisely the expanse of America and Europe and the greater time span of this novel that make its particular solution possible.

Anniversaries begins where the earlier work left off. The unknowability of the individual, his violation by political and social systems, the distortion of memory and the unreliability of language all have been forcefully demonstrated in the early novels. *Anniversaries* does not qualify such conclusions but brings us to the point of being able to live with them or in spite of them. Gesine learns to accept the unknowability of her own past and that of her family, as well as the subjective nature of all truth. In this framework, knowledge can be achieved only through instinctive trust and identification on the one hand, and through conjecture and speculation on the other. This is how D.E. defines Gesine's extraordinary capacity to recapture the people and places of the past, and her confidence in the assumptions according to which she lives, no matter how precarious they are:

> I'll never be able to say about my own mother that she was more
> than I could see, hear, listen to; yet you go and say: My father wasn't
> concerned with revenge, he didn't want to dirty his hands with the
> Nazis; which is actually an incomprehensible determination

because it can't be proven. And I believe it implicitly, as a truth with
which you go through life, often as the truth.*

Situated between Germany and America, the narrative is freed
from any deep involvement in any particular political system. The
juxtaposition of German and English, rather than German and
German, moreover liberates the novel from the trap of linguisitic
impotence and corruption.

It seems, at least in these first three volumes, that *Anniversaries*
presents the possibility of redeeming fiction as an instrument of
knowledge and a medium of communication. Its optimism is
tempered, however, by the uniqueness of the solution which I began
to outline above. Using Gesine and Marie as narrators is another key
to this redemption. Their discrimination, consciousness,
responsibility and integrity make them extraordinary people,
almost as elite as James' protagonists, but in a different sense.

That the relationship between author and reader has become
that of mother and daughter is a significant step toward overcoming
the structures of power and authority that characterize Rohlfs in
Jakob. In a suggestive study, Mark Boulby sees the Oedipal conflict
as the basis of Johnson's fiction: the conflict between child and
father is also that between the individual and the state.[9] The
protagonists of *Anniversaries*, eager to maintain independence,
reject the power of the father. When Gesine and Marie collaborate
on their story, no rigid hierarchy is maintained: they are talking
about their common past, their common ancestors. Their
knowledge is equally limited; their judgements are equally valid.
Their speculations and ours are based on the laws of plausibility and
not, if it can be avoided, on those of ideology. To render the multiple
and public nature of what might seem to be a private and singular
existence, Johnson develops a mixed fictional form that he agrees to
call a political novel; the story of an individual is thus already the
history of a collective group:

> It's a narrated story, I would say it's a political novel insofar as it is
> a biography and every person contains history and a person born in
> 33 contains even a very special kind of history. And I would say that
> all social relationships are already political ones, because a friend-

---

* Nie werde ich von meiner eigenen Mutter so bestimmt sagen können, sie sei mehr gewesen, als ich von ihr
geschen, gehört, angehört habe; du gehst hin und sagst: Meinem Vater ging es nicht um eine Rache, an den Nazis
machte er sich nicht die Hände schmutzig; was doch eine unbegreifliche Feststellung ist, weil nicht beweisbar.
Und ich glaube es dir aufs Wort, as eine Wahrheit mit der du dich durchs Leben bringst, oft als Wahrheit. (p. 817)

> ship, a love affair, a marriage contract will always depend on the
> social configuration, the political situation of the individual, that is
> the political preconceptions for the interaction of individuals.
> [*Interview*]

To arrive at the interrelationships between individual and political
events, Johnson crosses the boundaries of fiction and documentary
writing. The narrative tone itself often resembles that of reportage.
Moreover, the author relinquishes the control of his novel's
structure and allows it to be determined by the contingencies of a
year chosen at random. *Anniversaries* must end on August 19, 1968, a
date which coincides with the Russian invasion of Czechoslovakia:

> Insofar as I started on a certain day in August, I have been supplied
> with an ending which I did not quite desire, at any rate not for the
> book; that's the invasion of the Soviet troops in the CSSR. Well I
> have to adjust to the fact that I have this ending in particular, don't
> I? [*Interview*]

Newspapers, radio reports and other genuine documents play a
major role in the novel's composition. The climatic moments of the
novel are not private but public events which, of course, have repercussions on the private lives of the novel's protagonists; the crystal
night, the murders of Robert Kennedy and Martin Luther King are
examples.

Not only is *Anniversaries* open toward the circumstances of our
political reality but it is open formally as well. In the fragmentation
and juxtaposition of its elements it resembles *Mobile*. It is
ultimately the reader who is invited to define the connection
between 1933 and 1967, between Germany and America. He must
participate in the decisions Gesine finds so difficult to make. The
dialogue form of the novel includes the reader as well as Marie and
the other voices. In this respect, Marie serves as a model reader: she
is suspicious of contrivance, discriminating enough to insist on
difference as well as similarity. The novel's first paragraph suggests
the uniqueness of all that might seem related or equal; the Baltic is
different from the Atlantic. Marie is conscious of difference; she is
careful in her judgment, yet deeply involved in a story that is told for
her benefit. The usefulness of the narrative for a future generation
is clearly demonstrated in the novel itself and it is therein that the
difference between *Anniversaries* and *Passing Time* lies. I have
already indicated the solitary nature of Revel's quest. If Gesine finds
that the complex connections she tries to make are not as false and

specious as Revel's, it is partly because she approaches them with more awareness and cynicism, but more importantly because she has the help of Marie and others. Her narrative has immediate utility and purpose.

Many similarities between *Anniversaries* and *Mobile* have emerged in the course of the analysis. Both works aim at expansion and inclusiveness; both employ fragmentation, repetition and juxtaposition as techniques; both are attempts at an open form and use intertextuality. Both are historics rather than stories and they stress, therefore, not the individual event by the configuration of personal and public events. *Anniversaries*, however, retains the presence of a subject and, with an individual at its center, it commands a different form of interest and involvement. The particularity of the individual moment, although ultimately subservient to the organization of the whole, is still a vital focus of the novel.

Here, as in Johnson's earlier novels, the individual has the role of a spy: standing between different systems, different time periods, different languages, standing between "alternative realities," the individual experiences relativism in a most personal manner. In serving both systems, the individual would be annihilated. Spying to get at the truth, yet realizing that each truth is relative to the position of each observer, the individual must accept the absence of truth, even while continuing to spy, as the marginal position dictates. The activity of spying is as essential as the necessity to avoid being coopted by an particular system. Johnson's protagonists are condemned to be perpetual outsiders; they have, like Cresspahl, an excuse that relieves them of responsibility and that maintains for them a core of inviolability.

It is not surprising that nearly a decade after the publication of its third volume, *Anniversaries* should still be unfinished. The epic task Johnson has undertaken is a difficult one in an era no longer suited to the epic mentality, an era which has, perhaps, gone beyond the mentality of fiction as well. As he was writing the novel, Johnson himself felt he was reaching an impasse not unlike that of Jacques Revel:

> It was supposed to be 365 days and since I went to the beach on an August day in 1967. . . . I asked when should I start if not tomorrow? And so I wanted to describe the 20th of August on the 21st,

then the 21st on the 22nd and so with a lot of luck I should finish in
exactly one year. . . . . This couldn't be done. I needed, for example,
more information about the Weimar Republic than the New York
Public Library could provide, . . . and it turned out that I didn't yet
know the year that was still ahead of me in the future. One obstacle
was that while I wrote, the daily reality of the city eluded me; I
couldn't have it, but I needed it for the book. [*Interview*]

Johnson expresses here an incongruity which I have found
throughout my reading of *Anniversaries* and which takes us back to
Henry James with a vengeance. The competing planes of the novel
lead Gesine and Marie more and more to immerse themselves in the
creation of their history, at the expense of their own lives.
Fictionmaking takes the place of living; tape recorders replace the
human voice; mother and daughter become part of a larger mythic
order but no longer have time to enjoy their friends and their
neighborhood. Their compensations, however, are not as much
personal as they are communal.

Conclusion: Beyond the Single Vision

Mobile and *Anniversaries* embody forms of expansion that go beyond single and multiple visions toward the acceptance, even the embracing, of a plurality in which the individual self is subordinated and submerged. In *Mobile*, the self is anonymous and that anonymity is cause for celebration because it presents a possible means of survival in a fragmented, chaotic, discontinuous universe. *Anniversaries*, despite its reliance on the content of one individual consciousness, that of Gesine Cresspahl, and on her dialogues with her daughter Marie, does subordinate the identity and present life of these characters to the story they are piecing together through memory, imagination and invention, and to the larger truth they are discovering. Gesine becomes a representative of her generation, the instrument by which the story of our century might be revealed, the optic by which New York is described.

Butor's more recent works, the geographical critiques of *Ou* and *Boomerang*, as well as the personal dream narratives of *Matière de rêves* represent an expansive movement toward the inclusion of greater and greater multiplicity within the literary text. The individual units of these texts as well as the entire texts themselves enact multiple interrelationships. Narrative is pushed to the edge of its possibility because it has to combine syntagmatic progression with the complex paradigmatic patterns of these texts. Butor says that dreams interest him precisely because they elude narrative and challenge its linearity. *Boomerang* is designed not to be read from one page to the next, but to evoke, on each page, so many references to so many other pages, that it needs to be read again and again in infinitely different ways.

Here Butor goes much further than in *Mobile* toward the creation of an alternate form of selfhood which might better account for the multiplicity in which it is forced to exist. Suprisingly, the individual self returns in these works, but, as in *Anniversaries*, not as a subject of study, not as the focus of introspection but as the agent of knowledge about the outside world. Here we see how the multiplicity celebrated in *Mobile* affects the single self, we see the emotional expansion and the physical dispersal demanded by the celebration. If the individual self returns to encounter and narrate its world, it does not do so until it has undergone visionary transformations, losing its physical and psychological boundaries in a mystical dream-like fusion with the world, until it has been exploded, dispersed, deconstructed.

Butor's deconstructed self and Johnson's submerged individuality represent more than a psychic revolution. Playing themselves out in literary terms, these transmutations represent a break with the literary structures which bolster and support the self as, in Leo Bersani's terms, an "ordered and ordering presence, a guarantee of wholeness and totality." "Literature," says Bersani, "give[s] structure and continuity to what may be fragmented and discontinuous in the history of our desires";[1] the experimentation with alternate forms makes possible the emerge of all that, according to Bersani, we have suppressed.

This redefined literary subject is both the creation and the creator of new fictional structures, as Roland Barthes suggests in *The Pleasure of the Text:*

> Then perhaps the subject returns, not as illusion, but as fiction. A certain pleasure is derived from a way of imagining oneself as *individual*, of inventing a final, rarest fiction: the fictive identity. This fiction is no longer the illusion of a unity; on the contrary, it is the theater of society in which we stage our plural: our pleasure is *individual*—but not personal.[2]

The individual subject does not disappear, but it is transformed and reconstituted. The self becomes, in Barthes' terms, the "theater of society"; we see one pole, the images of society, in *Mobile*, and the other, the individual, in *Anniversaries*. Yet the theater is the image that best describes both works. The locus of both fictions is not the individual character, but the larger social order that is no longer either unified or coherent. Both works are directed toward a reader who is compelled to participate in their construction.

In a world where meanings are multiple and heterogeneous, complex and contradictory, in a world therefore that demands to be charted, the quest for knowledge, the act of reading, remains the only legitimate individual activity. The reader who makes an itinerary through these works, coping with fragmentation and disjunction, contradiction and illogic, who pieces a story together out of fragmentary scraps of questionable information, is, as Barthes suggests, a hero in the adventures of our culture. In order to cope, as we have seen, the reader must abandon individuality in favor of a multiple form of selfhood, in favor of an anonymity that gives him a different power. Barthes describes this new Monsieur Teste:

> Imagine someone (a kind of Monsieur Teste in reverse) who abolishes within himself all barriers, all classes, all excusions, not by syncretism but by simple discard of that old specter: *logical contradiction*; who mixes every language, even those said to be imcompatible; who silently accepts every charge of illogicality, or incongruity. . . . Such a man would be the mockery of our society: court, school, asylum, polite conversation would cast him out: who endures contradiction without shame? Now this anti-hero exists: he is the reader of text at the moment he takes his pleasure. Thus the Biblical myth is reversed, the confusion of tongues is no longer a punishment, the subject gains access to bliss by the cohabitation of languages *working side by side*: the text of pleasure is a sanctioned Babel.[3]

Not only Butor's and Johnson's recent works, but also all six of the texts analyzed in this study, offer their readers worlds to explore which are analogous to those in which he makes his way every day. Their novel experimental structures present to the reader accustomed to the traditonal novel difficulties of orientation similar to those posed by Paris, Bleston or New York. Both from the point of view of the character and from that of the reader, the process of knowledge and orientation is redefined in all these works. As knowledge is no longer mastery, but participation, creation and discovery, the knowing self changes its contours and outlines. Yet the expansion I described above and the concomitant threat of submersion is actually no less present in *The Ambassadors* than it is in *Mobile* or *Anniversaries*. In their awareness and acceptance of plurality and multiplicity, division and fragmentation, in their search for cognitive instruments and fictional structures that could embrace this multiplicity, bridging gaps and reconstructing fragments, all six of these works function within a dialectic: the affirmation of selfhood, individuality and unity and its submersion, the resistance to the self's absorption by the world and the celebration of this absorption.

Two early modernist statements of how art responds to a plurality of viewpoints and perspectives might illustrate how this dialectic comes about. The first is a quote from Proust and it concerns Marcel's admiration for his favorite artists, Elstir and Vinteuil; it is quoted by Butor in an essay on Proust:

> The only genuine journey, the only Fountain of Youth, would not be to seek out new landscapes, but to have other eyes, to see the universe with the eyes of another, of a hundred others, to see the hundred universes which each of them sees, which each of them is; this we can do with Elstir, with a Vinteuil; with their kind we truly fly from star to star.[4]

Yet for Proust, the function of this multiplicity of viewpoints is to throw light on one single entity, the individual self; the hundred universes discovered in the work of other artists are no more than instruments of self-discovery:

> True readers of themselves, my book being merely a kind of magnifying glass like those of the optician of Combray offered to purchasers; my book by means of which I shall furnish them the means of reading in themselves.[5]

For Proust *any* journey is a journey into the self, *any* knowledge is self-knowledge, *any* discovery self-discovery. Marcel's imagination has absorbed the worlds of Combray, Balbec, Paris and Venice.

In a frequently cited passage from the Preface of *Portrait of a Lady*, James offers a different response to the need to integrate a variety of viewpoints in the single art work:

> The house of fiction has in short not one window, but a million—a number of possible windows not to be reckoned, rather; every one of which has been pierced or is still pierceable, in its vast front, by the need of the individual vision and by the pressure of the individual will. These apertures, or dissimilar shape and size, hang so, all together, over the human scene, that we might have expected of them a greater sameness of report than we find. They are but windows at the best, mere holes in a dead wall, disconnected perched aloft; they are not hinged doors opening straight upon life. But they have this mark of their own that at each of them stands a figure with a pair of eyes, or at least with a fieldglass, which forms, again and again, for observation, a unique instrument, insuring to the person making use of it an impression distinct from every other. ... Tell me what the artist is, and I will tell you of what he has *been* conscious. Thereby I shall express to you at once his boundless freedom and his 'moral' reference.[6]

Interestingly, James' emphasis in these multiple perceptions is different from Proust's. Both are intent upon the individual mark of each perspective, upon their distinctive dissimilarity from each other. Yet James speaks not of "a hundred universes" which correspond to a hundred eyes, as does Proust, but of one human scene to which the artist is related at once by "boundless freedom" and by a "moral reference." Whereas the Proustian artist is creator and simultaneously part of the world he sees, the Jamesian artist is removed from it, "perched aloft" as a safe observer, and therefore neither a creator nor a participant. As we move toward the annihilation of the observer in Butor and Johnson, it is important to see that the Jamesian artist, in his responsibility to an external scene, is equally threatened by extinction.

Thus, Lambert Strether's supreme individuality is affirmed only tenuously and in opposition to all those forces of contemporary society that threaten it and are therefore removed from the work. *The Ambassadors* expresses forcefully the strong conflict between the inner and outer realms and ultimately I see his (partial) withdrawal into the mind as a response to those social and political realities that are suppressed in his work. The physical *donnée* is always there and cannot be ignored. Behind the smooth cerebral surface of his novels is the threat of plurality, division, alienation and, worst of all, anonymity. James represents the confrontation of the individual and his culture, the interaction of individuals and cultures. If individuality is asserted, it is done in a way which attests to James' recognition of the precariousness of that assertion. Self-transcendence is the response to a fear of self-annihilation.

Strether leaves Paris having gotten, as he says, nothing for himself, a comment that certainly seems ironic when one compares Strether to Revel, but that might not be so blind when one considers his inability to be engaged in the reality of either Paris or Woolett, to relate to either Maria or Mme. de Vionnet or Mrs. Newsome. Not so unlike Revel, Strether might well be seen as the creator destroyed by his creation. Having absorbed all of the contradictory images of Paris and Woolett, he loses a sense of himself as a participating human individual, in favor of himself as the originator of a vision, of the moral reality of Europe. Strether becomes his prodigious imagination, as vision is affirmed and life denied. His mind becomes, as Barthes says, the "theater of society."

Maggie Verver operates under the same threat, illustrated so well by Charlotte Stant who has lost all individuality in her effort to conform to two cultures and to absorb contradictory gestures, manners and morals. Yet Maggie refuses to choose vision over life; she aims to develop a vision that will be in the service of life, to become a participant rather than the field where cultural forces interact with one another. Maggie's knowledge enables her to try this, at least, but in her final appeal to her husband, Maggie reveals all her vulnerability and thereby almost destroys herself. It is up to the Prince and to the reader to preserve her integrity for Maggie as she does for Amerigo. The inquisitive activity of fiction threatens to annihilate both the knower and the object to be known. Knowledge seems to require either the sacrifice of Lambert Strether or the corruption of Maggie Verver; secrecy alone guarantees the protection of the individual self.

Butor's Revel becomes an element in a complex set of relations that he struggles to understand. The self is no more than a point of view, the field where the cultural conflict plays itself out; the self is the culture's voice and expression. Yet Jacques Revel suffers from his faulty anthropomorphic preconceptions and fights to make a place in the center, a significance for himself. No longer himself the "mirror of miraculous silver," he merely attempts to make his journal a mirror by which the hostile city might be captured: "this mirror trap by which to capture you." As a recorder of the city, Revel is anonymous and entirely in its service; the cultural conflict, or, more generally, the culture he tries to understand does not feed but subsumes his individuality. He is defined by his function in relation to the city.

For Butor, knowledge does demand the sacrifice of the single seeker. Rather than leading to even the tenuous self-enrichment of Strether, it results in the diminution of Revel as an individual. To know them, he must live the patterns of Bleston and participate in its corruption, its murders, its fires, its dirt. Moreover, his optic is false and insufficient; it requires a major readjustment that results in his self-effacement. The sacrifice of Revel's individuality is the painful abandonment of humanism and anthropocentrism and *Passing Time* demonstrates again and again to us as readers our dependence on traditional forms and myths of centralization and individualism.

In *Mobile*, that sacrifice is no longer necessary, as the individual knower disappears. Here knowledge becomes a collaborative effort of composition; its materials are the fragments of the American past and present which emerge not as plots but as patterns for us to recognize, interpret, recompose. Some of the work is already accomplished by previous writers and Butor includes the results of their efforts. Revel's humility results in a new form of being, the collective: the individual knower becomes a participant in a collective effort at knowledge.

This defeat of the individual subject leads Butor to give it up as a unit of reference in *Mobile* and to substitute a collective form of being for it. While we lose particularity and depth in comparison to James, we gain a breadth, an expansion of vision that the limited anthropocentric novel could not approach.

Yet even in *Mobile* and in Butor's more recent works where our traditional conception of selfhood is redefined and transmuted, both individuality and the plot structures that bolster it can still be recuperated, as I have shown. In *Où*, *Matière de rêves* and *Boomerang* the traveler is and remains always Michel Butor; through all his transformations and metamorphoses, through all his frustrating and unsuccessful attempts to understand places rarely before visited by Europeans—an act of understanding which demands the anonymity of the individual seeker—he never forgets his identity as Michel Butor.

In Johnson's work, as well, the individual is merely one in a complex set of relations, yet Johnson emphasizes that one element and brings the individual voice to the foreground. The threats to the primacy of the individual self and the efforts to resist those threats form the subject of his novels. By asserting the self's essential unknowability, he guarantees its inviolability. Thus even Jakob's closest friends are unable to penetrate the truth of his story and his character. Gesine cannot even understand her own father and mother. National and political systems, however, most strongly threaten to co-opt the self. Every aspect of life must be defended against supra-personal systems that define human motive and action. The assertion of individual over national identity, the very possibility of individuality has become extremely problematic. Johnson's novels express a nostalgia for the free individual of James and cannot help questioning the possibility of salvaging even a part of it.

For Johnson knowledge is based on conjecture; only the surface can be seen, but the truth lies beneath the surface, at the ineffable center of each individual. It is the meaning of human action in the shifting cultural and poltical codes that is so difficult to interpret. Moreover, the knower in Johnson's novels is handicapped not only by the insufficiency of his tools, such as perception, memory, interpretation, but also by the violation that is inherent in the process of "truthfinding": the knower threatens the integrity of the object to be known. To diminish that violation, Johnson suggests the possibility of another form of knowledge, not analytic but of one piece, not cerebral but intuitive. Again, it involves the humility of the knower, his self-effacement and generosity toward the human object of his quest.

In *Anniversaries*, however, where there is, as in *The Ambassadors*, essentially one individual seeker, that protection no longer works; Gesine is exposed to larger forces she cannot even begin to control and is swallowed by her story. Yet in comparing these two works, the first and the last of this study, it becomes apparent that Johnson's self-effacement is only the other side of James' self-assertion. There is in the entire process of what Johnson calls "truthfinding," in the process of knowledge and fictionmaking something terribly threatening to the coherence and the stability of the individual knower. The three writers studied here all acknowledge the threat, though they deal with it in different ways: in *The Ambassadors*, James affirms the power of the self, the imagination of the knower, bolsters the human capacities of perception by protecting Strether from the involvement in "messy life" and by eliminating from his fiction those socio—cultural forces that threaten his elitism. In *The Golden Bowl*, Maggie is less protected and more implicated; the risks are taken. Butor celebrates self-annihilation as a means to a more accurate perception of a multiple and chaotic universe and as the only means of survival in it. At the same time, there is, throughout his work, a nostalgia for coherence and unity and the pain of relinquishing the values of humanism upheld so desperately against all odds. Johnson offers an alternative to James' self-assertion and Butor's self-annihilation; his self-preservation essentially involves the abandonment of fiction and "truthfinding." In *Anniversaries*, however, he recognizes, as much as the other two writers, knowledge as a supreme value and storytelling as the necessary means by which to obtain it.

In his fascinating account of our need for fictions as instruments of knowledge, *The Sense of an Ending*, Frank

Kermode identifies the position of the modern individual as being "in the middest," cut off from beginning and end, yet craving order, pattern and meaning. According to Kermode, the only means by which we can deal with the chaos that surround us are our "fictive powers," the plots that organize contingency, that relate past and present to a projected future and thereby order what might otherwise remain fragmentary and chaotic.[7]

In all of these works, fictional plots are examined and repeatedly questioned for their potential as instruments of knowledge and tools for ordering our world. The plot of *The Ambassadors* which unfolds linearly with the help of one central intelligence and some "ficelle" characters concerns the human mystery of Lambert Strether and his learning process—a process the reader follows and in which he shares. The plot of *The Golden Bowl* does not unfold linearly because, centered in two central consciousnesses, it plays itself out in their interaction. Here the reader's role is that of a mediator who might contribute to the meeting and thereby might earn a share of it. The failure of plot is demonstrated in *Passing Time* and non-human pattern replaces plot in *Mobile*. Here the reader is the only one who perceives the patterns and who must respond to them. *Speculations about Jakob* depicts the collective efforts to build a plot out of the fragments of Jakob's story and illustates the failure of plots to penetrate a human truth. In their use of the detective story form, both *Passing Time* and *Jakob* redefine the whole notion of an innocent plot. Johnson's intuitive form of knowledge is essentially non-narrative, as plot and story inevitably result in falsification. *Anniversaries*, however, shows us our need for fictions as ordering processes, our inability to perceive the connective patterns within our lives without the help of plots.

Besides being incapable of accounting for either the breadth or the depth of reality, narrative forms have been shown as potentially exploitative to the object of knowledge in all these works. These fictional experiments, as we have seen, aim not only at improving the power of fiction as an epistemological tool, but they also move toward the diminution of authority and authorship; they attempt to broaden their vision through a collaborative process of discovery. James often speaks of literature in general as an object of consumption. His greedy authorial figures use their knowledge to enrich themselves and grow as a result. Butor and Johnson take fiction out of the capitalist-consumptive position it occupies in

James' work and continue to redefine its forms as well as its social function.

Johnson's novels depend on collaboration. In their openness toward the future and toward the reader, in their use of dialogue, they search for a broader basis of knowledge, a supra-personal, communal form of truth. They search for a language that might reunify what was severed, or that might help us to understand the division. In his open mobile structures, Butor aims at overcoming the acquisitive form of learning that James exemplifies. If the artist can be redeemed at all, it is because of his service to the community, his donation of a hardearned knowledge to others. In Butor's post-fictional works, knowledge is arrived at through collaboration and the process of learning itself becomes the basis of a collective form of being. Thus these books could be the locus for a new community, although by giving up fiction, Butor takes a radical step in which not many of us are willing to follow him.

I would like to return to one of the oldest fictions that we have invented to impose some order and meaning on our lives, in order to illustrate the difference between knowledge as a commodity to acquire and knowledge as a gift to share with others so that a new community might become possible. Kermode sees the book of *Revelation* not as fulfillment but as prophecy and its prophetic tone is in keeping with the prophetic voices of James, Johnson and Butor:

> Then I saw another mighty angel coming down from heaven. He was wrapped in cloud, with the rainbow round his head; his face shone like the sun and his legs were like pillars of fire. In his hand he held a little scroll unrolled. His first foot he planted on the sea, and his left on the land. Then he gave a great shout, like the roar of a lion; and when he shouted, the seven thunders spoke. I was about to write down what the seven thunders had said; but I heard a voice from heaven saying, 'Seal up what the seven thunders have said; do not write it down.' Then the angel that I saw standing on the sea and the land raised his right hand to heaven and swore by him who lives for ever and ever, who created heaven and earth and the sea and everything in them: 'There shall be no more delay; but when the time comes for the seventh angel to sound his trumpet, the hidden purpose of God will have been fulfilled, as he promised to his servants the prophets.'
>
> Then the voice which I heard from heaven was speaking to me again, and it said, 'Go and take the open scroll in the hand of the

angel that stands on the sea and the land.' So I went to the angel and asked him to give me the little scroll. He said to me, 'Take it, and eat it. It will turn your stomach sour, although in your mouth it will taste sweet as honey.' So I took the little scroll from the angel's hand and ate it, and in my mouth it did taste sweet as honey; but when I swallowed it my stomach turned sour.

Then they said to me, 'Once again you must utter prophecies over peoples and nations and languages and many kings.'[8]

Several things concern us here. The angel who bridges land and sea, heaven and earth, fire and water holds in his hand a scroll that contains the totality of knowledge, the ultimate fulfillment. John of Patmos is the witness; he writes down his complete testimony so as to preserve if for posterity. Why, then, is he bidden not to write down the thunders' response to the angel's great shout? Could it be that this response must remain a mystery so that John's future audience might be involved, might be challenged to interpret and perhaps to duplicate this response? Similarly puzzling is the consumption of the little scroll. The process of eating must be reversed if this is to be understood. Thus the scroll turns John's stomach sour because understanding this knowledge alone, i.e. without help, is difficult and involves sacrifice. Moreover its digestion is selfish and un-rewarding. Once he has understood and digested the scroll, John must share his knowledge. The mouth is the medium of communication and the scroll tastes sweet as honey there. He must utter prophecies that will unify peoples, nations, languages and kings.

We, like John of Patmos, are deeply anchored in the processes of storytelling. Fictions are the means by which we think about our lives; we can alter them, question them, modify them, but we cannot do away with them. This book has been an attempt to show that even when fiction appears bankrupt and introverted, trapped in a prison cell or in an insane asylum, it regenerates itself to the point of helping us cope with the realities of our lives. We are all readers of fictions, we are all creators of fictions; we all participate in the everchanging processes of fiction-making and those processes themselves form the richness of our lives.

NOTES TO THE INTRODUCTION

1. In the last chapter of *The English Novel: Form and Function* (New York: Harper & Row, 1953) Dorothy Van Ghent motivates the interiorization of the novel's focus similarly.

2. New York: Harcourt, Brace, Jovanovich, 1959, pp. 99-170.

3. *Theory of the Novel*, Anna Bostock, trans. (Cambridge, Mass.: M.I.T. Press, 1971), pp. 56, 66.

4. *Ibid.*, p. 80.

5. Heller, pp. 87-98.

6. Chicago: University of Chicago Press, 1978.

7. *Répertoire* II (Paris: Minuit, 1964) p. 44. Unless otherwise indicated, all translations are my own.

8. Paris: José Corti, 1973, pp. 65-66.

9. *Inventory* (New York: Simon and Schuster, 1968), p. 26.

10. *Ibid.*, p. 30.

11. Henry James, *The Portrait of a Lady* (New York: Signet, 1963), p. 55.

NOTES TO CHAPTER 1

1. *The Art of the Novel* (New York: Scribner, 1934), pp. 198-216.

2. *Ibid.*, p. 203.

3. For an interesting study of the phenomenology of knowledge in James' work, see Paul B. Armstrong, "Knowing in James: A Phenomenological Perspective," *Novel*, 12, No. 1 (1978): pp. 5-20.

4. Christof Wegelin in *The Image of Europe in Henry James* (Dallas: Southern Methodist University Press, 1958), charts James' developing vision of Europe against the background of other contemporary Americans who have dealt with Europe. The following quote from "Portraits of Places" illustrates James' own development beyond the national and provincial: "If you have lived about you have lost that sense of absoluteness and the sanctity of your fellow patriots which once made you so happy in the midst of them. You would have seen that there are a great many *patriae* in the world, and that each of these is filled with excellent people for whom the local idiosyncracies are the only thing that is not rather barbarous. There comes a time when one set of customs, wherever it may be found, grows to seem to you about as provincial as another."

5. Page numbers in parentheses refer to the Riverside edition of *The Ambassadors* (Cambridge, Mass.: 1960).

6. For a fuller treatment of this aspect of James' work, see John Paterson, " 'The Language of Adventure' in Henry James," rpt. in *The Ambassadors*, ed. S.P. Rosenbaum (New York: Norton, 1964), pp. 458-465.

7. See Arnold Weinstein, *Vision and Response in Modern Fiction* (Ithaca: Cornell University Press, 1974), p. 71: "The plot of *The Ambassadors* can be seen as a backdrop for the protagonist's thinking processes." Weinstein's reading of *The Turn of the Screw* investigates the moral implications of James' "literature of perception."

8. Charles Feidelson in "James and 'The Man of Imagination,' " *Literary Theory and Structure*, eds. Frank Brady, John Palmer, and Martin Price (New Haven: Yale University Press, 1973), speaks of the harmony of living and seeing as the ideal of Paris outlined in Gloriani's garden.

9. For an interesting discussion of this confusion, see F.O. Matthiessen, *"The Ambassadors"*, from *Henry James: The Major Phase*, rpt. in Rosenbaum, p. 433: "James makes such a magnificently functional use of his architectural details that his hero is persuaded—and thousands of his countrymen have had the same yearning belief—that the life which goes on behind those windows and that balcony must also be characterized by tact and taste, by 'the fine relation of part to part and space to space.' "

10. Butor explores the notion that at the origin of every city there is murder and bloodshed. See chapter 2.

11. Rosenbaum, p. 334.

12. The novel that just preceded *The Ambassadors* is *The Sacred Fount* and there are numerous parallels between the two novels. The theory developed by the narrator of *The Sacred Fount* is based on the observation of the magnificent growth of one member of a couple and the horrible diminution of the other. In fact, the horribly destructive potential of imagination creating in a vacuum is dramatized more fully in this earlier work than in *The Ambassadors*.

13. In *Henry James and the Requirements of the Imagination* (Cambridge, Mass.: Harvard University Press, 1971), Philip Weinstein deals with the fear of experience shared by James' characters and with James' refusal to present a convincing image of experience; Chad, of course, is discredited at the end of the novel.

14. "The First Paragraph of *The Ambassadors*: An Explication," rpt. in Rosenbaum, pp. 465-484.

15. James' first-person protagonists are among his most obsessed and ambiguous: the governess in "The Turn of the Screw," the publishing scoundrel of "The Aspern Papers," and the narrator of *The Sacred Fount*. Strether becomes one of James' most sympathetic characters partly as a result of the definition and protection afforded him by the external narrator.

16. For a contrary view of this "narrated monologue" technique, see Dorrit Cohn, *Transparent Minds* (Cambridge, Mass.: Harvard University Press, 1978), pp. 99-140.

17. In the article cited above, Charles Feidelson discusses James' desire to "do a man of imagination." He speaks of Strether as a romantic hero whose imagination is "fed by every contact and every appearance and feeding in turn every motion and every act." According to Feidelson, James has achieved a precarious balance between the romantic and the social realist, suggesting the beauty of things discovered through thought and reflection while yet saving the hero and his story from "the darkest abyss of romance."

18. See Laurence Holland, *The Expense of Vision* (Princeton: Princeton University Press, 1964), for very convincing parallels between Strether and Chad.

19. May Bartram of "The Beast in the Jungle" is a very similar figure in this respect.

20. This phrase is reminiscent of Conrad's artistic credo in his preface to *The Nigger of the Narcissus*: "My task which I am trying to achieve is, by the power of the written word to make you hear, to make you feel—it is, before all, to make you see."

21. See Laurence Holland for some convincing parallels between Strether and James. Holland sees a similar kind of exploration as the basis of James' aesthetic.

22. Cited in Rosenbaum, p. 387.

23. For a treatment of *The Ambassadors* as a social novel, see John Cawelti, "Vision into Form," in *Literature and Society*, ed. Bernice Slote (Lincoln: University of Nebraska Press, 1964).

24. Rosenbaum, *loc. cit.*

25. *Ibid.*, p. 398.

NOTES TO CHAPTER 2

1. *Répertoire* (Paris: Minuit, 1960) p. 272.

2. *Ibid.*, p. 249.

3. *Répertoire II* (Paris: Minuit, 1964), p. 49.

4. *Répertoire*, p. 11.

5. *Répertoire II*, p. 49.

6. *Ibid.*, p. 60.

7. *Michel Butor ou le livre futur* (Paris: Gallimard, 1964).

8. *Répertoire*, p. 249.

9. For an interesting exploration of the human "eclipse" in modern fiction, see A. Weinstein, *Vision and Response in Modern Fiction*, especially Chapter 4: "Kafka, Joyce and Michel Butor." My own reading of *Passing Time* owes a great deal to Weinstein's with whom I have had occasion to discuss this novel at length.

10. See the essays of Alain Robbe-Grillet, *Pour un nouveau roman* (Paris: Gallimard, 1963), especially "Nature, humanisme, tragédie" for a more detailed sense of the new novelists' attack of Western humanistic values and preconceptions.

11. Page numbers in parentheses refer to *Passing Time*, translated by Jean Stewart (New York: Simon and Schuster, 1960). The French text is *L'Emploi du temps* (Paris: Minuit, 1957).

12. *Répertoire*, p. 134.

13. *Vision and Response*, p. 211.

14. *Répertoire II*, p. 212.

15. *Ibid.*, p. 72. For Butor, this new form of selfhood has important consequences on the novel form. In an unpublished interview, "Le Nouveau Roman," he says: "The characters of novels and their adventures have become formal devices".

16. George Charbonnier, *Entretiens avec Michel Butor* (Paris: Minuit, 1967), p. 189.

17. See my "Interview with Michel Butor." *Contemporary Literature* 19, 3(1978), 271: "If you imagine the self as a kind of container, then it is obvious that you cannot put everything in it. That would be gluttony."

18. See Weinstein, *Vision and Response in Modern Fiction*, for an extensive explanation of the experience of reading *Passing Time*.

19. Andre Hélbo, *Michel Butor: Vers une littérature du signe* (Bruxelles: Complexe, 1975), develops a similar notion of what he calls a "réalisme phenoménologique." See especially pp. 31-33. Hélbo's semiotic study of Butor's work insists on the structural integration of the text in its context.

20. *Répertoire*, pp. 251-252.

NOTES TO CHAPTER 3

1. Henry James. *The Art of the Novel,* pp. 330-331.

2. In *A Future for Astyanax* (Boston: Little, Brown and Co., 1976).

3. Page numbers in parenthesis refer to the Meridian edition of *The Golden Bowl* (New York, 1972).

4. In the chapter of *Moby Dick* called "The Whiteness of the Whale," Melville brings out the terror of white: it misleadingly indicates that that which is hidden is beneficent. The reference in the scene itself is to Poe's *Gordon Pym.*

5. In a wonderful article, "Symbolic Imagery in the Later Novels," rpt. in *Discussions of Henry James,* ed. Naomi Lebowitz (Boston: Heath, 1962), pp. 96-105, Austin Warren speaks of the modes of knowledge in James' novels and characterizes the intuitive and imaginative way to arrive at truth in *The Golden Bowl.* The richness of these images displays not only the characters' imaginative superiority, but also their loneliness. According to Warren, images characterize those entities which cannot be talked out, and therefore are not available to the dialectic mode of arriving at truth.

6. In recent years, the reader has received a great deal of critical attention, as well as a number of different appellations. This is an essay in "objectivist" reader criticism. I have taken the term *implied reader* from Wolfgang Iser, *Der Implizite Leser* (München: Wilhelm Fink Verlag, 1972), translated as *The Implied Reader* (Baltimore: Johns Hopkins University Press, 1974), although I use the term somewhat differently than Iser. I am referring not to an actual consciousness which mediates between author and reader, but to a property of the text itself; the term *encoded reader* suggests this tight connection to the text. See also Iser's *Der Akt des Lesens: Theorie aesthetischer Wirkung* (München: Wilhelm Fink Verlag, 1972), translated as *The Act of Reading* (Baltimore: Johns Hopkins University Press, 1978). I agree with Tzvetan Todorov who, in *The Fantastic: A Structural Approach to Literary Genre* (Ithaca: Cornell University Press, 1975), p. 31, speaks of the "implicit reader" and argues that "the perception of this implicit reader is given in the text with the same precision as the movements of the characters." The most useful distinction is that made by Gérard Genette in *Figures III* (Paris: Seuil, 1972), pp. 265-267. His "narrataire

intradiégétique," the second person addressed within the text, Marlow's friends in *Heart of Darkness*, for example, has only limited applicability to the actual reader. His "narrataire extradiégétique" or "lecteur virtuel" is the figure I am referring to here, the figure the text postulates indirectly as the receiver of its message, and with whom the actual reader identifies. See also Gerald Prince's "Introduction à l'étude du narrataire," *Poétique 14* (1975), a semiotic study of the "narratee," the text's counterpart of the narrator. Another useful term, the "ideal reader," is one often used by structuralist critics: it also refers to a reader implied within the text: see Robert Scholes, "Cognition and the Implied Reader," *Diacritics*, (Fall 1975), 13-15. In contrast to these "objectivist" critics, Stanley Fish, *Self-Consuming Artifacts of Literary Response* (New York: Oxford University Press, 1974), and Norman Holland, *The Dynamics of Literary Response* (New York: Oxford University Press, 1968), and *Five Readers Reading* (New Haven: Yale University Press, 1975), base their analysis on actual readers reading texts, placing the text's meaning in the subject.

7. *The Negative Imagination* (Ithaca: Cornell University Press, 1968).

8. *The Ordeal of Consciousness in Henry James* (Cambridge, England: Cambridge University Press, 1963).

9. In the preface, however, James insists on the novel's symmetry, the equality of the Prince's and the Princess' roles in the novel's structure. It is this insistence on symmetry that makes the novel's imbalance all the more disturbing.

10. "Love and Knowledge: *The Golden Bowl*," rpt. in Lebowitz, p. 80

11. See William H. Gass' article, also reprinted in Lebowitz, called "The High Brutality of Good Intentions," which deals, as the title indicates, with this constraint imposed by consideration.

12. While numerous critics have remarked on the false basis of Charlotte and Amerigo's passion, most have somehow managed to distinguish it from the "real" passion that develops between Maggie and Amerigo. I, on the contrary, am trying to show that all intimacy in this novel is subjected to the structures of possession and manipulation, and that Maggie is far from exempt.

13. Leo Bersani points out this misunderstanding between Fanny and Bob in a different context.

14. When compared to such miserable failures as Robert Acton and John Marcher, Maggie emerges as someone who is able to accept, understand, and incorporate the Other. Other "failures,"—Isabel, Strether, Maisie, Nanda Brookenham, and

especially Fleda Vetch,—demonstrate the integrity that comes of renunciation and show up Maggie's ravenous hunger for all that life has to offer.

15. Henry James, "The Novels of George Eliot," *Atlantic*, 18 (October 1866): 485.

16. *The Language of Fiction* (London: Routledge and Kegan Paul, 1966), p. 197. See also William James' famous statement:

"You can't skip a word if you are to get the effect and 19 out of 20 worthy readers grow intolerant. The method seems perverse: 'Say it out, for God's sake,' they cry, 'and have done with it.' And so I say now, give us *one* thing in your older directer manner, just to show that, in spite of your paradoxical success in this unheard-of method, you *can* still write according to accepted canons. Give us that interlude; and then continue like the 'curiosity of literature' which you have become. For gleams and innuendos and felicitous verbal insinuations you are unapproachable, but the *core* of literature is solid. Give it to us *once* again." (4 May, 1907 in *The Letters of Williams James*, II, p. 278).

17. In an excellent analysis of *The Golden Bowl* which constitutes the major part of her *Language and Knowledge in the Late Novels of Henry James* (Chicago: University of Chicago Press, 1976), Ruth Bernard Yeazell stresses the "irremediable division between husband and wife" who "do not speak the same language, nor see in the drama they have enacted the same 'moral' " (p. 125). Yeazell provides a thorough review of critics' judgments of Maggie, as well (pp. 131-132).

18. See Bersani's assertion that Maggie's silence and passivity threaten the basis for storytelling. "Her patience requires that his [the Prince's] appreciation of her mature to the point where his interest in interpretation will have died" (p. 151). I have found Bersani's reading extremely provocative and helpful, although I disagree with his vision of James as an artist exclusively interested in composition. We agree, however, that fiction is finally surpassed in favor of life, or as Bersani puts it, "a single, insistent passion" (p. 155).

NOTES TO CHAPTER 4

1. The S-Bahn runs through both East and West Berlin. Before the wall was built, it was possible to get off at any stop and most people leaving the East chose this route.

2. *Merkur*, 15 (August 1961): 728.

3. *Ibid.*, p. 732.

4. *Writing Degree Zero and Elements of Semiology* (Boston: Beacon Press, 1967), p. 24.

5. Johnson, *loc. cit.*

6. *Ibid.*, p. 733.

7. Quoted by Wilhelm Johannes Schwarz, *Der Erzähler Uwe Johnson* (Bern: Francke Verlag, 1970), p. 93.

8. Johnson, *loc. cit.*

9. *Loc. cit.*

10. *Loc. cit.*

11. Page number in parentheses refer to *Speculations about Jakob*, trans. by Ursule Molinaro (New York: Harcourt Brace Jovanovich, 1963); the German references are to *Mutmassungen über Jakob* (Frankfurt: Fischer, 1962).

12. Quoted by Reinhard Baumgart, *Über Uwe Johnson* (Frankfurt: Suhrkamp, 1970), p. 132.

13. For a discussion of the reader's role, see Manfred Durzak, *Derdeutsche Roman der Gegenwart* (Stuttgart: Kohlhammer, 1971), p. 184.

14. In her interesting essay, "Johnsons Darstellungsmittel und der Kubismus," in Baumgart, Ingrid Riedel gives us a useful framework in which to speak about the

structural characteristics of Johnson's novels. Fragmentation, disjunction and recomposition, multiple angles, foregrounding, montage and collage are all devices that link Johnson to the cubist movement. Both in his work and in cubist painting these devices serve an impulse toward an accurate, "realistic" portrayal of modern reality.

15. For an excellent discussion of this syntatic device, see Herbert Kolb, "Rückfall in die Parataxe," *Neue deutsche Hefte*, 10 (1963): 42-74.

16. "The First Paragraph of *The Ambassadors*: An Explication," rpt. in Rosenbaum, pp. 465-484.

17. *Ibid.*, p. 475.

18. "Uwe Johnson: A Critical Portrait," *Ventures*, 10, 1 (1970): 53.

NOTES TO CHAPTER 5

1. *Inventory: Essays by Michel Butor*, Richard Howard, ed. (New York: Simon and Schuster, 1968), p. 28.

2. Quoted by St. Aubyn, "Entretien avec Michel Butor," *French Review*, XXXVI (Oct. 1962), 20, 21.

3. *Répertoire II*, p. 87.

4. "An Interview with Michel Butor," conducted by Marianne Hirsch, 268.

5. *Ibid.*, 269.

6. Georges Charbonnier, *Entretiens avec Michel Butor*, p. 198.

7. *Ibid.*, p. 199.

8. See, for example, R.M. Albérès, *Butor* (Paris: Ed. Universitaires, 1964), p. 94.

9. *Essais Critiques* (Paris: Ed. du Seuil, 1964), pp. 175, 177.

10. Page numbers in parentheses refer to *Mobile*, translated by Richard Howard (New York: Simon and Schuster, 1963). The French edition cited is the 1962 Gallimard edition.

11. Charbonnier, p. 170.

12. *Ibid.*, pp. 188-197.

13. See Roland Barthes' suggestion that "a text's unity lies not in its origin, but in its destination," in "The Death of the Author," *Image/Music/Text* (New York: Hill and Wang, 1977), p. 148.

14. Charbonnier, pp. 189, 190.

15. (Columbus: Ohio State University Press, 1978).

16. St. Aubyn, 429, 430.

17. Charbonnier, p. 170.

18. *Michel Butor ou le livre futur*, p. 37.

19. *Pour une sociologie du roman* (Paris: Gallimard, 1964), p. 29.

20. From *Last Year at Marienbad*.

21. Hirsch, "Interview," 272.

22. *Ibid.*, 273.

23. This is a typical Brechtian alienation device, and Butor expects the same kind of attentive and thoughtful response from his reader as Brecht aims for in his theater. See also St. Aubyn, 434, 435.

24. Hirsch, "Interview," 279.

25. See Mary Lydon, "Michel Butor: Monstre de lecture," *French Review*, *LII*, 3 (Feb. 1979): 423-431.

26. *Loc. cit.*

27. *Répertoire III*, p. 19. See also Umberto Eco's *L'oeuvre ouverte* (Paris: Seuil, 1965) and Roland Barthes' outline for the writerly text, the "texte scriptible," in *S/Z* (Paris: Seuil, 1970).

28. Hirsch, "Interview", 278.

29. *Image/Music/Text*, p. 146.

30. Charbonnier, p. 24.

31. *Répertoire III*, p. 8.

32. *Loc. cit.*

33. Danielle Bajonnée, "8 Questions à Michel Butor," *Marche Romane*, Tome XXI. 1 & 2 (1971): 37-39.

34. Charbonnier, p. 228.

35. St. Aubyn, p. 435.

NOTES TO CHAPTER 6

1. Three volumes have appeared to date and a fourth is projected. My analysis is based on a reading of the first three volumes (Frankfurt am Main: Suhrkamp, 1970, 1971, 1973). The English translation, *Anniversaries*, tr. Leila Vennewitz (New York: Harcourt, Brace, Jovanovich, 1975), encompasses volume 1 and part of volume 2. Subsequent translations are my own.

2. Interestingly, each of the three volumes begins with a description of a body of water: the ocean, a swimming pool, and a lake, respectively.

3. From a personal unpublished interview with the author held on May 29, 1974, in Berlin. Subsequent references to the interview will be made in the text.

4. Cited by Hans Bienek, *Werkstättgesprache mit Schriftstellern* (München: 1962), p. 108.

5. Interview with Zimmer, *Die Zeit* (November 26, 1971).

6. Cited by Rée Post-Adams, "Antworten von Uwe Johnson: Ein Gespräch mit dem Autor," *German Quarterly* 50 (May 1977): 243.

7. *Uwe Johnson* (Berlin: Colloquium Verlag, 1973), p. 68.

8. Post-Adams, 243.

9. *Uwe Johnson* (New York: Frederick Ungar, 1974), see esp. pp. 96-126.

NOTES TO THE CONCLUSION

1. *A Future for Astyanax: Character and Desire in Literature,* p. 10.

2. Richard Miller, trans. (New York: Hill and Wang, 1975), p. 62.

3. *Ibid.,* pp. 3, 4.

4. Quoted in "The Imaginary Works of Art in Proust," *Inventory,* p. 184.

5. *Loc. cit.*

6. *The Art of the Novel* pp. 46-47.

7. London: Oxford University Press, 1970.

8. *The New English Bible* (New York: Oxford University Press, 1971), Revelation 10. I am grateful to John Erwin for calling my attention to this passage.

A SELECTED BIBLIOGRAPHY

I. By Henry James

The Ambassadors. Ed. L. Edel. Cambridge, Mass.: Riverside, 1960.

The Ambassadors. Ed. S.P. Rosenbaum. New York: Norton, 1964.

The American. New York: Rinehart, 1949.

The American Scene. Bloomington: Indiana University Press, 1968.

The Art of the Novel. Ed. R.P. Blackmur. New York: Scribner, 1934.

The Future of the Novel. New York: Random House, 1956.

The Golden Bowl. Ed. J. Halperin. New York: Meridian, 1972.

Lady Barberina and Other Tales. New York: Universal Library, 1961.

The Portrait of a Lady. New York: Signet, 1963.

Selected Fiction. Ed. L. Edel. New York: Dutton, 1953.

Theory of Fiction: Henry James. Ed. James E. Miller, Jr. Lincoln: University of Nebraska Press, 1972.

Three Novels. (The Europeans. The Spoils of Poynton, The Sacred Fount). New York: Harper & Row, 1968.

The Turn of the Screw. New York: Norton, 1966.

The Wings of the Dove. New York: Dell, 1965.

II. About Henry James

Anderson, Quentin. *The American Henry James.* New Brunswick: Rutgers University Press, 1957.

Armstrong, Paul. "Knowing in James: A Phenomenological View." *Novel* 12, 1 (Fall, 1978): 5-20.

Bayley, John. *The Characters of Love: A Study in the Literature of Personality.* London: Constable, 1960.

Beach, Joseph Warren. *The Method of Henry James.* (1918), rev. ed. Philadelphia: Albert Saifer, 1954.

Bersani, Leo. "The Jamesian Lie." *Partisan Review,* XXXVI, 1 (Winter, 1969): 53-83.

Cargill, Oscar. "The First International Novel." *PMLA,* LXXIII (Sept. 1958): 418-425.

_____. *The Novels of Henry James.* New York: MacMillan, 1961.

Cawelti, John G. "Form as Cultural Criticism in the Work of Henry James." *Literature and Society.* Ed. Bernice Slote. Lincoln: University of Nebraska Press, pp. 202-212.

Chatman, Seymour. *The Later Style of Henry James*. Oxford: Basil
    Blackwell, 1972.

Dupee, F.W. Ed. *The Question of Henry James: A Collection of Critical
    Essays*. New York: Holt, 1945.

Edel, Leon. Ed. *Henry James: A Collection of Critical Essays*. Englewood
    Cliffs: Prentice Hall, 1963.

Feidelson, Charles. "Henry James and the Man of Imagination." *Literary
    Theory and Structure*. Eds. F. Brady, J. Palmer, M. Price. New Haven:
    Yale University Press, 1972.

Greenstein, Susan M. "*The Ambassadors:* The Man of Imagination
    Encaged and Provided for." *Studies in the Novel* 9 (1977): 137-153.

Holland, Laurence Bedwell. *The Expense of Vision: Essays on the Craft of
    Henry James*. Princeton: Princeton University Press, 1964.

Krook, Dorothea. *The Ordeal of Consciousness in Henry James*.
    Cambridge, Eng.: The University Press, 1962.

Krupnick, Mark. "*The Golden Bowl:* Henry James' Novel about Nothing."
    English Studies 57 (1977): 533-540.

Leavis, F.R. *The Great Tradition: George Eliot, Henry James, Joseph
    Conrad*. New York: New York University Press, 1967.

Lebowitz, Naomi. Ed. *Discussions of Henry James*. Boston: Heath, 1962.

_____. *The Imagination of Loving: Henry James' Legacy to the Novel*.
    Detroit: Wayne State University Press, 1965.

Lubbock, Percy. *The Craft of Fiction*. New York: Viking, 1957.

Matthiessen, F.O. *Henry James: The Major Phase*. London: Oxford
    University Press, 1946.

McMahon, Joseph. "Paris for Expatriates." *Yale French Studies* 32 (1964):
    144-158.

Mlikhotin, A.M. *Genre of the International Novel in the Works of
    Turgenev and Henry James*. Los Angeles: University of Southern
    California Press, 1971.

Pearson, Gabriel. "The Novel to End all Novels: *The Golden Bowl*." *The
    Air of Reality: New Essays on Henry James*. Ed. John Goode. London:
    Methuen, 1973.

Powers, Lyall. *Henry James and the Naturalist Movement*. East Lansing:
    Michigan State University Press, 1971.

Rimmon, Shlomith. *The Concept of Ambiguity: The Example of Henry
    James*. Chicago: Chicago University Press, 1977.

Sears, Sallie. *The Negative Imagination: Form and Perspective in the
    Novels of Henry James*. Ithaca: Cornell University Press, 1968.

Segal, Ora. *The Lucid Reflector: The Observer in Henry James' Fiction*.
    New Haven: Yale University Press, 1969.

Tanner, Tony. "The Watcher from the Balcony: Henry James' *The
    Ambassadors*." *Critical Quarterly* VIII (1966): 35-52.

Vitoux, Pierre. "Le Récit dans *The Ambassadors.*" *Poétique* 24 (1976): 460-478.

Wegelin, Christof. *The Image of Europe in Henry James.* Dallas: Southern Methodist University Press, 1958.

_____. "The Internationalism of *The Golden Bowl.*" *Nineteenth Century Fiction* XI (Dec. 1956): 161-181.

_____. "The Rise of the International Nove." *PMLA*, LXXVII (June 1962): 305-310.

Weinstein, Philip. *Henry James and the Requirements of the Imagination.* Cambridge, Mass.: Harvard University Press, 1971.

Wilson, Edmund. "The Ambiguity of Henry James." *The Triple Thinkers.* New York: Oxford University Press, 1948.

Yeazell, Ruth Bernard. *Language and Knowledge in the Late Novels of Henry James.* Chicago: Chicago University Press, 1976.

III. By Michel Butor

L'Arc, Numéro 39 (1969).

Boomerang: Le Génie du lieu 3. Paris: Gallimard, 1978.

Description de San Marco. Paris: Gallimard, 1963.

L'Emploi du temps. Paris: Minuit, 1957. Transl. as *Passing Time* by Jean Stewart, New York: Simon and Schuster, 1960.

Le Génie du leu. Paris: Grasset, 1958.

Matière de rêves. Paris: Gallimard, 1975.

Mobile: Etude pour une représentation des Etats-Unis. Paris: Gallimard, 1962. Transl. as *Mobile* by Richard Howard. New York: Simon and Schuster, 1963.

La Modification. Paris: Minuit, 1957.

Où: Le Génie du lieu, 2. Paris: Gallimard, 1971.

Passage de Milan. Paris: Minuit, 1954.

Répertoire. Paris: Minuit, 1960. Transl. as *Inventory* by Richard Howard. New York: Simon and Schuster, 1968.

Répertoire II. Paris: Minuit, 1964.

Pépertoire III. Paris: Minuit, 1967.

Répertoire IV. Paris: Minuit, 1974.

Second Sous-Sol. Paris: Gallimard, 1976.

6 810 000 litres d'eau par seconde: Etude stéréophonique. Paris: Gallimard, 1965.

Troisième dessous. Paris: Gallimard, 1977.

IV. About Michel Butor

Albérès, R.M. *Michel Butor.* Paris: Ed. Universitaires, 1964.

Bajonnée, Danielle. "Huit questions à Michel Butor." *Marche Romane* XXI, 1-2 (1971): 37-39.

Barthes, Roland. "Littérature et discontinu." *Essais Critiques*. Paris: Seuil, 1964.

Chapsal, Madeleine. *Les Ecrivains en personne*. Paris: 10/18, 1960.

Charbonnier, Georges. *Entretiens avec Michel Butor*. Paris: Gallimard, 1967.

Dällenbach, Léon. *Le Livre et ses miroirs dans l'oeuvre romanesque de Michel Butor*. Paris: Archives des Lettres Modernes, 1972.

Helbo, André. *Michel Butor: Vers une littérature du signe*. Bruxelles: Complexe, 1975.

Hirsch, Marianne. "An Interview with Michel Butor." *Contemporary Literature* 19, 3 (1978): 262-279.

Janvier, Ludovic. *Une Parole exigeante*. Paris: Minuit, 1964.

Lydon, Mary. "Michel Butor: Monstre de lecture." *French Review* LII, 3 (Feb. 1979): 423-431.

McWilliams, Dean. *Michel Butor: The Writer as Janus*. Columbus: Ohio State University Press, 1978.

Mercier, Vivian. *The New Novel, from Queneau to Pinget*. New York: Farrar, Straus and Giroux, 1971.

Oseki, Inès. "Les Recherches formelles dans l'oeuvre de Michel Butor." Unpublished dissertation. Aix-en-Provence.

Pouillon, Jean. "Les Règles du 'je.'" *Les Temps Mondernes* 134 (April 1957): 1591-1598.

Raillard, Georges. *Michel Butor*. Paris: Gallimard, 1968.

Roudaut, Jean. *Michel Butor ou le livre futur*. Paris: Gallimard, 1964.

_____. "Parenthèse sur la place occupée par l'étude intitulée *6 810 000 litres d'eau par seconde* parmi les autres ouvrages de Michel Butor." *NRF*, XXVIII, 165 (December 1966): 498-509.

Roudiez, Léon, S. *French Fiction Today*. New Brunswick: Rutgers University Press, 1972.

_____. "Gloses sur les premières pages de *Mobile* de Michel Butor." *MLN*, LXXXVII, 6 (1972): 83-95.

_____. *Michel Butor*. New York: Columbia Essays on Modern Writers, 1965.

_____. "The Problem of Point of View in the Early Fiction of Michel Butor." *Kentucky Romance Quarterly* XVIII, 2 (1971): 145-149.

Spencer, Michael. *Michel Butor*. New York: Twayne Publishers, Inc., 1974.

Spitzer, Leo. "Quelques aspects de la technique des romans de Michel Butor." *Archivum Linguisticum* XIII (1961): 171-195 and XIV (1962): 49-76.

St. Aubyn, F.C. "A propos de *Mobile*: Deuxième entretien avec Michel Butor:" *French Review* XXXVIII, 4 (1965): 427-440.

_____. "Michel Butor: A Bibliography of His Works: 1945-1972." Part I. *West Coast Review* 12, 1: 43-49.

_____. "Michel Butor's America." *Kentucky Foreign Language Quarterly* XI (1964): 40-48.

Sturrock, John. *The French New Novel: Claude Simon, Michel Butor, Alain Robbe-Grillet.* London: Oxford University Press, 1969.

Weinstein, Arnold. "Order and Excess in Butor's *L'Emploi du temps.*" *Modern Fiction Studies* XVI, 1 (1970): 41-55.

Wolfzettel, Friedrich. *Michel Butor und der Kollektivroman; von "Passage de Milan" zu "Degrés."* Heidelberg: C. Winter, 1969.

V. By Uwe Johnson

Berliner Sachen: Aufsätze. Frankfurt: Suhrkamp, 1975.

"Berliner Stadtbahn." *Merkur* 15 (August 1961): 722-733.

Das dritte Buch über Achim. Frankfurt: Fischer, 1969.

Jahrestage: Aus dem Leben von Gesine Cresspahl. Frankfurt: Suhrkamp. Vol. 1, 1970. Vol. 2, 1971. Vol. 3, 1973. Volumes 1 and part of 2 transl. as *Anniversaries* by Leila Vennewitz. New York: Harcourt, Brace, Jonanovich, 1975.

Karsch und andere Prosa. Frankfurt: Suhrkamp, 1966.

Mutmassungen über Jakob. Frankfurt: Fischer, 1962. Transl. as *Speculations about Jakob* by Ursule Molinaro. New York: Harcourt, Brace, Jovanovich, 1963.

Zwei Ansichten. Frankfurt: Rowohlt, 1968.

VI. About Uwe Johnson

Baumgart, Reinhart. *Über Uwe Johnson.* Frankfurt: Suhrkamp, 1970.

Bienek, Horst. "Werkstattgespräch mit Uwe Johnson." *Frankfurter Hefte* XVII, 5 (1962): 333-342.

Boulby, Mark. *Uwe Johnson.* New York: Ungar, 1974.

Demetz, Peter. "Uwe Johnson: A Critical Portrait." *Ventures* X, 1 (1970): 48-53.

Detweiler, Robert. "*Speculations about Jakob*, The Truth of Ambiguity." *Monatshefte* 58 (1966): 25-32.

Diller, Edward. "Uwe Johnson's Karsch: Language as a Reflection of the Two Germanies." *Monatshefte* LX, 1 (Spring 1968): 35-39.

Durzak, Manfred. *Der deutsche Roman der Gegenwart.* Stuttgart: Kohlhammer, 1971.

Friedrichsmeyer, Erhard. "Quest by Supposition: *Speculations about Jakob.*" *Germanic Review* 42 (1967): 215-226.

Good, Colin H. "Uwe Johnson's Treatment of Narrative in *Mutmassungen über Jakob.*" *German Life and Letters* 24 (1971): 358-370.

Hatfield, Henry. *Crisis and Continuity in Modern German Fiction.* Ithaca: Cornell University Press, 1969.

Hye, Roberta. *Uwe Johnson's "Jahrestage": Die Gegenwart als variierende Wiederholung der Vergangenheit.* Bern: Peter Lang, 1978.

Jackiw, Sharon Edwards. "The Manifold Difficulties of Uwe Johnson's *Mutmassungen über Jakob."Monatshefte* LXV, 2 (Summer 1973): 126-143.

Kolb, Herbert. "Rückfall in die Parataxe." *Neue Deutsche Hefte* 10 (1963): 42-74.

Osterle, Heinz. "Uwe Johnsons *Jahrestage:* Das Bild der USA." *German Quarterly* 48: 505-517.

Phillippi, Klaus-Peter. "Parabolisches Erzählen: Anmerkungen zu Form und möglicher Geschichte." *Deutsche Vierteljahrsschrift* 43 (1969): 297-332.

Piwitt, Hermann Peter. "Chronik und Protokoll."*Sprache im technischen Zeitalter* 1 (1961): 83-86.

Post-Adams, Rée. "Antworten von Uwe Johnson: Ein Gespräch mit dem Autor." *German Quarterly* 50: 241-247.

——————. *Uwe Johnson: Darstellungsproblematik als Romanthema in "Mutmassungen über Jakob" und "Das dritte Buch über Achim."* Bonn: Bouvier, 1977.

Riedel, Nicolai. *Uwe Johnson: Bibliographie 1959-1975.* Bonn: Bouvier, 1976.

Rühle, Jürgen. "Schwierigkeiten der Verständigung: Die Interpretation der ostzonalen Wirklichkeit." *Der Monat* 136 (1960): 70-77.

Schwarz, Wilhelm Johannes. *Der Erzähler Uwe Johnson.* Bern: Francke Verlag, 1970.

Steger, Hugo. "Rebellion und Tradition in der Sprache von Uwe Johnsons *Mutmassungen über Jakob." Zwischen Sprache und Literatur. Drei Reden.* Goettingen: Sachse and Pohl, 1967: 43-69.

Wunberg, Gotthart. "Struktur und Symbolik in Uwe Johnsons Roman *Mutmassungen über Jakob." Neue Sammlung* 2 (1962): 440–449.

Zehm, Günther. "Ausruhen bei den Dingen." *Der Monat* 14 (1962): 69-73.

VII. General

Alter, Robert. *Partial Magic: The Novel as Self-Conscious Genre.* Berkeley: University of California Press, 1975.

Bersani, Leo. *A Future for Astyanax: Character and Desire in Literature.* Boston: Little Brown and Co., 1976.

Barthes, Roland. *Le Degré zéro de l'écriture.* Paris: Seuil, 1953.

——————. *Image/Music/Text.* New York: Hill and Wang., 1977.

——————. *The Pleasure of the Text.* Richard Miller, trans. New York: Hill and Wang., 1975.

——————. *S/Z.* Paris: Seuil, 1970.

Blake, William. *The Poetry and Prose of William Blake.* Ed. David V. Erdman. New York: Doubleday, 1965.

Booth, Wayne. *The Rhetoric of Fiction.* Chicago: The University of Chicago Press, 1967.

Cohn, Dorrit. *Transparent Minds*. Cambridge, Mass.: Harvard University Press, 1978.

Culler, Jonathan. *Structuralist Poetics*. Ithaca: Cornell University Press, 1975.

Eco, Umberto. *L'Oeuvre ouverte*. Paris: Seuil, 1965.

Edel, Leon. *The Modern Psychological Novel*. New York: Grosset & Dunlap, 1964.

Fish, Stanley. "Literature in the Reader: Affective Stylistics." *Self-Consuming Artifacts*. Berkeley: University of California Press, 1972: 383-427.

Frank, Joseph. "Spatial Form in Modern Literature." *The Widening Gyre*. Bloomington: Indiana University Press, 1963: 3-62.

Genette, Gérard. *Figures III*. Paris: Seuil, 1972.

Goldman, Lucien. *Pour une sociologie du roman*. Paris: Gallimard, 1964.

Heller, Erich. *The Artist's Journey into the Interior and Other Essays*. New York: Harcourt, Brace, Jovanovich, 1959.

Holland, Norman. *The Dynamics of Literary Response*. New York: Oxford University Press, 1974.

Iser, Wolfgang. *The Act of Reading*. Baltimore: Johns Hopkins University Press, 1978.

_____ *Der implizite Leser: Kommunikationsformen des Romans von Bunyan bis Beckett*. München: Wilhelm Fink Verlag, 1972.

Kahler, Erich. *The Inward Turn of Narrative*. Richard and Clara Winston, trans. Princeton: Princeton University Press, 1973.

Kermode, Frank. *The Sense of an Ending: Studies in the Theory of Fiction*. London: Oxford University Press, 1968.

Krieger, Murray. *The Tragic Vision*. Chicago: University of Chicago Press, 1966.

Lodge, David. *The Language of Fiction*. London: Routledge and Kegan Paul, 1966.

Lukács, Georg. *The Theory of the Novel*. Transl. Anna Bostock. Cambridge, Mass.: M.I.T. Press, 1971.

Nelson, Lowry, Jr. "The Fictive Reader and Literary Self-Reflexiveness." *The Disciplines of Criticism: Essays in Literary Theory, Interpretation, and History*. Eds. P. Demetz, T. Greene, L. Nelson. New Haven: Yale University Press, 1968.

Robbe-Grillet, Alain. *Pour un nouveau roman*. Paris: Minuit, 1963.

Rousset, Jean. *Narcisse romancier: Essai sur la première personne dans le roman*. Paris: José Corti, 1973.

Sarraute, Nathalie. L'Ere du soupçon. Paris: Gallimard, 1956.

Scholes, Robert, and Kellogg, Robert. *The Nature of Narrative*. London: Oxford University Press, 1968.

Scholes, Robert. *Structuralism in Literature*. New Haven: Yale University Press, 1974.

Van Ghent, Dorothy. *The English Novel; Form and Function.* New York: Harper & Row, 1953.

Watt, Ian. *The Rise of the Novel.* Berkeley: University of California Press, 1967.

Weinstein, Arnold L. *Vision and Response in Modern Fiction.* Ithaca: Cornell University Press, 1974.

Williams, William Carlos. *In the American Grain.* New York: New Directions, 1956.

INDEX